CATHOLIC MORAL PHILOSOPHY
IN PRACTICE AND THEORY

CATHOLIC
MORAL
PHILOSOPHY

in Practice & Theory

AN INTRODUCTION

BERNARD G. PRUSAK

Paulist Press
New York / Mahwah, NJ

Cover art: *At the Theshold*, © 2011 Brian Whelan
Cover design by Lightly Salted Graphics
Book design by Lynn Else

Library of Congress Cataloging-in-Publication Data

Prusak, Bernard G.
    Catholic moral philosophy in practice and theory : an introduction / Bernard G. Prusak.
        pages cm
    Includes bibliographical references and index.
    ISBN 978-0-8091-4978-0 (pbk. : alk. paper) — ISBN 978-1-58768-591-0 (ebook)
    1. Christian ethics—Catholic authors. I. Title.
    BJ1249.P786 2016
    241`.042—dc23

                                                                    2015030646

ISBN 978-0-8091-4978-0 (paperback)
ISBN 978-1-58768-591-0 (e-book)

Published by Paulist Press
997 Macarthur Boulevard
Mahwah, New Jersey 07430

www.paulistpress.com

Printed and bound in the
United States of America

For H. M. P. and A. M. P.,
and in gratitude to my father

"Business!" cried the Ghost, wringing its hands again.
"Mankind was my business. The common welfare was my
business; charity, mercy, forbearance, and benevolence were all
my business."
—Charles Dickens, *A Christmas Carol* (1843)

CONTENTS

PREFACE

After graduating from college, I had the very good fortune to go on a pilgrimage across France and Spain. It's not always clear what to do after going on such a pilgrimage! I then had the good fortune to work for a year at *Commonweal* magazine in New York, for which I thank Peggy Steinfels, the magazine's editor at that time, and Paul Baumann, the magazine's editor since 2003. My time at *Commonweal* drew me into the conversations of Catholic intellectuals, and eventually I learned to write for the magazine and to contribute to those conversations in print. Several of the chapters of this book originated as articles in *Commonweal*, with which I'm proud to be associated.

The president of Paulist Press, Father Mark-David Janus, CSP, invited me to write this book after reading my reviews and articles for some years in *Commonweal*. I thank him for his initiative and his trust in me, and as well for employing such a fine editor as Christopher Bellitto, whose work has benefited my own and who has been an encouraging voice from the beginning of this project. It also pleases me both to acknowledge that Chris was the editor of my father's book for Paulist, *The Church Unfinished* (2004), and to remember with gratitude my years worshiping at the Paulist Center in Boston while I was doing my graduate studies in philosophy.

My debt to my father is acknowledged, but faintly, by the dedication of this book to him. I also dedicate this book to my wonderful daughters in hopes that, with the Spirit's help, it might contribute toward keeping faith a live possibility for them as they grow and mature.

What I hope this book will do for my daughters I likewise hope it will do for other readers, young and old. Catholic moral philosophy ought to be exciting and fire the mind!—for the good of the tradition and the faith it seeks to support. I wrote this book with my former students at Villanova University in mind; in intent at least, it's the book that I wanted but couldn't find for the introductory ethics courses I offered then. My current students at King's College inspired my choice of the book's epigraph from Charles Dickens's *A Christmas Carol*. It's been gratifying to teach so many good people who are quick to acknowledge—and to remind me of—what old Marley had to learn the hard way.

Generous colleagues read and commented on the manuscript of this book. Greg Bassham, Lydia Moland, Dennis O'Brien, Tom Shannon, and my father worked through every chapter. They noted grammatical mistakes, which I've fixed, and raised critical, searching questions, which I've sought to address. They also expressed valuable enthusiasm for my project. In addition, Peg Hogan sharpened my thinking in chapter 1; John Zeis raised crucial questions for chapters 2 and 3; Patrick Ryan, SJ, saved me from a blooper in chapter 4; and Gabriel Gross brought her critical, well-informed eyes to chapter 5. I thank all these persons heartily. Institutional support from King's College also made this book possible. I thank in particular Joe Evan, Neal Bukeavich, Barry Williams, and Bill Irwin. In the library, Kenya Flash, Emily Sisk, and Adam Balcziunas not only got me what I needed, but brought verve, somehow, to book acquisition and interlibrary loan. King's has been a grace-filled place for me, which I attribute to the Congregation of Holy Cross there and our new-found friends, especially Regan Reitsma; Beth Admiraal; Margarita Rose; Greg Bassham; Tom Looney, CSC; and Dan Issing, CSC.

My wife Margaret's enthusiasm for this project was second to none. I express my boundless thanks to her with joy.

The chapters in this book draw not only from several articles and reviews of mine published originally in *Commonweal*, but from papers that appeared in the *American Catholic Philosophical Quarterly*, *Theoretical Medicine and Bioethics*, the *Proceedings of the American Catholic Philosophical Association*, and the *Journal of Catholic Social Thought*. With the exception of what appears in chapter 3, everything has been extensively rewritten. I am grateful to the editors of these publications for seeing value in my original work. Finally, I thank Wendy Roseberry and Brian Whelan for permission to use Brian's "At the Threshold" on this book's cover. Title, subject, and style struck me as perfect for this book's purposes. What's more, what work of philosophy couldn't use a burst of artistic vitality?

INTRODUCTION
Why This Book and What It's About

The author of a book proposing to introduce readers to Roman Catholic moral philosophy has a lot of explaining to do. Not only is it fair to wonder whether his bark is bigger than his bite, or his eyes bigger than his belly; it is also a good question to ask just what he means to sink his teeth into. For just what is Roman Catholic moral philosophy? For example, is it moral philosophy done by persons who happen to be Roman Catholics? If that's all it is, why not just edit a collection of writings by these persons, writings that may or may not show common philosophical interests and positions? Or maybe Roman Catholic moral philosophy is in fact a misnomer, or even a contradiction in terms. To spell out this last thought, what could the adjective *Roman Catholic* really mean here but that Roman Catholic moral philosophy is, at bottom, a form of theology? Accordingly, one might speculate darkly about why it refuses to say its proper name....

This book speaks to these questions. But there are other questions that also must be recognized. Grant that such an animal as Roman Catholic moral philosophy exists, which is to say that it's not a misnomer, or an oxymoron, or a wild fantasy. If so, surely it has been adequately studied already; what, then, does this book do that's different? Further, if not finally, who cares, or has reason to care? Is there today a healthy population of readers—whether young or old, in college or out of school—who have the ears to hear? Or has the Roman Catholic tradition, after the pedophilia and other scandals of recent years and the accumulated burdens of centuries, lost not only all claim to authority, but the privilege of being accorded a respectful hearing on matters of morality? (By the way,

1

I do not distinguish in this book between morality and ethics. For my purposes, ethics is simply the Greek for which morality is the Latin. Both have to do with the way to live: with the good life and the obligations we must observe in seeking it—see more on this in chapter 7.)

That I have written this book attests to my hope and faith, supported thankfully by some experience, that there are plenty of people who already do care about the fate and fortunes of Roman Catholic moral philosophy.[1] Moreover, I also believe, again with some experience in support of my conviction, that there are yet more people, in particular young people, who can be brought to care about Catholic moral philosophy, or maybe more precisely be shown that there are reasons to care and that they in fact share these reasons. The book's publisher evidently shares my hope and faith. But I am not Pollyannish about the current conditions of Roman Catholicism in the United States, or about the institutions of higher education—more likely than not Roman Catholic—in which younger readers may encounter this book.[2] Not to put too fine a point on it, but in recent years, the nuns of Catholic school lore have given way, with really amazing rapidity, to the "nones" of no religion.[3] Roman Catholic philosophers from but a century ago now seem to have been living and thinking within a deeply foreign cultural milieu.

On a personal note, I am myself a product, so to speak, of the last fifty years' great changes within the church: my father was a Rome-educated diocesan priest, my mother a Benedictine sister, before they married and had and raised me and my sister.[4] Despite this background, the American Catholic subculture that shaped my parents is familiar to me only through anecdote and historical research. In very brief, there has been a sea change within American Catholicism since Vatican II (1962–65), and it does not seem like a tendentious reading of the sociological data to claim, as one contemporary theologian has, that the voices of younger Catholics often "sound remarkably like the tides of the culture," more mainstream American than distinctively Catholic.[5]

YOU, THIS BOOK'S READER, AND THE TRADITION TO WHICH YOU BELONG

It is nonetheless my expectation that the majority of readers of this book will be at least nominally Catholic. Some might be readers of magazines like *America*, *Commonweal*, and *First Things* and follow relevant discussions in other national publications. Many, if not most, however, will never have heard of these magazines and will be little acquainted with the latest on the inner workings of the Vatican, or the state of Catholic institutions of higher education, or what have you. In any event, this book is addressed, primarily, to persons *within the Catholic tradition*, whether by reason of the mere fact that they are enrolled in Catholic schools, or by reason of the fact that they were raised in practicing Catholic families, or by reason of the fact that they understand themselves and existence as a whole in more or less Catholic, Christian terms.

By *tradition*, I have in mind what the Scottish Catholic philosopher Alasdair MacIntyre calls a living tradition: "An historically extended, socially embodied argument, and an argument precisely in part about the goods which constitute that tradition."[6] In other words, to belong to a tradition is *not* to have what one is to think and do all laid out for one. Instead, it's to be a participant in a back-and-forth conversation, sometimes friendly, sometimes heated, about the point, value, and direction of the beliefs, practices, and institutions that have constituted the tradition over time. As MacIntyre also writes, "Traditions, when vital, embody continuities of conflict."[7]

MacIntyre's basic insight is of great importance: to put it somewhat differently, a tradition is dead when none of its members care enough about it to argue with one another about what it's fundamentally about— what it calls us to, what it rules out, what it demands. Such "members" have ceased to belong to a living whole. But MacIntyre's understanding of tradition is open to criticism for failing to recognize that while conflict can reflect the vitality of a tradition, it can also fragment a tradition, with splinter groups defining themselves in disagreement with one another and feeling a deep antagonism toward one another.[8] This antagonism is characteristic of what the German sociologist Georg Simmel (1858–1918) called a conflict between intimates, typically the most intense kind of conflict because it involves, in Simmel's terms, the totality of our being.[9] In such a conflict, everything that we're about is at stake, which can prove too much to cope with dispassionately.

The upshot is that, in some circumstances, conflict indicates that a tradition is in trouble, not that it's thriving. Arguably, this is the case for the American Catholic Church today, polarized with respect to cultural conflicts over women's social roles, contraception, same-sex marriage, the destruction of human embryos for potentially life-saving research, and what ought to be the law regarding abortion, among other vexing matters.[10] Arguably again, the Roman Catholic Church more generally is currently in an unhealthy state of conflict, divided by struggles over the meaning of Vatican II, perhaps most centrally over how to stand toward, represent, and manage change and continuity in the church's teachings and structures.[11] In this regard, Pope Francis's joint canonization of Popes John XXIII (1881–1963) and John Paul II (1920–2005) on April 27, 2014—in the popular imagination, the popes of liberalization and restoration, respectively—can be understood as symbolizing his desire to move the church beyond its divisions into a deeper appreciation of the joy of the gospel and its radical yet liberating demands.

WHAT MAKES THIS BOOK DIFFERENT

This book is a humble effort to follow in Francis's path. One lesson to learn from him, as from John XXIII, is to resist despair over the conditions of our age.[12] In theological terms, this despair is a sin against the Holy Spirit, at work in every age. Another lesson I have tried to heed is that "time is greater than space," which Francis characterizes as a principle that can help us patiently endure adversity.[13] The contrast he draws is with trying to dominate space: "Giving priority to space means madly attempting to keep everything together in the present, trying to possess all the spaces of power and of self-assertion....Giving priority to time means being concerned about *initiating processes rather than possessing spaces*."[14]

In accord with this lesson, this book is structured, as compared to the typical book in moral philosophy, upside down. More precisely, I do not begin by laying out a moral theory that I then apply to various controversies. Think of that method as trying to dominate space, seeking to set the terms for all subsequent discussion. Instead, I begin with a handful of controversies—and only a handful—that I invite readers to reflect on with me as a means of entry into moral theory (which otherwise can feel unmotivated, as if it fell fully formed from the sky). Each chapter ends, accordingly, with several questions for further critical reflection. To use language closer to Francis's, this book is intended to initiate processes among its readers: with luck or inspiration, to enable and encourage readers to enter into the twists and turns of the tradition of Catholic moral philosophy; to find it *exciting*; to become more reflective; and to agree and disagree even vehemently, but with greater appreciation of the tradition's depths and complexities.

A third lesson that I take from Francis is that it is a distortion of the Catholic moral tradition, theological and philosophical alike, to "insist only on issues like abortion, gay marriage, and the use of contraceptive methods."[15] To quote him further, "When we speak about these issues, we have to talk about them in a context,"[16] in brief that of the good news of God's saving love and mercy.[17] Separated from this context, "the moral edifice of the church," in Francis's striking words, "is likely to fall like a house of cards."[18]

Against this background, it may appear ironic that this book's first chapter focuses on abortion, a culture-war topic if ever there was one. But the church's opposition to abortion reaches deep in its history—see in this regard the late first- and early second-century *Didache* (or *Teaching of the Twelve Disciples*)[19]—and Pope Francis himself has stated explicitly that the church's defense of unborn human life is not "subject to alleged reforms or 'modernizations,'" as if it could be "'progressive' to try to resolve problems by eliminating a human life."[20] How to argue against abortion, however, which is to say on what grounds and in light of what considerations, is a different matter. Here, I propose, Catholics and other persons of good will may well hope for progress. But progress can come only if we situate the controversy over abortion in a much wider and richer context, as Francis insists.

PHILOSOPHY AND THEOLOGY, FAITH AND REASON

With all this theological talk, and all my invocations of the pope, the question of the relationship of philosophy and theology, and faith and reason, can't be put off any further. Readers eager to begin grappling with moral controversies might turn at this point to chapter 1. Readers who still wonder if such an animal as Catholic moral philosophy really exists should keep on.

Some years ago, the great Polish poet Czesław Miłosz (1911–2004) urged the American monk and man of letters Thomas Merton (1915–68) "not only [to] understand and deplore the modern gnashing of teeth, but to have some complicity with it"—like the seventeenth-century Catholic mathematician, philosopher, and theologian Blaise Pascal (1623–62), to pay attention to atheists and perhaps even the atheist in himself.[21] Miłosz's letter to Merton suggests one understanding of what distinguishes the philosopher from the theologian and likewise philosophy from theology: the philosopher, when he or she is doing philosophy, is God-less, unlike the theologian who, when doing theology (God-talk and God-study), speaks precisely of what we have come to know or believe about God through God's self-revelation.

This understanding of the difference between the philosopher and the theologian, and philosophy and theology, has had its distinguished proponents, but it's not my understanding in this book. It is right that what might be called the question of God simply does not arise in many areas of philosophy; and it is also right that the philosopher, in doing philosophy, may reason herself out of the faith she once had. But it is no less a live possibility that the theologian might lose her faith in doing theology. It has been argued, in fact, that modern atheism originated with modern theologians![22] I think we also have to reckon with the claim that, as Pope John Paul II wrote in his 1998 encyclical *Fides et Ratio* (*Faith and Reason*), "faith purifies reason. As a theological virtue, faith liberates reason from presumption, the typical temptation of the philosopher."[23] Put aside for a moment what is to be understood by reason, or, for that matter, faith (or theological as opposed to natural virtues, that is, excellences of character). The important point for present purposes is that, just as it is imaginable that the philosopher might lose his or her faith through philosophy, it is likewise imaginable that the faithful philosopher might be skeptical of a philosophical argument that cuts against his or her faith precisely for this reason. For, he or she might think, who is the mere mortal philosopher to presume to have everything and everyone figured out, including the God of Abraham, Isaac, and Jacob? The atheist philosopher Friedrich Nietzsche (1844–1900) saw such an attitude as a sickness born of priest craft,[24] but the believing philosopher would want at the very least a second opinion.

A THEOLOGICAL-PHILOSOPHICAL TALE

Consider the following tale. You have been made to do a deed that will burden you forever with guilt, cover you forever with blood, compromise you to your core, thus establishing a bond of complicity between you and your persecutor that will make it impossible for you to return to the community that reared you and the way of life that you once knew.[25] For example, this happens, horribly, with child soldiers today in parts of Africa, Asia, and South America: at the age of ten you were abducted, together with a number of your friends, and made to gather in a public space with the village's younger children, parents, and elders. There your friend who refused to shoot his mother was shot himself. So was another friend, and another. But not you, and not those whom your persecutors chose after you: after seeing what happened to your friends, you all shot your mothers and so were not shot yourselves. The effect of this ordeal, however, was to make you and your fellow child soldiers feel irredeemably corrupted, outcasts to your community, bound to your abductors.[26]

But you have since experienced inexplicable, unwarranted, overwhelming grace, mercy, and forgiveness. Your soul has been redeemed from the dead. New life has flowered in you. You have had a taste of life that is stronger than death, that death could not overcome, that vanquished death. Somehow, you have encountered the crucified but risen Christ. And before this encounter, you did not appreciate how deeply, deeply lost you were. What, now, can human wisdom seem to you but

7

foolishness (1 Cor 3:19)? A power beyond the powers of this world has freed you from sin and death (Rom 8:2; 1 Cor 15:56). The immutable givens of this world now seem to you subject to a higher power of a different kind and order—a Creator to whom all the world is answerable. And the world now appears to you precisely as created in light of your experience of being re-created, summoned from nothingness into being again. Will clever words be able to deprive you of your newfound conviction? Will you let it go so easily and cheaply? Or, under pressure to defend yourself, will you not be moved to say, with the ancient theologian Tertullian (ca. 160–220) in one of his more dyspeptic moods, "What indeed has Athens [that is, philosophy] to do with Jerusalem [that is, faith]? What concord is there between the Academy and the Church?...We want no curious disputation after possessing Christ Jesus, no inquisition after enjoying the gospel!"[27]

You probably would be so moved, or at least tempted, but in a calmer moment and a more contemplative mood, you might think twice, as Tertullian himself did on occasion.[28] To extend the tale just a little further, in Christ Jesus, you have come to know the saving power and love of a "god" entirely different from the gods of ancient polytheism. These gods, as we know from the ancient myths, stand within the world. They are part of, and reflect, the order of what is. The "god" you have come to know is distinct from the world as its Creator.[29] The world, accordingly, reflects God's greatness—*God* as opposed to the *gods*, to indicate (how inadequately!) the abyss of difference between powerful beings in the world (as the gods of ancient polytheism appeared) and the being (if we can apply our earth-bound language to God) from whom all being springs and lives and moves and has its being (Acts 17:28): let us say, if we must, the being of beings.[30]

How much theology is compressed in these affirmations! Understand by *faith* here a cleaving to what you have come to know through God's action or revelation—though it should be noted that what revelation means calls for reflection itself and that even the three so-called Abrahamic religions, namely, Judaism, Christianity, and Islam, explain the concept differently.[31] The person of faith is then faithful *by keeping faith*, even through periods of darkness when God seems distant or absent. Understand by *theology* disciplined, rigorous reflection on God's self-revelation, which for Christians is concentrated in the person of Christ, through whom Christians read the Jewish Tanak or Bible anew.[32] On this account, the theologian is a person of faith who seeks to know God and make God known more deeply—and thereby to grow in faith and enable others to grow. A person need not become a theologian or study theology at all in order to be faithful. In fact, persons of simple faith sometimes can have much to teach theologians. But theology is in the service of faith—theology amplifies what faith knows—so that it might take roots and bear fruit.

Here is just a little bit of theology, drawing from my tale above. If God is good (after all, God saves) and if God is Creator (after all, God saves from death: God has power even to summon being from nothingness), how can we not confess the goodness of Creation, which is to say, the natural world? Of course we know it to be wounded or fallen (for recall the need to be saved), but that God would care to save it—that God would become present to it in order to save it, which is expressed in Christianity in the doctrine of the incarnation—suggests that the created natural world is both redeemable and worth redeeming. In other words, it suggests that the created natural world has value itself. Otherwise, why would God bother?

ATHENS AND JERUSALEM, TAKE TWO

This last affirmation has implications for the Greek practice of philosophy (etymologically, the love of wisdom). In his First Letter to the Corinthians, the Apostle Paul (ca. 5–ca. 67) presents the doctrine of Christ crucified—in other words, of the God who is known through death and resurrection, the God whom my tale has concerned—as foolishness to the Gentiles, that is, Greeks, who sought the right way to live through the cultivation of reason, the practice they called philosophy (1 Cor 1:23). Understand by *philosophy* here the free, rigorous, and methodical exercise of the mind in search of truth, more concretely by reflection on intellectual and experiential evidence, developed through logical argumentation.[33] Understand by *reason* the natural power of the human mind to construct correct and coherent systems[34]—though it should be noted that what *reason* means varies from philosophical system to system. In other words, like most, if not all, key terms, it does not have one meaning that is constant across the history of philosophy.[35]

Importantly, philosophy in the ancient world was not merely an academic discipline, one subject among others to be learned in school. Instead, as Pope Benedict XVI observed in his 2007 encyclical *Spe Salvi* (*Saved in Hope*), "the philosopher was someone who knew how to teach the essential art: the art of being authentically human—the art of living and dying."[36] But what could be more absurd to the Greek lover of wisdom, schooled in argument, fixed on the intelligible, and dedicated to the mastery of his emotions, than the claim that the person of Jesus—an obscure Jew, born according to one account in the backwater town of Bethlehem, betrayed by his followers, crushed by the Romans—could be, as John's Gospel claims for him, the Way, the Truth, and the Life (14:6)? And so, as the French Catholic philosopher Étienne Gilson (1884–1978) observed, "we would not be wrong in summing up the thought of Saint Paul on this central point by saying that, according to him, the Gospel is not a wisdom but a salvation."[37]

Yet Gilson also notes that this interpretation is potentially misleading, for in dismissing Greek wisdom, Paul immediately substituted for it the person of Jesus, whom Christians very early depicted in the style of a philosopher.[38] Moreover, in his Letter to the Romans, Paul affirms that God's power and nature may be known through the natural world (1:19–20), and he appears to claim further that there is a natural knowledge of the moral law or, in other words, a natural law, knowable in some way through conscience (2:14–15). How can this be? For, to recall Tertullian's words, "what indeed has Athens [philosophy] to do with Jerusalem [faith]? What concord is there between the Academy and the Church?"

We shouldn't be surprised. If God is good and if God is Creator, and consequently if the created natural world has value itself, we shouldn't be surprised in the least to find in Paul's thought, and Christian thought more generally, this rapprochement between Athens and Jerusalem, faith and philosophy, which is nowhere more evident than in the Prologue to John's Gospel, composed around thirty years after Paul's letters. For reason—the natural power of the human mind, however it is to be explicated—belongs to the natural order; why then wonder that it too is good, that it too is worth exercising, that it too can be exalted? By contrasting Greek wisdom with the person of Jesus, Paul makes clear that reason may go astray and is in need of salvation itself, but, as created, reason too is redeemable and worth redeeming. Consistent with the Christian experience of salvation, God's grace does not destroy nature; according to the tale that I have told, grace heals, restores, and transforms nature. That's what makes it amazing. The upshot is that there can be Christian philosophy, philosophy within a Christian worldview, so to speak. Further, philosophy can even be considered one of the wonders or glories of God's Creation. For is it not an implication of the incarnation that a human being is most like God when she exercises her most human powers, such as reason, most fully?[39]

[handwritten margin note: philosophy makes us most human, most like God]

WHY PHILOSOPHY?

We have come a long way quickly. To take a look back, much of the ground that we covered was theological, which is to say uncovered by reflection on the experience of God's saving power manifest in Jesus, called for this reason the *Christ* or *Messiah*. Within this theological landscape, we also discovered that there is at least no inherent contradiction or necessary opposition between Athens and Jerusalem, faith and philosophy. The story may be different within other theological landscapes. The question of the relationship among philosophy, theology, faith, and reason can't be answered simply in the abstract, but has to be considered within some particular theological or philosophical framework, which is what we just did.

The attentive reader will have noticed, however, that the question of what Catholic moral philosophy is, if it exists at all, still has not been answered. What's more, it's not really much of a recommendation of philosophy to say that well, yes, the Christian may do it if she feels so called. Are there reasons for Christians positively to embrace philosophy, which is to say to study, advance, and teach it? Is there great work that Christianity may expect or hope from philosophy? As these questions suggest, we have both a bit more ground to cover and a little more lifting to do.

PHILOSOPHY IN THE TRADITION

There are several traditional answers to the question of Christianity's interest in philosophy. One is that philosophy may be useful in defending the faith against challenges and errors—alien philosophical systems and various heresies. These are the grounds on which Pope Leo XIII (1810–1903), in his 1879 encyclical *Aeterni Patris* (*Of the Eternal Father*), commended the thought of the great Thomas Aquinas (1225–74),[40] thereby giving rise to the movement known as neo-Scholasticism, also known as neo-Thomism, which thrived into the 1960s. Scholasticism was itself a tremendous movement of thought, taking shape in the twelfth and thirteenth centuries, associated with the great European universities likewise originating in that age. The Scholastics sought to bring systematic unity to the growing body of authoritative texts—biblical, classical, legal, philosophical, theological—that medieval Christianity had as its patrimony.[41] Aquinas, whom the reader will meet many times again in the following chapters, was a master systematician as well as a profoundly innovative thinker.

It is also a matter of long tradition—and a second answer to the question of Christianity's interest in philosophy—that theology must call on and make use of philosophy in order to construct and explain its account of faith. From this perspective, philosophy is *ancilla theologiae*: the handmaid or maidservant of theology, which is cast in the role of the higher science.[42] In *Fides et Ratio*, Pope John Paul II lists three reasons for theologians to call on philosophers: (1) "As a work of critical reason in the light of faith, theology presupposes and requires in all its research a reason formed and educated to concept and argument."[43] In other words, theologians must be as "tough minded" as philosophers. For much of the twentieth century, philosophers often regarded theologians as "tender minded."[44] The pope seems concerned that, with the relative demise of Thomism since the midcentury, philosophers and others have only more reason for this dismissive attitude. (2) "Moreover, theology needs philosophy as a partner in dialogue in order to confirm the intelligibility and universal truth of [theology's] claims."[45] Here, interestingly, the pope echoes the German philosopher Martin Heidegger's understanding of the relationship between theology and philosophy as he articulated it in 1927. According to Heidegger (1889–1976), theology needs philosophy *"as a corrective of the…pre-Christian content of basic theological concepts."*[46] In other words, theology needs philosophy in order to secure its scientific character—in order to develop in the right way, or in a word, correctly. For example, theology needs philosophy in order to make sense of a properly theological concept like sin, which is Heidegger's example. Sin, after all, is thought to affect human existence profoundly. The task of the theologian, from Heidegger's perspective, is to give an account of how our being-in-the-world is affected by sin. In order for this account to be accurate, however, it must be based upon a correct understanding of being-in-the-world, which is where Heidegger believes the philosopher needs to enter. (3) Yet further, the pope writes, "were theologians to refuse the help of philosophy, they would run the risk of doing philosophy unwittingly and locking themselves within thought structures poorly adapted to the structures of faith."[47] The pope does not give any examples here, but we might cite, in recent memory, warnings to Christian theologians not to be seduced by none other than Heidegger's thought.[48]

A third answer to the question of Christianity's interest in philosophy is no less traditional but potentially more inspiring. Philosophy may fire the mind. The ancient theologian Clement of Alexandria (ca. 150–215) spoke in this regard of philosophy as "a schoolmaster to bring the Greek mind to Christ."[49] Much closer to our day, the British theologian and historian John Henry Newman (1801–90) proposed that the church may expect "a momentous benefit" from philosophy: "rescue from that fearful subjection to sense [the 'evil of sensuality'] which is [man's] ordinary state." Philosophy thus offered "the first step…in the conversion of man and the renovation of his nature."[50]

We can restate Newman's point in happier terms. When I am doing philosophy well, or reading or listening to a very good philosopher, the experience is of discovering new, surprising, wonderful, and sometimes baffling depths and complications to existence, our lives, and our beliefs. Hardly a claim does not give way under its own pressure, calling for further thought and work. It can be exhausting, and it can be exhilarating. Philosophy, in brief, has the potential to awaken us from our dogmatic slumbers and to make us more alive to the mysteries, wonders, and complexities of being. For it is not only in children's stories and works of fantasy that marvels may be encountered. It is worth remarking that this is how philosophy figured in the life of the great theologian Augustine (354–430): his reading of the ancient Roman philosopher Cicero (107–44 BCE) fired him for truth and helped lead, after many twists, turns, and wanderings, to his conversion.[51]

CHRISTIAN PHILOSOPHY?

To anticipate an objection, it has to be acknowledged that the dogmas of faith—speaking of dogmatic slumbers—can certainly prove obstacles to philosophy; we saw already, with Tertullian, the temptation to oppose faith and philosophy. At the same time, the dogmas of faith can also prove obstacles to the development of faith itself. The defensive believer risks having a faith that is brittle and vulnerable to self-destruction should his or her defenses prove weak. And they will prove weak should the believer's strategy for defending his or faith be to eschew thinking it through. Much better is to risk theology, as in fact the tradition calls us to do (1 Pet 3:15). Philosophy likewise holds out the possibility of growth. Moreover, whereas earlier I observed that there is so much theology compressed in the affirmations of faith, now we can likewise exclaim, How much philosophy there is as well! The Christian who is called to philosophy cannot but marvel at how much there is thrown open for her to think through.

Consider our question of whether such an animal as Catholic moral philosophy exists, or the question of whether the gods exist. What does it mean to *exist*? We might say, as a first approximation, that a thing exists if it is "presentable as one thing over against the others it is differentiated from," as the Catholic philosopher Robert Sokolowski characterizes the thinking here of the ancient Greek philosopher Aristotle (384–322 BCE).[52] So we might affirm or deny that Catholic moral philosophy exists, or that the gods exist, depending on whether or not they present themselves to us as distinct from other things that, in various ways, already have impressed on us that they are. But let's think about what it means to exist against the background of the Christian experience and claim that God is Creator. Does God exist? Is God? Well, it's thinkable—Christians believe it happened—that God could become present, in the form of a created thing, against the background of other created things (that is, God could take on flesh). As Creator, however, God does not figure among the things against the background of which we determine whether or not things exist. For God is not a created thing among other created things, and so we do not find God present there in the way that other things are. We could say, then, either that God does not exist—though if we have faith in God, presumably we would want to say immediately that God likewise does not *not* exist!—or that God is "beyond being," though in this statement, it seems we would have to cross out the *is*, that is, somehow affirm and deny at once that God *is* "beyond being."

One way or the other, against the background of the doctrine of Creation, the things of the world and indeed the world as a whole appear in a new light: they do not have to exist or be at all. Further, existence or being itself—call it the existence of existence—becomes a theme for thought in a way that it was not for Aristotle and the Greeks. What it means to exist is thrown open anew. For how could God not be—or so it might appear we have to say if God is not "presentable as one thing over against the others it is differentiated from"—yet be the origin of being? And what sense can we make of the world's not being? What is it, in the end, to be? This line of thought eventually led Aquinas to speak of God as *ipsum esse subsistens*—subsisting being itself, pure actuality—and to develop a theory of being quite different from Aristotle's.[53] And so we might have expected. For, as Sokolowski has remarked, from the Christian perspective, what exists most truly is not this or that thing or the whole of things, but the "unforced generosity" (John speaks of God as love) that let and lets things be.[54]

There are other examples of philosophical topics that Christianity either cast in a new light or brought to awareness to begin with: among others, the freedom of the will, the nature of evil, embodiment, and the role of affectivity. I am thinking of Pascal's famous claim that "the heart has its reasons that reason does not know," which might be glossed as suggesting that intellectual inquiry presupposes affective commitment.[55] To the point for present purposes, the Christian philosopher, in thinking about these topics, does not cease to be a philosopher and become, instead, a theologian. Whatever else she may be, the philosopher is someone who needs, alas, to have next to everything explained to her—who seems to understand nothing on its face, beginning with what it is to exist![56]

We might call what the philosopher is doing *Christian philosophy*, however, inasmuch as Christian revelation (that is, what is revealed in and through Christ) opened or shaped the horizons of her thought. This concept of Christian philosophy was articulated a century ago by Étienne Gilson: "I call...Christian, *every philosophy which, although keeping the two orders* [of faith and reason] *formally distinct, nevertheless considers the Christian revelation an indispensable auxiliary to reason.*"[57] Commenting on Gilson's formulation, the Catholic philosopher and theologian Jean-Luc Marion has recently claimed that "the 'auxiliary' brought by revelation not only assists in providing a new interpretation of phenomena that are already visible, but also makes visible phenomena that would have remained invisible without it."[58] In the first case, to use Marion's terminology, revelation serves as a "hermeneutic," directing our interpretation of the phenomena in question. In the second case, revelation serves as a "heuristic," uncovering hidden phenomena.[59]

CATHOLIC MORAL PHILOSOPHY, AT LAST

So, what does the author of this book mean to sink his teeth into, to recall my question of long ago? This introduction allows us to answer, in the end, as follows.

Catholic moral philosophy is a species of Christian philosophy. Like all Christian philosophy, Catholic moral philosophy operates in a "space" opened or shaped by Christian revelation. Catholic moral philosophy does not, however, take what is revealed in and through Christ as its object; that's what Catholic theology does.[60] Nevertheless, the Catholic moral philosopher sees the world in a way that is clearly marked by the Christian experience of God and its theological articulation.

That the horizon of thought of the Catholic moral philosopher has been shaped or opened by the Christian experience of God is most evident, I think, in the role that the concept of *nature* has played in the tradition, in particular in the elaboration of the moral theory of the natural law. According to the natural law tradition, to characterize it simply for now, through our natural reason, we can gain a basic understanding of the goods of human life and discern, through reflection upon experience and dialogue with others, precepts or rules corresponding to human needs and fulfillment.[61] Natural law theory both predates Christianity—it seems that Paul was alluding to it above in his Letter to the Romans—and figures in other faith traditions, Jewish as well as Islamic; but it was greatly developed by medieval Scholastics like Aquinas and is the subject of lively discussion, debate, and further development within Catholic circles to this day. As the contemporary Catholic moral theologian Jean Porter has observed, the Scholastic theory of natural law reflected a fundamental faith commitment to the goodness of Creation, rooted in the Old Testament's witness "to God's work as Creator and provident Sustainer of the visible world."[62]

Other Christians (and Jews and Muslims), of course, share this faith commitment, but in the aftermath of the sixteenth-century Reformation and Counter Reformation, postdating Aquinas by several centuries, the natural law tradition has been strongly associated with Roman Catholicism. Part of the explanation may be the importance and authority of Aquinas in the Catholic tradition.[63] Another part of the explanation may be that popes have traditionally appealed to the natural law in promulgating moral teachings.[64] Finally, hewing to the doctrines of Creation and the incarnation, Catholics have tended, more than theologians in the Reformed traditions, to insist on "the fundamental scholastic view," quoting Porter once more, "that human nature reflects the goodness and wisdom of its Creator."[65] From this perspective, there is accordingly "natural goodness apart from Christian revelation," meaning virtue may be expected in all the nations, an echo of Paul's Letter to the Romans.[66] By contrast, following the great Swiss theologian Karl Barth (1886–1968), moral theologians in the Reformed traditions have recently stressed the distinctiveness of Christian ethics, centered on the example and radical teachings of Jesus.[67]

This contrast between the Catholic and Reformed traditions, it should be acknowledged, can be overdrawn: since Vatican II, Catholic moral theology has seen a debate over the adequacy of the natural law and the role of biblical ethics.[68] While the contrast can be overdrawn, however, it can also be underplayed. It is nothing if not Catholic to see the divine in the material, the Word in flesh, the invisible present in the visible.[69] Think of the Catholic belief in the real presence of Christ in the Eucharist; or, if you know it, of Counter Reformation Baroque architecture; or of the "sacramentality" of language in Catholic poetry, signs that body forth what they signify.[70] The natural, in Catholic imagination and thought, has theological depths and resonance.

POPES, BISHOPS, AND PHILOSOPHERS

So far I have claimed that Catholic moral philosophy is (1) Christian in that the horizons of its thought may be seen as opened or shaped by what is revealed in and through Christ, and (2) distinct from other Christian traditions—that is, distinctively Catholic—in its concern with the concept of nature, elaborated in the moral theory of the natural law. For his own natural law theory and for various historical reasons, Aquinas is to this day a key figure for the tradition of Catholic moral philosophy, which in recent decades has also rediscovered his theory of the virtues (which, for him, was of a piece with his theory of the natural law—about which more later). It should be emphasized, however, that as Pope John Paul II wrote, "the Church has no philosophy of her own nor does she canonize any one particular philosophy in preference to others."[71] At the same time, the pope recognizes "the incomparable value of the philosophy of St. Thomas" and commends him as "an authentic model for all who seek the truth"—yet commends him precisely as a *model*, which apparently may be approximated by other methodologies.[72]

I think it is also right to say (3) that Catholic moral philosophy is philosophical inasmuch as, and only if, it engages alternative positions, which is to say puts itself in dialogue with currents of thought and thinkers outside the framework of Catholic, Christian faith (for example, utilitarians, Kantians, contemporary virtue ethicists, and at the limit Nietzscheans—terms that most courses in ethics will introduce). Doing so might seem risky, and indeed it is; but if Christians really believe that

Christ is the Way, the Truth, and the Life, they have reason likewise to believe, as John Paul boldly claimed, that "the human search for truth—philosophy, pursued in keeping with its own rules—can only help to understand God's word better."[73] In other words, they have reason to believe that philosophy offers a way deeper into faith, even if that way isn't always easy or clear.

Now there is no doubt that the Catholic moral philosopher, and likewise the Catholic reader, is enjoined as a Catholic to what has traditionally been called *obsequium religiosum*, which appears as well in the documents of Vatican II.[74] But how to translate the term *obsequium* from the Latin, which is to say just what it means, is a matter of some controversy.[75] One viewpoint is that Catholics must *submit* to all papal teachings, whether infallible or noninfallible, ruling out any dissent unless some papal teaching of greater authority changes the landscape.[76] Another is that Catholics must *respect* all papal teachings, allowing for the possibility of dissent from at least some teachings after the rigorous examination of conscience.[77] By contrast, the distinguished canon lawyer Ladislas Orsy has argued that "the discussion whether [*obsequium*] means precisely 'respect' or 'submission' works on a wrong assumption, which is that the Council indeed meant it in a specific and precise way."[78] According to Orsy, what is called for in all cases is "the virtue of religion," namely, an attitude of "love of God and love of His Church," which will be in need of specification in every concrete case. Sometimes submission could be called for, sometimes respect, "depending on the progress which the Church has made in clarifying its own beliefs."[79]

This point is important for clarifying the vocation of Catholic moral philosophy. On a visit to a Jesuit university, I was once asked whether I agreed with the statement of the local bishop that the Catholic professor at a Catholic college or university is obliged to understand and embrace, and to lead students to understand and embrace, the moral teachings of the magisterium—meaning, in this question, all statements and documents by the pope, who at this time was John Paul II. It was clear that the Jesuit asking this question wished to hear the answer yes. On John Paul's account of the role of the Catholic philosopher, however, yes appears not altogether correct. For, according to John Paul, philosophy not only stands to be enriched by theology, but at times may have a critical though constructive role to play with respect to it, thereby enriching it in turn.[80] It clearly would be wrong to hold that the Catholic moral philosopher could dissent from deeply rooted Catholic commitments like the goodness of procreation, which follows from the basic faith commitment to the goodness of Creation itself. Dissent from *some* teachings—infallible or noninfallible, what matters is whether they belong to Christian faith in fundamental ways—would rightly raise the question of whether the Catholic moral philosopher was in fact any longer Catholic. But not every teaching is so deeply entrenched, and it is in these instances that human intelligence and ingenuity—in a word, philosophy—may be so bold to query, though respectfully, even the magisterium.

In this regard, we do well to remember that the church once thought quite differently about religious freedom and slavery, to choose only the two most striking examples.[81] Some have wanted to deny that church teachings have changed over the millennia, but arguably this denial is misguided on theological as well as historical grounds. Drawing on theology, the American jurist and historian John Noonan has proposed that "to think it necessary to conceal the mistakes made in the past or to hide the changes going on in the present" is in fact a "way of doubting the divine dimension of the Church"—that the Spirit is alive in it today no less than in centuries past. He explains,

> Divinity needs no devices to hide human error or progress in the apprehension of truth. The divinity of the Church sustains a body composed of people—you and me—who make mistakes and make progress. There is no need to deny the truth of corrections when they are made, or of an advance when it occurs.[82]

This book proposes that Catholic moral philosophy can help in the progress of truth. Now, with the following chapters, to see if this is so!

CHAPTER 1

A RISKIER DISCOURSE

*How Catholics Ought to Argue
about Abortion*

In this book's introduction, I quoted Pope Francis's remark that it is a distortion of the Catholic moral tradition to "insist only on issues like abortion, gay marriage, and the use of contraceptive methods."[1] And so I also noted that it might seem ironic for this book's opening chapter to focus on abortion. Why, other than alphabetically, begin there?

Here's my answer. Opposition to abortion is basic to the Catholic moral tradition both because defense of innocent human life is basic and because, since the early days of Christianity in the ancient Greco-Roman world (where abortion and even infanticide were freely practiced), abortion appeared obviously wrong.[2] Many Catholics, among others, were accordingly baffled and shocked by the United States Supreme Court's 1973 decision *Roe v. Wade*, which claimed that, in light of "the wide divergence of thinking on this most sensitive and difficult question," the right of personal privacy located in the Fourteenth Amendment protected "a woman's decision whether or not to terminate her pregnancy" through its first two trimesters.[3] That there was "wide divergence" on the morality of abortion fell as a sudden blow.[4]

In this chapter, I propose that it's possible to argue productively about abortion—but not as most Catholic philosophers now do, at least if we want to address the problem of abortion as it really is. What's needed is to expand the terms in which the Catholic case against abortion is made. I proceed as follows: first, I review the argument as it's been conducted to date; second, I show that it's reached an impasse; and third, I propose a new way forward.

TERMS OF THE DEBATE

In his excellent book *The Ethics of Abortion*, the Catholic philosopher Christopher Kaczor characterizes "the status of the human being in utero" as the main question on which "the critic and defender of abortion disagree."[5] And, sure enough, Catholic philosophers have tended to focus on just this question. Patrick Lee, in his *Abortion and Unborn Human Life*, makes a strong case that "the human being is essentially a physical organism, and the organism comes to be at conception," with the conclusion following (after the relevant premises have been brought forth) that "it is wrong to kill a human being whether he or she is two years outside the womb, one month past conception, or three days past conception."[6] In *Embryo: A Defense of Human Life*, Robert George and Christopher Tollefsen make the case for the newly conceived, arguing, "Human beings in the embryonic stage are already, and not merely potentially, human beings."[7] According to George and Tollefsen, the embryonic, fetal, infant, child, and adolescent stages are all alike "developmental stages of a determinate and enduring being who comes into existence as a single-celled human organism and develops, if all goes well, into adulthood by a gradual and gapless process over many years."[8]

Now, all these claims are vigorously contested. It is by no means agreed by all that human beings are essentially physical organisms—rather than, say, minds or souls, or for that matter, merely brains. It is by no means agreed by all, even granting that human beings are essentially physical organisms, that they come into existence at conception—rather than, say, after twinning and fusion are no longer possible, or after the development of critical organ systems, or that of the higher nervous system.[9] It is by no means agreed by all that human beings ought not to be killed in virtue of the kind of thing they are, rather than in virtue of this or that attribute or set of attributes that they come to have—say, self-consciousness. And, finally, it is by no means agreed by all, even granting that human beings come into existence at conception and have value in virtue of the kind of thing they are, that it is wrong intentionally to kill a human being in utero. For some hold that a fetus has no *right* to the use of its mother's body, and that a woman who elects to expel the fetus through the methods of abortion is then within her own rights to do so.[10]

Recent Catholic literature on abortion is well aware of these points of contention, however, and the several books that I have cited anticipate and counter, at length and with sophistication, the many predictable objections. Whether these replies suffice to answer the objections I leave to readers to determine for themselves. In any event, I am myself convinced of the full humanity of the fetus at least from the phase of development called gastrulation, after which twinning and fusion can no longer occur.[11] But here is the thesis of this chapter: though it is necessary, in order for Catholic opposition to abortion to be well-grounded, that Catholics hold that abortion kills human beings, this way of carrying on the argument is too limited. The Catholic argument need not rest here, and what's more *cannot* rest here if it's to speak to people to whom the full humanity of the fetus is not likewise evident. Instead, the Catholic argument against abortion on demand ought to be recast so that it addresses not only the status of the unborn, but the proper attitudes to have toward developing human life, whether the fetus is a full human being from conception or not.

INTUITIONS

The first claim to establish is that, while the case for the full humanity of the fetus is a strong one, it cannot honestly be considered the only plausible position. My aim in making this claim, to be clear, is not to undermine Catholic opposition to abortion on demand, but to indicate that the terms of this opposition need expanding.

We can begin by considering a paper by the Catholic philosopher and lawyer Andrew Peach arguing against what is called the developmental, gradualist, or process theory of the coming into existence of a human being, which is the theory that, in one form or another, defenders of abortion often hold.[12] This theory takes its start from the widely shared intuition (or feeling or sense) that "later is worse than earlier"—in other

23

words, that a late-term abortion is more seriously wrong than an early-term abortion. It's a further question whether this intuition has the facts going for it, but any account of the morality of abortion that simply dismissed it out of hand, or couldn't explain it, would have at best a shaky hold on us.

As Peach writes, "In arguments in favor of abortion rights, the intuition that there are moral differences between late- and early-term abortions has been cited as evidence that an early-term abortion is somehow a different *kind* of act from a late-term one because of an alleged change in the moral standing of the fetus."[13] Such arguments hold that, prior to some point in development, the fetus is neither a person nor a full human being (the terms of the arguments vary), with the upshot that an early-term "abortion is some type of action other than murder,"[14] albeit an action that is morally significant enough to require justification in a way that removing a mere mass of tissue does not.

Consider, by way of example, the following argument by the American philosopher Warren Quinn (1938–91). Quinn begins by articulating "two intuitions that," he tells us, "I have long found persuasive" and a third "that sometimes strikes me as equally compelling": (1) "a very early abortion stands in need of moral justification in a way that the surgical removal of a mere mass of tissue does not"; (2) "abortion occurring early enough in pregnancy, at least before all the organ systems of the fetus are complete, is not morally equivalent either to the killing of an adult or the killing of an infant"; and (3) "as pregnancy progresses abortion becomes increasingly problematic from the moral point of view," such that "more, and perhaps considerably more, is required to justify an abortion at six months than at one month."[15]

Quinn goes on to develop what he calls "two alternative metaphysical theories of the status of the fetus and the nature of fetal development in which these moral intuitions could be seen as satisfied."[16] (By *metaphysical* here, understand an account of the being of things: what things really, most fundamentally are.) For present purposes, the relevant theory is Quinn's second, the process theory, according to which "an individual human being gradually comes to exist."[17] On this view, a fetus is indeed a human being—that is its so-called *substance sortal*, which means the sort

24

of thing it is—but a fetus may not be a fully realized human being at a given time: it may be, instead, a human being *in the making*, only partly realized. For a different, much less controversial example, a house under construction is indeed a house—it makes perfect sense for someone to refer to his or her house under construction *as a house*, which is its substance sortal—but it is, plain to see, a partly and not fully realized house.

THE PROCESS THEORY

We now need to do a bit of work. To make sense of "the idea that some human beings or houses are incompletely real at a given time," Quinn introduces a distinction between two kinds of substance sortals.[18] Some, so-called *complex* substance sortals, have two-part extensions: two classes of things can fall under such concepts, namely, fully realized instances of the thing in question and partly realized instances of the thing. (A concept's *extension* is what it covers, or from another point of view, what falls under it.) Take, by way of example, houses, beer, and wine. Beer that is not done brewing is still beer—that's its substance sortal, the thing that it is—but it still has a ways to go before it's finished becoming what it is, before it's *really* beer, as we might say. By contrast, *simple* substance sortals have only a one-part extension: these concepts do not admit of or break down into two classes of things, one fully realized and the other partly realized. Take here, by way of example, paper, sea shells, currency, and musical notes. A thing simply is or isn't an instance of one of these things. There is no kinda, sorta paper, sea shell, currency, or musical note, by contrast to houses, beer, wine, and doubtless many other examples.[19]

The implications of the process theory for the morality of abortion should not be surprising: according to this theory, abortion is always morally significant since it is the killing of a human being rather than the removal of a mere mass of tissue, but an early-term abortion is less morally charged or objectionable than a late-term abortion, because in an early-term abortion, it is a *partly realized* human being that is killed, not the equivalent of a child or an adult whose killing would in most circumstances constitute murder. Finally, the seriousness of abortion increases as the fetus develops, such that to kill a fetus with a functioning higher nervous system is in most circumstances murder, as such a fetus is, by Quinn's lights, a *fully realized* human being. These implications for the morality of abortion should not be surprising because, after all, the process theory was constructed to have precisely these implications, corresponding to the several intuitions that Quinn articulated at the beginning of his argument.

A DIFFERENT ACCOUNT

Peach's response to the process theory is twofold. First, according to him, "it is difficult not to feel that such accounts...have been engineered for no other reason than to justify abortion."[20] One can see where this feeling is coming from, but it would be more accurate to say that such accounts have been constructed to accommodate intuitions about the moral differences between early-term and late-term abortions. After all, we do seem reluctant to call a very early abortion *murder*, whereas we are willing to do so for a very late abortion, so long as it is not performed to save the life of the mother.[21] Also, someone who disagreed with Peach might counter that it's difficult not to feel that accounts according to which the unborn are fully realized human beings from conception have likewise been "engineered" to rule out abortion. After all, while it's the case that a person's a person no matter how small, is an embryo the size of a period, "so small that it could rest on the head of a pin,"[22] clearly a person or a human being when it has no brain or capacity to think and feel and has the appearance of a ball of cells?[23] Or consider the first-trimester loss of a vanishing twin. Was its loss the loss of a fully realized human being, or the loss of a human being in the making, who sadly did not come to be?

As the New Zealand–born philosopher Rosalind Hursthouse has observed, "The familiar biological facts" about pregnancy do not include philosophical theories about the status of the fetus.[24] Reasonably well-informed persons know that, again in Hursthouse's words, "the premature termination of a pregnancy is, in some sense, the cutting off of a new human life,"[25] but whether this new human life is better understood as a fully realized human being from the beginning, or as a human being in the making until some point in its development, is to ask more than most persons know what to do with. Of course, here is where the philosophers enter, typically with "the desire to solve the problem of abortion by getting it to fall under some general rule such as 'You ought not to kill anything with the right to life but may kill anything else.'"[26]

Though Peach agrees with the Catholic philosophers cited earlier in this chapter on the status of the unborn, he does not question the basic assumption of the process theory: substances admit of degrees or grades. Questioning this assumption might cast some doubt on the process theory, but the intuitions that underlie it would go untouched. So instead, as his second response to the process theory, Peach offers an alternative account of the grounds of the intuition that "later is worse than earlier." Whereas proponents of the process theory develop this intuition into the position that "an early term abortion is somehow a different *kind* of act from a late-term one because of an alleged change in the moral standing of the fetus,"[27] Peach holds that it is consistent to regard all direct abortions "as acts of murder and inherently wrong" while acknowledging that abortions can differ in moral gravity according to the *circumstances* in which they are performed.[28] (By *direct* abortions, which is a technical term, understand for now abortions done with the express intent of killing the fetus.)

Consider what Peach calls, following Thomas Aquinas, the circumstances "touching the act," which is to say such considerations as when, how, and to whom or what the act is done. Peach proposes that it makes sense to consider the act of a late-term abortion *worse* than that of an early-term abortion because of "the greater likelihood of the fetus feeling pain" in the second and third trimesters.[29] Also, in the second and third trimesters, "the possibility of the [fetus's] living outside the womb increases," with the upshot that "the decision to abort, as opposed to having the child merely removed and incubated, should be regarded as more wanton...than the decision to abort a previable fetus."[30] There is no implication here that the act of aborting a previable fetus is *not* wrong. Instead, the point is that aborting a viable fetus is generally *more wrong* in the sense of graver and more objectionable, provoking the moral outrage that many people feel, for example, over so-called partial-birth abortions.

Late-term abortions provoke outrage and sometimes even disgust not only on account of the circumstances of the *act*, however, but toward the *agents* who would do such things. "Other things being equal," Peach writes, "it is possible that, in the earliest stages of a pregnancy, a woman, as well as the father of her child, may be [inculpably] ignorant of the moral standing of the developing human life."[31] To abort the child would be wrong, but the woman and man in question might deserve pity rather than condemnation. By contrast, "to deny the humanity and personhood of the fetus at later stages of the pregnancy," Peach goes on, "almost certainly must involve some active cooperation on the part of the agents involved," in a word, negligence if not malice.[32] Hence the feeling that later is worse than earlier. We can also understand that "when a woman first becomes aware of [a] pregnancy," she might well feel a wash of passions: "dread of the burden of carrying the baby…, apprehension and anxiety at the notion of being a parent…, fear of being financially and emotionally abandoned by the biological father, etc."[33] So her decision to have an early-term abortion, while still wrong, can be forgiven as done of out weakness rather than malice. Yet, Peach observes, "Should a person (or persons) endure the initial onslaught of emotion and, after ample time for deliberation and investigation into the nature of the being in the womb, still decide to abort in the later stages of pregnancy, one may more reasonably suspect"—other things being equal—"that the parties in question have a wanton disregard for human life."[34] Hence, again, the feeling that later is worse than earlier.

Peach has more to say, but the point is already clear: there is reason to find late-term abortions more objectionable than early-term abortions—but this is not, on Peach's account, reason to judge early-term abortions a different *kind* of act, which is to say *not* murder (the intentional killing of an innocent human being). In sum, we might say that, on Peach's account, the difference between early-term abortion and late-term abortion is that, other things being equal, the latter is typically murder under aggravating circumstances, the former murder under mitigating circumstances.

OBJECTIONS AND REPLIES

Now, how are we to decide between the way that the process theory accounts for the intuition that later is worse than earlier and the way that Peach does? Peach recommends his account by deriding the process theory as giving us "a dubious account of personhood,"[35] and Patrick Lee has claimed, "Being a certain kind of substantial entity is an either/or matter—a thing either is or is not a human being."[36] Similarly, it might be objected that Quinn's analogy with a house is weak. A house moves from being partly realized to fully realized through no doing of its own, but wholly by the work of builders who intend to build it. By contrast, a human being in the embryonic and fetal stages develops by an active natural potency of its own, which seems to suggest that it has been really, fully a human being from the beginning, or at least from early on. After all, *it* is working to make itself.

Finally, it might also be objected that there is no clear, nonarbitrary point at which we could say a human being in the making becomes a fully realized human being, with the full moral standing of children and adults. Quinn proposes, "It is natural to think that the becoming process is over when the higher nervous system is developed enough for the organism to start learning, in the fashion of the normal neonate, the ways of the world"[37]—but why is it natural to think so? This word *natural* is doing a lot of work here, without any argument to support it. And are we really to conclude that mentally disabled infants who themselves cannot learn "in the fashion of the normal neonate" do not constitute full human beings with full moral standing? In Quinn's support, it ought to be remembered that he does not think that, say, a six-month-old fetus, even if still a human being in the making, is *not* a human being at all and may be killed simply at will. Instead, serious justification would be needed for this decision to pass moral muster. But what reasons would count as serious justification Quinn leaves "gladly…aside."[38] To quote the last sentence of his paper, "How the complex web of moral forces vectors out in particular situations is, as Aristotle would say, what the wise man knows."[39]

Such a conclusion is hardly satisfying. We want to know what the wise know!—though of course this is more easily said than done. Quinn's distinction between complex and simple substance sortals, however, certainly seems plausible, and so it seems that Lee's claim that "being a certain kind of substantial entity is an either/or matter—a thing either is or is not a human being"—is either too simple, or at least not obvious. And while the analogy between a house and a human being in the embryonic and fetal stages is indeed weak, its imperfection does not mean, without further ado, that the concept human being does not have a two-part extension, covering both fully realized instances and partly realized instances. What's more, the analogy is not quite so imperfect as might be thought. Popular culture has it that the DNA of an organism is sufficient for it to develop all on its own so long as the environment does not stand in the way. The contemporary science of epigenetics, however, teaches that the maternal environment contributes to the *construction* of the organism, with the upshot that, at least arguably, its development cannot be understood as exclusively self-directed.[40] Finally, while it seems right that there is no clear point at which we can say that a human being in the making becomes a fully realized human being, the conclusion does not follow that we must abandon this distinction altogether. Is there a clear point at which a house in the making becomes a finished house? Or, to use the classic examples, is there a nonarbitrary point at which the addition of one more grain of wheat makes a heap? At what number of hairs does a man become bald? Clearly, these very imperfect analogies do not *establish* that human beings come into being gradually, but the analogies do make this proposition intelligible, such that it can't simply be dismissed.

Perhaps, in the end, the critical question on which the morality of abortion turns is whether substances do in fact admit of degrees or grades. But this suggestion ought to strike us, I think, as amazing. Does the rightness or wrongness of a decision to abort, say, a fourteen-week old fetus turn exclusively on this question of metaphysics? How striking it would be if the rightness or wrongness of a decision whether or not to bear a child to term—that most earthy, physical deed—should turn exclusively on such an abstract, disembodied consideration. As Hursthouse has remarked, it is

a most bizarre aspect of nearly all the current philosophical literature on abortion…that, far from treating abortion as a
unique moral problem, markedly unlike any other, nearly
everything written on the status of the fetus and its bearing on
the abortion issue would be consistent with the human reproductive facts (to say nothing of family life) being totally different from what they are.[41]

The process theory is not the Catholic theory. The great majority of
Catholics, including myself (and a good many pro-life, feminist women),
reject the process theory's implications. But why? It might be thought—
the Catholics philosophers whom I have cited seem to think—that
Catholic opposition to abortion on demand stands or falls with metaphysics. So far as I can tell, however, the jury is out and is likely to stay
out for some time to come on such metaphysical questions as whether
substances admit of degrees or grades. In defense of the Catholic philosophers I have cited, it is certainly important to have arguments supporting
the full humanity of the fetus. Otherwise, Catholic opposition to at least
first-trimester abortions would not make much sense. But there is no
need for the argument to rest there, and I take myself to have established
that it cannot, given the apparent plausibility of the process theory.

THE VALUE OF HUMAN LIFE

So how ought the argument against abortion be expanded if it is to
speak to persons to whom the full humanity of the fetus is not evident? I
propose to come at this question by considering a concrete example. An
August 2011 *New York Times Magazine* article, "The Two-Minus-One
Pregnancy," looked at the phenomenon of so-called pregnancy reductions. Developed in the 1980s as an emergency medical intervention in
response to megabirth pregnancies created by fertility treatments, the
practice "has quietly become an option for women carrying twins," with
one fetal twin receiving a fatal injection of potassium chloride while the
other is carried to term.[42] There is typically no medical indication for the
procedure; it is done because the woman or couple simply does not want

twins. In the words of one woman who chose to abort one of her two fourteen-week-old fetuses, "Things would have been different if we were 15 years younger or if we hadn't had children already or if we were more financially secure."[43]

Predictably, the procedure is controversial, even among obstetricians who have no qualms about megapregnancy reductions or aborting singletons, healthy or not. One doctor is quoted as reflecting rather defensively, "In a society where women can terminate a single pregnancy for any reason—financial, social, emotional—if we have a way to reduce a twin pregnancy with very little risk, isn't it legitimate to offer that service to women with twins who want to reduce to a singleton?"[44]

Now, how should Catholics—or anyone else for that matter—argue against this practice? To begin with, reasons should be given for believing that a fetus is a full human being from conception, or at least from the point when twinning and fusion are no longer possible. The objections that I raised against Quinn's process theory are all relevant here. First and foremost, is there really a nonarbitrary point at which a human being in the making becomes a fully realized human being? Isn't appealing to viability, or the development of the higher nervous system, a baseless prejudice that we might call "adultism," judging whether a being counts as a full human being on the basis of how much it approximates an *adult* human being—which, note, is a phase that human beings pass through, not the substance they are? But surely this is not all there is to say, and it seems doubtful that arguments along these lines would make much of an impression on persons who would even consider "reducing" to a singleton. So there is a second set of considerations that I think is just as important. Even if the fetus is regarded as *merely* a developing human being, it is no way to greet new human life—it is a deeply callous way to greet new human life—to reject one of two on grounds of inconvenience: that one had hoped to have only one child at this time, not two, and the second should not have come along to make life more difficult than it has to be. To abort a fetus on such grounds is to exhibit the wrong attitude toward the value of human life.

It's not difficult to anticipate the reply: Who is anyone to say for anyone else what is or is not the right attitude toward the value of human life?

But this reply is thoughtless. For it's no minority opinion that human life is precious; we know that it is. What's more, the position that human life is precious need not be explicated or grounded in terms of this or that faith tradition. On this point, secular and faith traditions come together in an overlapping—and overwhelming—consensus.

Consider another, more controversial example: deciding whether to abort a fetus found to have developmental defects or challenges. The philosopher Shelley Burtt, who is now the executive director of the Camphill Foundation serving people with disabilities, writes,

> The question is not whether it is right to desire a "normal" child, but how one ought to respond when genetic testing reveals that desire has been thwarted. To take steps at that point to abort the fetus and "try again" is not just to decide against being pregnant or in favor of "controlling one's life." It is to decide in advance and for another that a certain sort of life (a female one, a physically handicapped one, a mentally retarded one) is not worth living….Postponing an abortion decision until one knows what sort of child has been created places relative weights on human beings: some are more worthy of living, of being cared for, of being cherished, than others.[45]

And such an attitude toward human life is surely wrong to have—not the attitude that a wise, caring, mature person would exhibit.

THE MORAL ARGUMENT AND THE LAW

In the United States, after *Planned Parenthood v. Casey* (1992), it is the law of the land that states may not place "undue burdens" on women electing to have abortions within the first two trimesters of pregnancy. That a person has a legal right, however, does not mean that he or she is always *right*—meaning virtuous as opposed to callous, self-indulgent, or cruel—to exercise it.[46] The moral argument over abortion extends beyond the legal argument and need not be limited to its terms.

What is lacking about the way that most Catholic philosophers argue about abortion, I think, is precisely that they limit themselves to the question whether the unborn constitute persons or full human beings. Soon after *Roe*, Catholics and others began comparing it to the 1857 *Dred Scott* decision, which denied black Americans membership in the political community (citizenship) inasmuch as, it was claimed, they did not fall under the words *We the people* in the Constitution. The comparison of abortion to slavery is now common in the literature opposing abortion: just as slavery was premised on a denial of the personhood or full humanity of blacks, it is proposed, abortion is premised on a denial of the personhood or full humanity of the unborn.[47] Accordingly, there has recently developed a movement to pass amendments to state constitutions declaring a fertilized human egg a legal person, responding to *Roe* much as the Fourteenth Amendment to the U.S. Constitution responded to *Dred Scott*.

But it is naïve to think that the problem of abortion can be solved in this way. What is needed is an approach that focuses on the meaning and function of abortion in the living, breathing context of people's lives. Referring to *Roe*, Chicago's Cardinal Joseph Bernardin (1928–96) remarked in 1984, "What the decision did *not* change was the substantial, broad-based, and solidly grounded view of American citizens across the land that abortion on request is not a satisfactory way to address the real problems individuals and families face in this delicate area of respecting human life."[48] Note that Bernardin does not deny but affirms that there are "real problems individuals and families face" here. The question to consider—which the terms of the legal debate tend to obscure—is how to address these real problems, from lack of nutrition, housing, and health care (in a word, poverty) to "broken families; drug abuse...; abusive relationships; incomplete education; fear of public humiliation; antagonistic partners; failed love," as Christopher Kaczor extends the list.[49] To quote Bernardin again, abortion is surely not "a satisfactory way" to address any of these all too real problems, and it is difficult to imagine people of good will disagreeing with this claim. But simply outlawing abortion, on the grounds that the unborn constitute persons, also would not address these problems—the very problems that drive many women to abortion and that motivate women and men to defend abortion rights.[50]

It may be that Catholic philosophers tend to focus on the status of the fetus partly from a worry that Catholics might otherwise have to accede to abortion in some circumstances. For it's easy enough to say that relatively well-to-do couples who decide to abort a healthy twin exhibit the wrong attitude toward developing human life, but what about a poor, bone-tired woman who has already borne, say, nine children and whose husband or partner can be counted on only to want more sex? Would she show a lack of reverence for human life by seeking an early-term abortion by whatever means at her disposal? It may be difficult to know how to answer this question, and many other hard cases, such as pregnancy after rape and incest, could no doubt be brought forth.

My basic claim is that, while it may be difficult to come to terms with such hard cases and questions, this is a difficulty that Catholics must take on in order both to address the problem of abortion as it really is and to be able to talk about abortion with people to whom the full humanity of the fetus is not evident. If Catholics cannot make the case that abortion is never properly regarded as a "blessed escape" from the real problems that pregnancy may throw at people,[51] then there seems little chance of seeing abortion rates significantly decline even if *Roe* were overturned. The American sociologist Kristin Luker has observed in this regard that "although the pro-life movement often compares itself to the Abolitionist movement, it may more aptly be compared to the Temperance movement that produced Prohibition."[52] The reason is *not* because the gravity of the pro-life movement's cause is similar to that of the temperance movement; instead, the reason is that, in current circumstances, the effects of a national antiabortion law would likely be similar to the effects of the Eighteenth Amendment ratified in 1919, repealed in 1933. In light of the facts that public opinion strongly opposes overturning *Roe*,[53] that there was strong support for abortion even before *Roe*, and that generations have now come of age presuming the legality of abortion, a national antiabortion law would likely produce, in Luker's words again, "a Prohibition-like situation" in which abortions would be more expensive, harder to come by, and perhaps more dangerous, but remain nearly as numerous.[54]

MAKING THE CASE

There are currently around 1.2 million abortions per year in the United States; one in five pregnancies ends in abortion.[55] If a national antiabortion law is not likely, how else might these numbers be reduced?

To begin with, it is important to understand that the sorts of attitudes that people can sustain, or even comprehend, depend on the conditions of people's lives. In medieval and even early modern Europe, for example, child abandonment was widespread—not because no one cherished children then, but because subsistence economies often did not produce enough food for the many children women bore.[56] The upshot is that an argument concerned with the proper attitudes toward developing human life cannot concern itself only with developing human life, which fortunately is now often recognized in discussions of abortion. Attention must be given as well to the living conditions on the other side of birth, for these living conditions help determine how a new life will be greeted. As Cardinal Bernardin insisted, "Our lack of moral vision in protecting unborn children" is connected with "our lack of social vision in the provision of basic necessities for women and children."[57] Any legal policy that would be pro-life and not simply antiabortion must reckon with the fact that most of the women now having abortions are poor and relatively powerless.[58] Having an abortion is not, for these women, about liberation to pursue professional ambitions; instead, it's about *not* "falling even further into poverty or economic dependence on men or the state."[59]

Attention must also be given—as Pope John Paul II saw—to the *culture* in which we live. For it is not only poor living conditions that may lead people to see abortion as a blessed escape. Say a woman is single and in her twenties and finds herself pregnant after failed contraception. It is certainly understandable that she might see abortion as a blessed escape, for we can imagine how reluctant she might be to go through nine months of pregnancy and have a child at this point of her life and in these circumstances.[60] What are we to say to such a woman? In order to know that, we have to be able to listen to her first. Why don't other ways of coping with a crisis pregnancy appear much more, well, life-giving to the woman and child alike? For example, is there a problem with the way that

36

we imagine and talk about adoption, such that "giving a baby up" is too painful to consider? And why might people disagree, even vehemently, with Shelley Burtt regarding whether to abort or bring to birth babies with developmental defects or challenges? Arguably, part of the problem is with the way we imagine and understand what makes for a successful, worthwhile life. Against this background, it is hardly surprising that "the resources to aid parents with handicapped children are scant, and the burden could easily seem intolerable."[61]

THE SOCIOLOGY OF MORALITY

A way to summarize these points is that we need to take seriously what might be called the sociology of morality—in simpler if not too simple terms, the fact that people's social surroundings, living conditions, and life experiences all factor into how they think about abortion. This is not to deny that people have *reasons* for what they think, or to claim that social surroundings and the rest wholly explain why people think what they do, as if people's thinking were merely a function of these factors. Instead, the claim, roughly, is that people's vision of the world includes or more precisely inclines people to a view of abortion, as on the other hand coming to see abortion in a different light might change how people see and relate to the world, which is to say the wider context in which they live.

Kristin Luker makes an argument along these lines in her oft-cited book *Abortion and the Politics of Motherhood*, which has itself been described as a sociology of morality.[62] Luker claims, on the basis of her research, that "participants in the abortion debate…are defending a *world view*—a notion of what they see as sacred and important—as well as a view of the embryo."[63] More concretely, how people see abortion is bound up with how they understand and envision—normally in ways that prove quite difficult to articulate—family life, motherhood, and children.[64] Luker now and again overstates her thesis: for example, while "it is the embryo's fate that seems to be at stake, the abortion debate is actually about the meanings of *women's* lives."[65] This claim—in the words of one of her critics, that "the prolife movement is not what it appears because its deepest motives have nothing to do with the fetus" and everything to do with the place of women[66]—is not supported by data showing that, over the last several decades, people have become both somewhat less supportive of abortion and much more supportive of gender egalitarianism.[67] Other recent sociological research, however, suggests that Luker's basic thesis is right: people come to see abortion as wrong because it is the killing of a person, but they come to see it as the killing of a person because in turn they find meaning and value in a vision of the world in which pregnancy may call for even heroic virtue.[68]

Practically, as the American theologian and legal scholar Cathleen Kaveny has observed, the challenge for pro-life Catholics and others is to go about "identifying and creating the sort of legal and social systems likely to lead women to act virtuously, even heroically, with regard to...unplanned and unwanted unborn offspring"[69]—no small challenge, to say the least. As a small step, Caveny suggests that Catholic colleges have on staff "an advocate specifically designated for women with problem pregnancies, someone who will facilitate the arrangement of alternative housing and medical care, run interference with professors and deans, organize a support network, and provide financial counseling"[70]—a position that does not exist at the Catholic colleges where I have worked.

Theoretically, the challenge is likewise formidable: to articulate and defend, in terms and a style compelling to modern women and men, the vision of the world to which being pro-life belongs and that it helps support. A premise of the following chapters is that considering other practical controversies will both clarify this more general vision and begin to suggest what all there is to say for it.

QUESTIONS FOR FURTHER REFLECTION/PAPER QUESTIONS

(1) Edward Vacek, SJ, commented several years ago in an article in the magazine *Commonweal*, "Fortunately, the abortion debate has more and more turned toward the question of whether the fetus possesses the properties that constitute personhood."[71] Is this turn of the debate fortunate? In

other words, is focusing on the properties or capacities of the fetus the right way to argue about the morality of abortion?

Either be Vacek and write another article for *Commonweal* critically responding to the argument of this chapter in defense of your own position, *or* write a long letter to the editor, in your own voice, countering Vacek's claim by drawing from and elaborating the argument of this chapter. In the first case, affirm that the "turn" in the abortion debate toward the question of properties is the way to go; in the second, point out the limits of this way of framing the controversy. One way or the other, be sure to anticipate and counter objections.

(2) One claim this chapter makes is that the moral argument over abortion extends beyond the legal argument and need not be limited to its terms. To which one might reply, Fine and well, but what then should the law be? It's clear enough what policies and legislation correspond, ideally, to the position that the human being in utero has full moral standing from the time of conception. What policies and legislation correspond to the moral argument that this chapter has put forth?

Research Charles Camosy's proposed "Mother and Prenatal Child Protection Act,"[72] and read Cathleen Kaveny's paper "Toward a Thomistic Perspective on Abortion and the Law in Contemporary America,"[73] or George McKenna's article "On Abortion: A Lincolnian Position,"[74] among other resources.[75] Then write a memo on the legal and policy implications of this chapter's argument. Address your memo to your senator or congressperson. You might imagine further that you work in this representative's office.

(3) Your friend has just discovered that she's pregnant. She's not married to the father and has no intention of marrying him. She's also scared and really not feeling up to having a baby at this point of her life. She told you all this and more

in a rushed conversation. Now you've had some time to think. What do you want to tell your friend? Drawing from this chapter and the various readings it cites, either write your friend a long, thoughtful letter, or write a dialogue between the two of you. Gently but firmly make the case that you think ought to be made. Be sure to anticipate and speak to objections.

CHAPTER 2

DOUBLE EFFECT, ALL OVER AGAIN

Casuistry in the Catholic Tradition

The *Oxford English Dictionary* defines the word *casuistry*, derived from the Latin for *case*, as

> that part of Ethics which resolves cases of conscience, applying the general rules of religion and morality to particular instances in which "circumstances alter cases," or in which there appears to be a conflict of duties. Often (and perhaps originally) applied to a quibbling or evasive way of dealing with difficult cases of duty; sophistry.[1]

The claim that the word "often (and perhaps originally) applied to a quibbling or evasive way of dealing with difficult cases of duty" is supported by the quotations that the *Dictionary* lists showing its early uses. For example:

> *c*1740 Visct. Bolingbroke *Idea Patriot King* xi. 100 Casuistry… destroys by Distinctions and Exceptions, all Morality, and effaces the essential Difference between Right and Wrong.
> 1836 *Penny Cycl.* VI. 359 The science of casuistry…has been termed not inaptly the "art of quibbling with God."[2]

One of the word's earliest uses in English is in Alexander Pope's satirical epic poem *The Rape of the Lock*, first published in 1712. (Pope lived 1688 to 1744.) Whereas the occasion of the Trojan War recounted in Homer's *Iliad* was Paris's absconding with Helen to Troy, what occasions the dispute in Pope's poem is the unauthorized cutting of a piece of hair—the lock in the poem's melodramatic title. Pope's use of the word *casuistry* suggests, alas, that it is a rather dull, if not useless, business. "The Lock," we read,

> obtain'd with Guilt, and kept with Pain,
> In ev'ry place is sought, but sought in vain....
> Some thought it mounted to the Lunar Sphere,
> Since all things lost on Earth, are treasur'd there.[3]

But it turns out those things include such junk as

> The Courtier's Promises, and Sick Man's Pray'rs,
> The Smiles of Harlots, and the Tears of Heirs,
> Cages for Gnats, and Chains to Yoak a Flea;
> Dry'd Butterflies, and Tomes of Casuistry.[4]

This chapter concerns both a recent case of conscience and an old staple of the tradition of casuistry, the so-called rule or doctrine or principle of double effect. I would lay odds that some readers will come away from this chapter thinking that casuistry's bad reputation is well deserved. Pack it away with cages for gnats, chains to yoke a flea, and dried butterflies! But the heartrending tragedy of the case in question also shows why we need casuistry—even stronger, why, when it is properly understood and practiced, it deserves to be "treasur'd," though its value can sometimes be difficult to appreciate. So, in any event, I claim at this chapter's end.

By the way, there is some tough going in this chapter. The American essayist Ralph Waldo Emerson (1803–82) once called "the Temperance-question...a gymnastic training to the casuistry and conscience of the time."[5] Think of the twists and turns of this chapter's many arguments as gymnastic training for the mind.

FIRST APPEARANCES

In November 2009, the ethics committee of St. Joseph's Hospital in Phoenix, Arizona, chaired by Sister Margaret McBride, RSM, permitted the abortion of an eleven-week-old fetus. The fetus's mother was suffering from acute pulmonary hypertension, which her doctors judged would prove fatal for both her and her previable child.[6] Pulmonary hypertension is a condition in which high blood pressure, brought on by abnormalities in the lungs, threatens heart failure—more precisely, cardiogenic shock, which is when the heart is unable to supply enough blood to the body's other organs, which quickly become hypoxic, meaning no longer oxygenated. Pulmonary hypertension can be medically managed, but it is much exacerbated by the demands of pregnancy, because pregnancy greatly increases blood volume pumped to the heart in order to support the fetus. The placenta—which grows entirely from the embryo's cells, not the mother's—establishes blood supply at ten to twelve weeks into pregnancy,[7] which then is a critical time for a woman with pulmonary hypertension. According to the facts of the case that have become public, both the woman and her child were dying in November 2009 because of "decrease in maternal cardiac output and decrease in blood oxygenation."[8] The doctors accordingly advised that she have an abortion, the mother reluctantly agreed (she was also the mother of four children at home), and so too did the ethics committee, in what the hospital later described as a "tragic case."[9] Yet, as Thomas J. Olmsted, the bishop of Phoenix, observed in a statement critical of the hospital and of Sister McBride, under the principles of Catholic moral thought,

> While medical professionals should certainly try to save a pregnant mother's life, the means by which they do it can never be by directly killing her unborn child....The direct killing of an unborn child is always immoral, no matter the circumstances, and it cannot be permitted in any institution that claims to be authentically Catholic.[10]

In support of this claim, Bishop Olmsted went on to cite both Pope John Paul II's encyclical *Evangelium Vitae*, which states, "Direct abortion, that is, abortion willed as an end or as a means, always constitutes a grave moral disorder, since it is the deliberate killing of an innocent human being,"[11] and the United States Conference of Catholic Bishops' *Ethical and Religious Directives for Catholic Healthcare Services*, which states,

"Abortion (that is, the directly intended termination of pregnancy before viability or the directly intended destruction of a viable fetus) is never permitted. Every procedure whose sole immediate effect is the termination of pregnancy before viability is an abortion."[12] Bishop Olmsted might also have cited the *Catechism of the Catholic Church*, which states "Direct abortion, that is to say, abortion willed either as an end or a means, is gravely contrary to the moral law."[13] In a statement posted on the diocese's Web site, as well as in a statement to the media, Father John Ehrlich, the diocese's medical ethics director, put the point briefly, in language drawn from Paul's Letter to the Romans (3:8): "No one can do evil that good may come."[14]

All this is the stuff of an introductory ethics course at almost any Catholic college, as well as at many secular institutions. So too is the principle under which, according again to media reports,[15] the ethics committee believed abortion to be permitted in this case: namely, the principle of double effect (hereafter PDE), though this nomenclature did not appear until the twentieth century.[16] Textbook formulations of this principle, which is descended from sixteenth- and seventeenth-century commentaries on Thomas Aquinas's theory of action,[17] typically identify four conditions that must be satisfied for an action to be morally permissible when it has two effects, one of which is evil while the other is good. (Hence the name: principle of *double* effect.) As the Jesuit moral theologian Joseph Mangan (1911–86) summarizes those conditions in an oft-cited discussion, they are the following:

(1) that the action in itself from its very object be good or at least indifferent;

(2) that the good effect and not the evil effect be intended;

(3) that the good effect not be produced by means of the evil effect;

(4) that there be a proportionately grave reason for permitting the evil effect.[18]

The *Ethical and Religious Directives for Catholic Healthcare Services*, which regulates all Catholic hospitals, incorporates the PDE as follows:

"Operations, treatments, and medications that have as their direct purpose the cure of a proportionately serious pathological condition of a pregnant woman are permitted when they cannot be safely postponed until the unborn child is viable, even if they will result in the death of the unborn child."[19]

Against the hospital ethics committee, however, the case in question does not appear to satisfy all the conditions of the PDE, perhaps most strikingly the third condition that the evil effect (here, the death of the fetus) may not be the means to the good effect (here, saving the life of the woman). In the committee's support, the procedure did not have the death of the fetus as its sole immediate effect; instead, the mother's life was also thereby saved. But, in the case in question, the abortion appears to have been *direct* inasmuch as it was "willed…as a means," to use the language of *Evangelium Vitae* and the *Catechism*.

The Phoenix case thus appears different from operations in which the death of a fetus is an inevitable, secondary consequence. The paradigmatic example of such a case cited by most commentators, and likewise the United States Conference of Catholic Bishops' Committee on Doctrine in a June 23, 2010, statement,[20] is surgery to remove a cancerous but gravid uterus—in other words, hysterectomy when a woman is pregnant.[21] In this case, it is claimed that the death of the fetus is not directly intended; instead, what is directly intended is the cure of the woman's serious pathological condition. After all, it is not the nature of, or an essential constituent to, a hysterectomy that it kill a fetus.[22] Unless, strangely, a hysterectomy is chosen as a nonstandard means of abortion, that it kills a fetus may be considered accidental to the procedure. These cases thus appear to fall clearly under the *Ethical and Religious Directives* while the Phoenix case does not. For the Phoenix case appears to violate Paul's rule—named by the Australian philosopher Alan Donagan (1925–91) as the Pauline principle[23] —that evil is not to be done that good may come.

ON SECOND VIEW

Sometimes, however, a little philosophy is worse than none. For, all this appearance of clarity—that some cases clearly satisfy the PDE, no questions asked, whereas the Phoenix case does not—is misleading. It takes pushing deeper into philosophy to see why.

A few further preliminary points are in order. First, it is a starting point of Catholic moral philosophy that some actions can never be anything other than evil or base. They are, in other words, *intrinsically evil* or wrong in themselves, never to be made right or good by circumstances or consequences. And so they should not be done. The ancient Greek philosopher Aristotle gives the examples of adultery, stealing, and murder:

> There is…never any possibility of getting anything right about them, but one always goes astray, nor is there doing anything well or not well about such things [say] by committing adultery with the right woman and when and in the way one ought, but simply doing any of these things is to go wrong.[24]

Now, it should be noted that an action may be called *right* in two senses. We might call an action right because it is the best course of action available in a given situation. Still, we might not want to commend this action; we might even regret deeply that the person in question has put himself in the situation where he has to act one way or the other. (Say the person has promised to marry two women, has made both pregnant, and has to decide what to do next. The "right" thing to do might be to marry one woman over the other—but the man is a lousy creep whether he does here the right thing or not.[25]) By contrast, we might also call an action right because we want to commend it—because it is the action that a virtuous or excellent person would take. The claim that some actions are intrinsically evil or wrong in themselves, never to be made right or good by circumstances or consequences, amounts to saying that there are some actions that can never warrant commending, as if adultery, stealing, or murder could be "well done!"

Against this background, we can begin to understand why casuistry is needed and important. For sometimes, even a person with a well-formed conscience—who knows quite well that adultery, stealing, and murder are wrong and can never be done right—might really not know what to feel, think, or do in a given case when it seems some evil cannot be avoided.

- The second jet is approaching the World Trade Towers on 9/11. Would it be right, morally permissible (meaning nothing stands in the way), or justified (meaning there is positive reason to go ahead) to shoot down this jet, thereby killing all the passengers aboard, in order to save the people in the towers?[26]
- Conjoined twins share a heart that can support only one, not two. Would it be right to separate the two, giving the heart to one by severing and closing off the blood vessels of the other so that the one might live?[27]
- A bomb is about to explode. Would it be right to throw yourself on it in order to save your fellow soldiers if otherwise you all will die?
- The enemy has placed its military installations close to hospitals and schools. Would it be right to bomb those installations in the pursuit of a just cause, despite the fact that many innocent persons will thereby die?

Then there are somewhat more contrived cases that are discussed again and again in the tradition.

- You are fleeing an unjust aggressor. To escape, you have to ride your horse at high speed across a narrow bridge. But there is a child in the way who would be trampled to death if you did so. Would it be right for you to ride across the bridge?[28]

Back to the case that this chapter is concerned with, would it be right to abort an eleven-week-old fetus when, otherwise, both the fetus and the mother (who has four children at home) would die? If it would be all right, should this action even be called an abortion, if, as Catholics hold, abortion falls into the category of actions that can never be anything other than evil?

Another preliminary point is that I am concerned in this chapter with the textbook formulation of the PDE. My focus falls on the textbook formulation because it was some semblance of this formulation that figured in the controversy over the Phoenix case.[29] In particular, controversy centered both on the first condition "that the action in itself from its very object be good or at least indifferent" and on the third condition "that the good effect not be produced by means of the evil effect."

A third point to note is that examples or cases do more than serve to clarify the PDE. Instead, they are needed to guide its application. Consider only the fourth condition, "that there be a proportionately grave reason for permitting the evil effect." In the contemporary literature, this so-called proportionality condition is interpreted quite differently.

On one common interpretation, what this condition calls for is weighing good and bad effects against one another; the condition is satisfied if there is reason to expect the good to compensate for the bad.[30] As the contemporary American philosopher Alison McIntyre has pointed out, however, a problem with this interpretation is that it situates the PDE within a consequentialist framework, that is, a framework within which it is *consequences* that determine the morality of an action. On this interpretation, the PDE brings to this framework a small yet, for a consequentialist, puzzling restriction: good effects must not come by way of bad effects.[31] But the agent to whom the PDE is addressed is not a consequentialist seeking permission to maximize good effects. Instead, the agent to whom the PDE is addressed is someone wondering, in good faith, whether an action that is normally prohibited on other than consequentialist grounds—for example, killing a human being, or exposing someone the risk of severe injury if not death—is likewise prohibited when it would be brought about in the pursuit of a good end. Such an agent is concerned, not simply with weighing good effects against evil effects, but with the *reasons* for the action in question, which is to say whether they are sufficiently serious to permit going ahead despite the evil that one foresees or at least risks doing.

Accordingly, the second common interpretation of the proportionality condition has more to recommend it: there must be "sufficiently serious moral reasons for doing what brings about such harms," as the Catholic philosopher Joseph Boyle puts it.[32] What this interpretation has going for it in terms of relevance, however, it lacks in terms of guidance, for according to what criteria are we to determine whether a given set of reasons counts as "sufficiently serious"?[33] The upshot, to reiterate, is that examples or cases do more than serve to clarify the PDE. It is not the case that the PDE could be understood perfectly well on its own, and examples and the like make it easier to grasp. Instead, without examples and the like to indicate what reasons count as sufficiently serious, the fourth condition of the PDE would leave us at a loss. This critical role of examples helps explain why a case like that involving Sister McBride generates such interest and controversy. What is at stake in such discussions is not only whether the facts of the case do or do not satisfy the conditions of the PDE; what is at stake is also our understanding of the PDE itself, with implications for many other cases as well.

HYSTERECTOMY, CRANIOTOMY, AND "PLACENTECTOMY"

As I have already noted, a commonly cited case in the literature on the PDE is surgery to remove a cancerous but gravid uterus: more fully, hysterectomy against uterine cancer even when a woman is pregnant.[34] This procedure is commonly thought to be permitted under the PDE since the object of the action—that is, the matter at hand to which it is directed,[35] removing the cancerous uterus—is good or at least indifferent (condition 1); the action is done with the right intention of preserving the woman's life (condition 2); the death of the fetus (which is understood to be not yet viable *ex utero*) is only foreseen and does not figure as the means toward preserving the woman's life (condition 3); and preserving the woman's life is a sufficiently serious reason to go ahead with the action despite the harm that it will also bring about and for which the agent is then responsible, though in this case not culpable (condition 4).

As for what qualifies saving the woman's life as a sufficiently serious reason, if we think of the doctors performing the hysterectomy as the woman's agents, we can perhaps invoke Aquinas's natural law justification of self-defense—though it has to be acknowleged that describing the hysterectomy as an act of self-defense is a bit of a stretch, because what one is defending oneself against is not another person but a pathology. In Aquinas's words, "An action of this kind, from which is intended the conservation of one's own life, does not have the character of being unlawful, since it is natural that one keep oneself in being as far as possible."[36] On this account, it is the prerogative of self-defense arising from the natural inclination to self-preservation that does the work of justifying the action in question.[37] Aquinas immediately adds, however, an important proviso: "Nevertheless, a particular action coming from a good intention can be rendered unlawful if it should not be proportionate to the end. And so if one uses greater violence than is necessary for defending one's life, it will be unlawful."[38] For Aquinas, in other words, the proportionality condition does not concern weighing effects against one another. Instead, what needs to be "rightly proportioned" is the act to the end; hence his statement that it is unlawful to use greater violence than is necessary to defend one's life. But he also writes yet further, lest he be thought to oppose all killing in self-defense, that it is not "necessary for salvation that a man omit an action of moderate self-defense [that is, an action proportioned to this end] in order to avoid killing another, because a man is more obliged to provide for his own life than the life of another."[39]

Hysterectomy against uterine cancer even when a woman is pregnant is commonly contrasted with fetal craniotomy in the course of labor gone tragically wrong.[40] This latter case is commonly thought *not* to be permitted under the PDE, as it appears not to satisfy both the first condition that the object of the action (puncturing, evacuating, and crushing the fetus's head) be good or at least indifferent and the third condition that the evil effect (the death of the fetus by puncturing, evacuating, and crushing its head) may not be the means to the good effect (saving the life of the woman). From this point of view, fetal craniotomy to save a woman's life, because it is done as a means, is the direct killing of an unborn child and as such gravely wrong. In brief, a hysterectomy against uterine cancer is permitted even when a woman is pregnant, but an abortion when a woman's life is endangered by complications of labor is forbidden. For, in the first case, the death of the fetus is, strictly speaking, not intended but only foreseen—it is then a so-called indirect rather than direct abortion, if it is properly called an abortion at all—whereas in the second case, the death of the fetus is intended, on the grounds that he who intends the end intends the means.

It has been suggested that the death of the fetus in the Phoenix case might likewise be categorized as an indirect abortion, or in other words as only indirectly intended. (By the way, the point of this terminology of direct and indirect intention, as Warren Quinn observed, appears to be to acknowledge the "linguistic impropriety in an agent's asserting, with a completely straight face, that a clearly foreseen harm or harming is quite *un*intended"[41]—which would be difficult to accept.) Writing in the Jesuit magazine *America* several months after the Phoenix case was made known, the bioethicist Kevin O'Rourke noted, "The hospital's ethics committee identified the pathological organ as the placenta," which "produces the hormones necessary to increase the blood volume in pregnant women" and in this case apparently had "put an intolerable strain on the woman's already weak heart."[42] Therefore, what the committee might have recommended, O'Rourke suggested, was removal of the organ in which the placenta is located, namely, the uterus, thereby making this case analogous to hysterectomy against uterine cancer even when a woman is pregnant. As a physician observed in a letter responding to O'Rourke's article, the committee might also have authorized, yet more precisely, removal of the placenta itself, a so-called placentectomy, "even though the procedure would indirectly result in the loss of the pregnancy."[43] Inasmuch as the death of the fetus would not serve as the means to saving the life of the woman—inasmuch as removing the placenta would do so—a placentectomy, too, might be cast as analogous to hysterectomy against uterine cancer and so permitted under the PDE.

At the behest of Bishop Olmsted, St. Joseph's Hospital procured an independent analysis of the case. The Catholic moral theologian Therese Lysaught was given privileged access to documentation. As it happens, according to her, "The intentional object of the procedure centered on the placenta which was medically and physiologically the cause of the crisis."[44] In other words, according to her analysis, it seems that the ethics committee *did* authorize a placentectomy. Lysaught does not claim, however, that the placenta was itself diseased. Instead, as she writes, "in this case, the normal functioning of an organ (the placenta) within a diseased network (of pulmonary arteries) created a lethal situation" not only for the mother, but for the fetus too, given that the placenta—the fetus's life-support system—was becoming hypoxic together with the mother's organs.[45]

Bishop Olmsted rejected Lysaught's analysis, and a good number of philosophers and theologians have done so as well. For example, after remarking that "the placenta is an integral organ of the fetus and not an organ extrinsic to him," despite the fact that the fetus is cut from it at birth, the moral theologian Nicanor Austriaco claims that "*pace* Lysaught, attacking the placenta *is* attacking the fetus, in the same way that attacking the fetal heart *is* attacking the fetus, and dismembering the placenta *is* dismembering the fetus, because the placenta is an integral member of the fetus," though temporarily.[46] The moral theologian Gerald Coleman claims similarly that, given that the placenta was "acting normally" and itself not pathological, the object of the procedure performed—dismembering the placenta through dilation and curettage—was "the removal of the baby and its maternal environment for the intention of saving [the mother's life]," amounting to a direct abortion comparable to a craniotomy.[47] Finally, while holding that a direct abortion was wrongly performed in this case, the moral theologian Kevin Flannery nonetheless holds out what he considers a possible solution. Though the placenta is not a shared organ like a single heart belonging to conjoined twins—unlike the twins, the mother does not need the placenta in order to live—Flannery proposes that the decidua basalis, which is the maternal interface of the placenta, might be considered part of the placenta itself, which would then be a feto-maternal organ, alone of its kind.[48] Because, on this proposal, "the decidua basalis belongs to the mother," Flannery suggests that it can be "the object of a legitimate medical procedure"—he has in mind microsurgery—on the grounds that its functioning, though normal, is killing the mother given her underlying condition.[49] And so we are back to the analogy, however extended, with the removal of the cancerous gravid uterus.

TWO PHILOSOPHICAL QUESTIONS

Let us put aside, however, the questions of whether the placenta is integral to the fetus, such that dismembering the placenta is dismembering the fetus; and whether the placenta is in fact a feto-maternal organ; and whether the analogy of placentectomy—whether directed at the placenta as a whole or only at the decidua basalis—is sufficiently analogous to a hysterectomy when a woman is pregnant such that, if the hysterectomy is permissible, the placentectomy should be too. I think one lesson that we can draw from the Phoenix case is that, so to speak, there are cases and there are cases—in other words, that cases that appear to fall clearly under this or that precedent might appear quite different after casuists have had a look! Another lesson, perhaps, is that casuistry's bad name is not altogether undeserved—at least insofar as it proceeds according to what has been called the geometric method, judging actions in view of whether they satisfy timeless, idealized, necessary conditions (like what makes a square a square, or an action a "fit" for the PDE) and seeking to justify a controversial action by examining whether it can be described in terms that satisfy the conditions in question.[50] At its best, casuistry aims to do justice to the particularities of each and every case, which earlier solutions to earlier cases might help with, but also to some extent might not.

In any event, we need to turn now to some philosophical questions that might have occurred to readers along the way. Bluntly, can we really make out a morally significant difference between the cases of hysterectomy and fetal craniotomy, such that the first would be permissible but the latter prohibited? Supporters of the hospital's decision liken placentectomy to hysterectomy (though, as we've seen, it's arguable that the analogy holds only if the surgery is directed at the decidua basalis); opponents liken it to craniotomy.

We come here to two hard philosophical questions. One hard question is what grounds the claim, in a paradigmatically permitted case like that of a hysterectomy, that the evil effect, in this case the death of the fetus, is *not* part of the intended means but instead only a foreseen side effect. Another hard question is what grounds that claim that so-called instrumental intending—intending a harm only as a means to an end—is in all cases objectionable.

FIRST PHILOSOPHICAL QUESTION: WHAT COUNTS AS MEANS?

Consider three criteria for determining what is to be counted as part of the means: a causal connection criterion (something is part of the means if it is causally connected to what is done toward an end); an inevitable connection criterion (something is part of the means if it is inevitably connected to what is done); and a "same action" criterion (something is part of the means if it is the same action as what is done).[51] The problem for the PDE is that, in a hysterectomy, as in an abortion when the woman's life is in danger, the fetus's death is *causally connected* to what is done (both the hysterectomy and the craniotomy/placentectomy cause the fetus's death); the fetus's death is *inevitably connected* to what is done; and what is done is the *same action* as killing the fetus inasmuch as an action is not just a bodily movement, but is identical "with the causing of each and every consequence to which the doer's agency in doing it extends."[52] If, then, the fetus's death is for any of these reasons an intended part of the means in an abortion when the woman's life is in danger, such as a craniotomy or a placentectomy, so too is the fetus's death in a hysterectomy. And this is a problem for the PDE because, if the case of a hysterectomy when a woman is pregnant violates the third condition of the PDE "that the good effect not be produced by means of the evil effect," what case could be permitted? The PDE would appear useless.

It might be objected that, as I remarked toward this chapter's beginning, it is not the nature of, or an essential constituent to, a hysterectomy that it kill a fetus, unless, strangely, it is chosen as a nonstandard means of abortion. By contrast, it is the nature of a craniotomy that it kill a fetus; miracles aside, craniotomies always do.

Now, it's correct that it is not the nature of a hysterectomy that it kill a fetus: it does not, after all, when a woman is not pregnant. But the problematic situation is when a woman *is* pregnant, and in this situation, it *is* the "nature" of a hysterectomy that it kill a fetus. Nicanor Austriaco, who, as we have seen, is a critic of the hospital ethics committee's decision, claims that there is "a real distinction between medical intervention where the death of the fetus is necessarily included in the choice of the physician [for example, both craniotomy and placentectomy], and intervention where the death of the fetus does not have to be included in that choice [for example, hysterectomy]."[53] But this distinction is fictional when a woman is pregnant and the physician knows she is.

A physician performing a hysterectomy in such a case could sensibly say that it was no part of what he *wanted* that a fetus die, and that he wasn't aiming for its death "directly," and that how to kill the fetus did not figure in his deliberations about how to proceed (what tools to select, etc.); but consider the following to see where the problem lies. Say that the fetus is not yet viable *ex utero*, but will be relatively soon. Say further that the woman's cancer is growing slowly, such that her life will not be at any greater risk if her hysterectomy is postponed until the fetus is viable. If her physician did *not* postpone the hysterectomy but performed it right away, not as a nonstandard means of abortion but still to save the woman's life (for she would need the hysterectomy at some point), could the death of the fetus be considered *accidental*, falling altogether outside the intention with which the physician acted, not "included in the choice" he has made? I think the answer is clearly not. The choice to perform the hysterectomy clearly includes the choice to kill the fetus.

In the case when the fetus soon will be viable and the woman's cancer is growing slowly, it seems, at least, that the proportionality condition of the PDE would not be satisfied if the hysterectomy were performed right away. Yes, saving the woman's life is a serious reason to act, but *the means in this case*—hysterectomy when she is pregnant with a fetus who will soon be viable—are surely disproportioned to the end: an act of greater violence is done than was needed in order to save the woman's life. But we need to be clear about what is done: hysterectomy when she is pregnant with a fetus who will soon be viable. *This* is the relevant description of the means, not just "hysterectomy." The "nature" of the hysterectomy is to kill the fetus. Accordingly, so, too, is the "nature" of a hysterectomy when a woman is pregnant but the circumstances are such that the surgery cannot safely be postponed. Under these different circumstances, however, the proportionality condition of the PDE does appear to be satisfied. That is, what is done does not appear to be an act of greater violence than was needed in order to save the woman's life.

It likely hardly needs saying at this point that the question of what counts as *means* in the third condition of the PDE (the good effect not be produced by means of the evil effect) quickly becomes complex. Consider, briefly this time, this further objection. It might be claimed that the death of the fetus in the hysterectomy cannot be the means to save the woman's life because the death did not itself save her life. In other words, the death did not itself have the *effect* of saving her life; instead, the hysterectomy did. This is correct, but it might be countered that the death of the fetus in a craniotomy likewise does not have the effect of saving the woman's life. A craniotomy might be needed even if the fetus has died already in the course of delivery. What saves the woman is the crushing of the fetus's skull, not the fetus's death as such, though crushing the skull does kill a fetus if it is not dead already. Similarly, it might be countered that what saves the woman dying from pulmonary hypertension is not the death of the fetus as such, but the placentectomy, which again could be needed even if the fetus had died already from lack of oxygen, though once more the procedure does kill a fetus if it is not dead already.[54] The upshot is that the three cases—hysterectomy, craniotomy, and placentectomy—once more appear more similar than different on closer examination.

MEANS, CAUSES, AND OBJECTS

One last argument needs attention before we can move on to our second philosophical question. So far, my discussion has quietly taken for granted that every cause of an effect counts as a means to that effect. In other words, my discussion has interpreted *means* in terms of *cause*. From this perspective, because a hysterectomy when a woman is pregnant, a craniotomy, and a placentectomy all cause the death of the fetus, they are *all* means, and so it appears they all run afoul of the third condition of the PDE that "the good effect not be produced by means of the evil effect," despite the common claim that a hysterectomy when a woman is pregnant is a paradigmatically permitted case. There is another interpretation of *means*, however, according to which there is likewise no necessary moral difference among these three procedures, but for the quite different reason that *none* of these procedures, though they all cause the

56

death of a fetus, necessarily count as means. On this interpretation, *while every means is a cause, not every cause is a means.* Instead, a means is an *intended cause* of an intended effect—that is, a cause that figures in what an agent proposes and then chooses to do.

The last couple of sentences need explaining. The interpretation of means that I have just presented is associated, in Catholic moral philosophy, with the school of thought known as the new natural law, articulated and defended in multiple articles and books by John Finnis, Germain Grisez, and Joseph Boyle, among others. The name *the new natural law* indicates that its proponents aspire to renew the natural law tradition advanced by Aquinas, but there is some debate whether they have retrieved Aquinas's thinking and saved it from several centuries of neo-Scholastic misinterpretation (as they sometimes claim), or developed a new theory with ties to Aquinas's thinking but significantly different from it. In any event, for Finnis, Grisez, and Boyle, it was a mistake of the neo-Scholastics of recent centuries both to reduce means to cause and to focus on what was most "immediately" and "directly" caused by an action.[55] To the contrary, "that a bad effect issues from an act more immediately and more directly than a good effect, or precedes and causes a good effect, does not by itself make the bad effect a means to the good."[56]

The key question for this school of thought is, instead, what the agent *proposes* and then chooses to do, which may not be evident from the point of view of an observer focused on cause-and-effect relationships. Finnis, an Australian-born Catholic philosopher and legal theorist, puts the point this way:

> What consequences, results, outcomes of one's choosing and doing are to be judged intended and what are to be judged side-effects [outside the intention] is not to be determined by considering which consequences…were physically immediate ("directly caused") and which not….It is settled simply by considering why one is doing what one is doing, counting as within the proposal one has adopted by choice everything which one wants for its own sake or for the sake of what one wants for its own sake.[57]

An example might help. Consider, as Finnis, Grisez, and Boyle ask us to do, a farmer who proposes to castrate a male calf "in order to change [its] hormonal constitution and thereby make it [both] fat and manageable."[58] The farmer then chooses to act on this proposal of his. Not being stupid, he foresees with certainty that the calf will also be made sterile by this action, and indeed directly and immediately so. Does the farmer intend to sterilize the calf, or does sterilizing the calf fall outside his intention, so to speak, and count instead as a side effect? Finnis, Grisez, and Boyle say that the farmer does _not_ intend to sterilize the calf, and doing so is not a means to his end. At the same time, a different farmer who goes through the same motions—that is, executes the same physical behavior—might act for different reasons, which is to say with a different intention, for example, precisely to sterilize the calf, this time foreseeing but not intending that the calf will become both fatter and more manageable.

We could also consider the differences, to take several other examples from Finnis, (1) "between jumping from the top of the World Trade Center on '9/11' to escape the oily fireball and jumping to commit suicide, (2) between shooting down a passenger plane to save a skyscraper full of people and shooting it down to kill the passengers," and (3) between craniotomy when the mother's life is at stake and partial-birth abortion elected for some different, much less pressing reason.[59] Finnis, Grisez, and Boyle claim that a surgeon performing a craniotomy to save the mother's life need not intend the baby's death as a means. Instead, what the surgeon proposes and chooses to do in such a case "is to reduce the size of the baby's head so that the baby or its corpse can be removed from the birth canal."[60] To the observer, the claim that the surgeon does not intend to kill the baby might well seem incredible. But Finnis, Grisez, and Boyle insist that the relevant point of view, for moral assessment, is that of the acting person, not that of the observer who sees only the physical behavior and can only infer, perhaps mistakenly, the intention that forms the action, or in other words, makes the physical behavior the human action it is. And they claim that

> a surgeon who performed a craniotomy and could soundly
> analyze the action, resisting the undue influence of physical

and causal factors that would dominate the perception of observers, could rightly say "No way do I intend to kill the baby" and "It is no part of my purpose to kill the baby."[61]

What is at issue here is not only what counts as means in the third condition of the PDE (that the good effect not be produced by means of the evil effect), but what counts as an *object* in the first condition of the PDE—"that the action in itself from its very object be good or at least indifferent." As I noted earlier in passing, the controversy in the Phoenix case centered on both these conditions. Following the *Catechism of the Catholic Church*, I also earlier characterized the object of an action as the matter at hand to which it is directed.[62] But I need now to say a bit more.

The new natural law's position on craniotomy is in tension with official church teaching dating from the late nineteenth century, but Finnis, Grisez, and Boyle, among others, believe both that this nineteenth-century teaching needs revision and that it is inconsistent with the best of the Catholic tradition, as reflected in more recent church teachings. In particular, they point to Pope John Paul II's 1991 encyclical *Veritatis Splendor* (*The Splendor of Truth*):

> *The morality of the human act depends primarily and fundamentally on the "object" rationally chosen by the deliberate will*, as is borne out by the insightful analysis, still valid today, made by Saint Thomas [citing *Summa theologiae* I-II, q. 18, a. 6]. In order to be able to grasp the object of an act which specifies that act morally, it is therefore necessary to place oneself *in the perspective of the acting person*....By the object of a given moral act, then, one cannot mean a process or an event of the merely physical order, to be assessed on the basis of its ability to bring about a given state of affairs in the outside world. Rather, that object is the proximate end of a deliberate decision which determines the act of willing on the part of the acting person.[63]

There are two key points here for our new natural lawyers: (1) it's only from "the perspective of the acting person" that the object of an act can be seen; (2) the *object* of an act is not merely what happens physically,

59

which is to say the motions or behavior that any observer could see. Finnis, Grisez, and Boyle think, then, that it's a mistake to hold that the first condition of the PDE rules out fetal craniotomy on the grounds that the object of the act is killing a fetus and accordingly evil. By contrast, for the new natural law, "for moral assessment and judgment, the act is just what it is...as intended, i.e. under the description it has in the proposal which the agent adopts by choice,"[64] with the upshot that "when someone chooses to do a craniotomy on a baby to save his or her mother's life in an obstetrical predicament, the morally relevant description of the act would not include killing the baby," but instead only removing the baby to save the mother's life.[65]

Needless to say, these claims are not lacking for critics; the new natural law's accounts of both *object* and *intention* have provoked long and vehement objections. Working through these objections and the new natural lawyers' replies would take us well beyond introductory philosophy and into the minutiae of medieval texts and the intricacies of action theory. So, instead, I present here my own much briefer criticism.

Some years ago, the British legal theorist H. L. A. Hart (1907–92) presented what he considered an objection to the PDE's prohibition of fetal craniotomy. "In such a case," Hart claimed, "it could be argued that it is not the death of the foetus but its removal from the body of the mother which is required to save her life," with the upshot that the death of the fetus in the course of removing it ought to be thought of "as a 'second effect,' foreseen but not used as a means to an end."[66] This claim should remind us of Finnis, Grisez, and Boyle's position. The British philosopher Phillipa Foot (1920–2010) countered, however, that Hart's claim "makes nonsense" of the PDE as there is no room, so to speak, between crushing the fetus's skull and killing it, and thus no conceptual space to apply the intend/foresee distinction (that is, to claim that the crushing of the fetus's skull was intended, but the fetus's death was strictly unintended and only foreseen).[67]

Now I think that Foot is perfectly right that there is no room between crushing the fetus's skull and killing it—crushing the fetus's skull *constitutes* killing it, such that one cannot conceivably aim at the former without aiming at the latter—but is there any more room between removing a woman's uterus and killing the previable fetus within it, such that one could conceivably aim at the former without also aiming at the latter?[68] It seems not. Perhaps it could be countered in turn that the death of the fetus does not form part of the plan in the case of a hysterectomy in the sense that the doctor performing the hysterectomy is not guided in his or her choice of instruments by the aim of killing the fetus;[69] but the doctor performing the fetal craniotomy could reply that neither is he or she guided by the aim of killing the fetus—it is the aim of removing the fetus from the woman that does the guiding in choice of instruments—and so again the hysterectomy case and the fetal craniotomy case collapse into one another. A final, oft-invoked way to distinguish the cases, the so-called test of failure, likewise fails. For example, "a good test of whether or not you intend a particular foreseen effect of an action is to suppose that, by some fluke or miracle, the action does not have the effect you foresee, and to ask whether you then consider your plan carried out and your purpose accomplished."[70] But, of course, both the doctor in the hysterectomy case and the doctor in the fetal craniotomy case could answer yes, plan carried out and purpose accomplished, should both the woman live, as the doctors had intended, and the fetus live, contrary to all expectations.

It must be admitted that there is reason to be uneasy with what might be called the picture of intention that Hart's objection operates with; I think there is, then, likewise reason to be uneasy with the new natural lawyers' account. To intend is to will an action for the sake of an end.[71] As the British philosopher J. L. Austin (1911–60) put it, roughly but as well as anybody, an intention is then "*as it were* a plan, an operation order…on which I am acting, which I am seeking to put into effect, carry out in action: only of course nothing necessarily…so full-blooded as a plan proper."[72] Now, an action counts as intentional only under the descriptions that an agent knows it falls under—so, for example, it is mistaken to claim that Oedipus intentionally killed *his father*, for Oedipus didn't know that the stranger he killed was in fact his father[73]—but this next point is just as crucial to understand: *an agent may not pick and choose which description, of those that she knows the action falls under, is to count as the one and only description under which her action is intentional.*

61

Instead, as yet another British philosopher remarked, the formidable Elizabeth Anscombe (1919–2001), "circumstances, and the immediate facts about the means you are choosing to your ends, dictate what descriptions of your intention you must admit."[74] Or again, "a man's intention in acting is not so private and interior a thing that he has absolute authority in saying *what* it is—as he has absolute authority in saying *what* he dreamt."[75] To claim otherwise is practically to invite the ridicule that Blaise Pascal, in the seventh of his *Provincial Letters* dating from 1656, heaped on casuistry, in particular on his fictional Jesuit's *grande méthode de diriger l'intention* (great method of directing the intention), permitting one to do otherwise prohibited actions on the condition that one is able to find for these same actions a licit "object."[76] From Pascal's point of view and Anscombe's as well (as arguably Aquinas's), it is a mistake to reduce the object of an action to what is physically done—John Paul II is right in *Veritatis Splendor* that "the object of a given moral act" is not just "a process or an event of the merely physical order"—*but it is equally a mistake* to reduce the object of an action to what the agent proposes to do, as if the specification of the object depended solely on the agent's purpose.[77] Yet this is just what Finnis, Grisez, and Boyle appear to do. By way of example, recall here Finnis's claim, quoted above, that "for moral assessment and judgment, the act is just what it is…as intended, i.e. under the description it has in the proposal which the agent adopts by choice,"[78] with the upshot that "when someone chooses to do a craniotomy on a baby to save his or her mother's life in an obstetrical predicament, the morally relevant description of the act would not include killing the baby."[79]

The problem here is that, in the words of a critic of the new natural law, "the object of the will is constituted *both* by the choice of the acting person *and* by the physical structure of the act"—not just its physical/material component, but also not just the acting person's purpose.[80] In other words, *what* you can say you intend is constrained by *what* it is you are physically doing, that is, the physical structure of your action. You can't reasonably and intelligibly say that, in choosing to set in motion a process or event that you know constitutes killing, what you're doing isn't killing because you don't intend to kill and have some other object in mind instead. As two other critics put it, "If realizing condition

A in and of itself entails, by virtue of the laws of nature, the realization of condition *B*, and the agent knows this, then *B* is certainly included in his intention to bring about *A*."[81] Yes, what an agent proposes to do matters morally. The same behavior might be suicide or not, murder or not. But what an agent physically does—take a fetal craniotomy—constrains his intentions and so matters morally as well. The upshot is that, from this point of view, fetal craniotomy violates both the first condition of the PDE (good or at least indifferent object) and the third condition (evil effect not a means to the good effect).

The picture of intention that Hart's objection operates with does not, then, have much to recommend it, and the new natural lawyers' account fares no better. Not pulling any punches, Anscombe calls "choosing a description under which the action is intentional, and giving the action under that description as *the* intentional act," *absurd.*[82] Yet it is not only defenders of the permissibility of fetal craniotomy who do this. So, too, do defenders of the permissibility of hysterectomy when they claim that the death of the fetus by way of the hysterectomy is, strictly speaking, not intended but only foreseen—as if one could pick and choose the descriptions under which one's action is to count as intentional. One can't. The upshot is that, if it is nonsense and bad faith for a doctor performing the fetal craniotomy to claim that she intends only to remove the fetus, which it certainly does appear to be, it appears to be equally nonsense and bad faith for a doctor performing the hysterectomy to claim that she intends only to remove the uterus. And so we are back to the same problem for the PDE that we saw earlier: if the case that is nearly always put forth as the paradigmatically permitted case under the PDE—hysterectomy when a woman is pregnant—does not in fact pass muster, what use is the PDE?

One last bit of business before we move on: recall that Finnis asks us to consider the differences (1) "between jumping from the top of the World Trade Center on '9/11' to escape the oily fireball and jumping to commit suicide, (2) between shooting down a passenger plane to save a skyscraper full of people and shooting it down to kill the passengers," and (3) between craniotomy when the mother's life is at stake and partial-birth abortion elected for some different, much less pressing reason. I

think we can make sense of the differences even if we reject the new natural law's account of intentional action. Take the first of Finnis's cases.
Does the person jumping from the top of one of the twin towers to escape
the fireball intend to commit suicide? Well, the person's *principal aim* in
jumping is certainly not to kill himself; it's to avoid being killed by the
fireball. But it's hard to imagine that the person does not intend to die in
a different way, namely, by falling one hundred floors. In other words, it
seems that, imagining the situation from the perspective of the acting person and taking into account what, physically, he does, we have to
acknowledge that, yes, he does intend to kill himself—he doesn't only
"foresee" that jumping one hundred floors will bring about his death—
though he hardly went out of his way to put himself in this situation
where he will die one way or the other. To put this point another way,
killing himself is not an aim that he brought with him to work, so to
speak, and had been looking to put into effect. He was not up to no good.
So, yes, he does intend to die, but not in the same way that a suicide does.
By contrast, the intention is, as it were, forced on him by the awful circumstances—which leads us to be unwilling to call what he does *suicide*,
though there is no sense in denying that he knows what he is choosing to
do is to kill himself. In her oft-cited book *Intention*, Anscombe speaks
once, rather cryptically, of circumstances that "in some way…contradict
the intention."[83] I come back to this notion toward the chapter's end.

SECOND PHILOSOPHICAL QUESTION: IS "INSTRUMENTAL INTENDING" ALWAYS OBJECTIONABLE?

Let us turn at last to the second philosophical question that I noted:
what grounds the claim that so-called instrumental intending—intending
an evil only as a means to an end—is in all cases objectionable. Some
counterexamples might lead us to think twice about this claim. Imagine
a dentist who intends to inflict temporary but not insignificant pain, not
as an end in itself, but as the only effective means to discover a patient's
areas of sensitivity (in other words, as a diagnostic tool).[84] Or imagine a

censor of obscene literature who, in order to detect the obscenities from which he intends to protect the reading public, must allow and even intend for illicit thoughts to arise in his mind, not for the prospect of the pleasure they provide, but as the only effective means to his end.[85] Is the dentist morally in the wrong on the grounds that evil effects may not be means to good effects? Is the censor? I assume that it is unlikely that we would want to say that the dentist is morally in the wrong. We might have qualms about the censor, but not I think because he is allowing himself pleasure as a means to his end, but because we might have qualms about the end of censorship. Of course, we would be highly critical, to say the least, of a dentist who sought to inflict pain as an end in itself—he would be a sadist!—and we might also be critical of a censor—in any event other censors likely would be—who did the job precisely for what might be called its side benefits. If nothing else, he would be a hypocrite. But here is the point: the third condition of the PDE does not, on its own, give us reason to think that instrumental intending—intending an evil only as a means to an end—is in all cases objectionable. Sometimes doing a lesser evil appears justifiable as a means of preventing a greater evil. We need to call on other moral principles to judge the actions in question.

Another, stronger counterexample can be taken from Aquinas.[86] Assuming that they are fighting for a just cause,[87] and that they are motivated by this just cause and not by malice,[88] soldiers may rightly aim to kill an enemy, not only because doing so may be necessary to the end of self-defense (that is, not only as a means), but as an independent end. In other words, soldiers in war may rightly kill enemies even when doing so is not strictly necessary for self-defense or for winning this or that battle. Taking the enemy prisoner is surely the better moral course when possible, but the enemy may refuse surrender and have a chance at escape. In that case, killing the enemy may be not only permitted (nothing stands in the way) but justifiable (there is, moreover, positive reason to proceed). The wider public interest of winning the war—otherwise put, the wider public interest of not *losing* the war, which would be a great evil— justifies the lesser evil of killing one's fellow man. I say more about Aquinas's argument on this point in the next chapter, and much more about war in chapter 4.

The contemporary American philosopher Thomas Nagel has claimed, in an oft-cited discussion, "To aim at evil, even as a means, is to have one's action guided by evil." Further, to be guided by evil is wrong, since "the essence of evil is that it should *repel* us" and thus move us to work "toward its elimination rather than toward its maintenance."[89] If the question, however, is why it is objectionable to aim at evil only as a means, then Nagel has not answered this question, but begged it by simply stating without explanation that even aiming at evil as a means is "to have one's action guided by [it]."[90] Moreover, as we have seen with my counterexamples, there is reason to doubt this claim: surely it is nonsensical to say that, for example, the dentist who inflicts pain only as a means is guided by evil in what he does, though this claim would be perfectly right for a dentist who inflicted the same pain as an end.[91]

Consider one last example in order to determine whether aiming at evil only as a means is to have one's action guided by evil. Imagine a case of self-defense where killing the attacker is "moderate" or "rightly proportioned" to the end of saving one's life. In such a case, assuming of course that one has not already been mortally wounded, killing the attacker is admittedly a means toward saving one's life, but killing the attacker is not a first, intermediate step in a succession of actions. We need to be careful here not to assimilate unlike cases. Unlike the destruction of human embryos for the purpose of curing disease sometime in the future, killing the attacker with the intention of saving one's life is not a means *prior to* the achievement of this end. Instead, killing the attacker and saving one's life are the same action, only differently described. For one does not kill the attacker (call this action 1) and then, thereafter, save one's life (call this action 2). Instead, killing the attacker is *immediately* saving one's life. It might be countered—rightly—that the killing is initiated before the saving of one's life is realized; but it is also right that the initiation of the killing is the initiation of the saving of one's life. From the point of view of the agent acting with the intention to save his or her life, there is not first one action (killing) and then another (self-defense). Instead, there is one, indivisible action guided by the intention of self-defense.[92] To claim, to the contrary, that the agent is guided here by evil seems simply false. Instead, it is the good end of saving one's life that does the guiding.

Accordingly, it is misleading to say that one is doing evil here that good may come. What one is doing is seeking to save one's life—full stop. There is no question, then, of contravening the authority of Saint Paul.[93]

REVISIONS

There are, to conclude, a number of further questions to consider. One is whether we should "do away" with the textbook formulation of the PDE,[94] seeing that it apparently does not withstand philosophical scrutiny. To be clear, I am *not* proposing in this chapter that we keep the PDE but simply throw out its third condition. Such a proposal would effectively reduce the PDE to the fourth proportionality condition, inasmuch as the third condition (evil effect not a means to good effect) may be understood as an elaboration of the second condition (rightful intention) and even the first (good or at least indifferent object). In other words, I am not at all advocating that the end always justifies the means—though I have proposed, in my counterexamples to the claim that instrumental harming is in all cases objectionable, that in fact an end may *sometimes* justify a means. On what grounds an end may justify a means, please note, is a different question! Here we must engage in what the historian and jurist John Noonan calls the business of line drawing, which "is the ordinary business of moralists and lawmakers."[95] Line drawing consists in saying that up to this or that point, "such-and-such a value will be preserved, but after that point another value will have play."[96]

I also am not suggesting that there is no difference between intention and foresight: more precisely, that to foresee an effect is necessarily to intend it. Not so! A doctor might intend to relieve a patient's symptoms by prescribing a particular medicine while foreseeing the likelihood of significant side effects. So long as there is good reason to prescribe the medicine nonetheless—so long as the patient's symptoms warrant the medicine, and there is no safer and similarly effective medicine the doctor might choose instead—the doctor is justified in going ahead, and he or she can rightly claim that what is intended is to relieve the patient's symptoms, not to inflict the side effects. But this chapter has been concerned with importantly different cases: where effects that an agent would rather not cause—like the death of a fetus—*necessarily follow*, or follow *by nature*, from what he or she chooses to do in the circumstances. In these cases, it is not open to the agent to say that he or she only foresees the death of the fetus, for example, and does not really intend it. At most, the agent could say that the death of the fetus is *indirectly intended*— terminology that, as I noted earlier, acknowledges the "linguistic impropriety in an agent's asserting, with a completely straight face, that a clearly foreseen harm or harming is quite *un*intended."[97]

Finally, I am not at all suggesting that there is no moral difference between, for example, (1) terror and obliteration bombing, on the one hand, and (2) so-called strategic bombing, on the other, or between (1) preparing a narcotic in order to kill a suffering man and (2) preparing a narcotic in order to relieve a man's suffering, with the foreseen effect of hastening his death. But the moral difference is not even partly explained by claiming that, in the second case of each of these examples, the evil effect is not part of the intended means. For we have not seen an argument that shows this to be so. And the moral difference is also not even partly explained by claiming that, in the first case of each of these examples, the evil effect is intended instrumentally. For we have not seen an answer to the question of why instrumental intending is in all cases objectionable.

A further question is how to judge the Phoenix case involving Sister McBride. The Phoenix diocese concluded that the hospital ethics committee's decision to permit an abortion could not be justified under the PDE in its textbook formulation. Given the problems with the PDE, however, we might well wonder what it matters whether the decision could or could not be justified in its terms.

So (1) should we do away with the PDE, and (2) how to judge the Phoenix case? What is needed to answer both these questions, I think, is some insight into the practice and development of casuistry, the tradition of moral reasoning from which the PDE issued. As its name suggests, casuistry is case-based: at its best, it proceeds not "geometrically," by subsuming cases under timeless principles, but "taxonomically," which is to say by comparing, contrasting, and evaluating "the contours of one case…against other cases" considered to be already successfully resolved.[98]

(Taxonomy is the practice of classification.) Over time, principles like the PDE may then arise, but the important point, as the Jesuit moral theologian James Keenan has put it, is that "the principle is a shorthand expression of the taxonomic relationship among a number of paradigm cases" and does not itself justify the decisions made in these cases, which have an independent, internal certitude that the principle rather reflects.[99] The Jesuit moral theologian John C. Ford made much the same point some years ago: the PDE is "not…a mathematical formula, nor an analytical principle. It is a practical formula which synthesizes an immense amount of moral experience, and serves as an efficient guide in countless perplexing cases"—so long as it is "applied by a hand well practiced in moral principles and moral solutions."[100]

Casuistry, however, is vulnerable to degeneration into moral legalism, with prudence or practical wisdom giving way to rote application of rules under the guidance of reputed ethics experts.[101] Whereas the PDE should have what Keenan calls "a heuristic and confirming function"[102]— suggesting that, if a new case satisfies its conditions, there is reason to think that we can be as certain about it as earlier thinkers were about the paradigm cases—what happens instead, when moral legalism prevails, is that the PDE is invested with authority of its own and made into the up-or-down test of a case's morality. To put the point somewhat dramatically, the moral wisdom reflected in the PDE is replaced by an image of itself, the principle so derived, with the danger of distorting our evaluation of new cases that do not satisfy this principle and might better be resolved by looking to other cases and principles altogether.

Another principle within Catholic moral thought is the principle of choosing the lesser evil. This principle has a long, controverted history in Catholic thought.[103] It is typically invoked nowadays when a person is set on doing an evil one way or the other. In such circumstances, it is considered permissible to urge that person to choose the lesser evil.[104] Call this the principle of lesser evil in its *narrow* form. So, for example, Pope Benedict XVI opined in 2010 that a male prostitute might use a condom, despite the fact that official church teaching condemns the use of artificial contraception, as "a first step in the direction of a moralization, a first assumption of responsibility, on the way toward recovering an awareness that not everything is allowed and that one cannot do whatever one wants."[105] The principle of lesser evil has also long been invoked in circumstances where an evil is bound to occur whatever one does, though *not* because one has committed a prior misdeed or is currently up to no good. In other words, the principle of lesser evil has also been invoked in situations of genuine moral perplexity, where one really can see no good way forward, and again *not* because one has gotten oneself into this box by doing wrong earlier or being up to no good now. Call this the principle of lesser evil in its *wide* form. There is no question here, it must be noted, of doing evil that good may come: in the circumstances in question, one is not free to do good, but only to choose between evils.

The fundamental question separating proponents and opponents of the principle of lesser evil in its wide form seems to be whether there are in fact such situations of genuine moral perplexity. Is the moral universe so broken that innocent persons might find themselves having to choose between two evils, with no good to be had? Would God allow such a situation to come to pass, or does God's providence ensure that the innocent, at least, will never face such a desperate choice? Deep theological waters surround this question, and they are likely best entered through literature, rather than systematic philosophy or theology.[106]

I am afraid that the Phoenix case in which Sister McBride became ensnared suggests to me that there are situations of genuine moral perplexity, where the choices come down to evil on one side (do nothing: mother and baby die) and evil on the other (perform a placentectomy: baby dies). Imagine that you are Sister McBride. If you believe that one must never intentionally do evil—if intentionally doing evil must absolutely be avoided—it seems you must say to the mother (in the hearing of her husband with four children at home and the doctors and nurses at her bedside), "Here you are called to martyrdom: that is, to witness to the truth that no one can do evil that good may come," or, "It is not right to do what God's law qualifies as evil in order to draw some good from it," or some sentence of this kind. Citing Pope John Paul's reflections on martyrdom in *Veritatis Splendor*,[107] one philosopher has in fact suggested that martyrdom was the only just choice in the Phoenix case,[108] and apparently that is what Bishop Olmsted and his advisors believed. But remember that, in the circumstances appropriate to what I've called the wide form of the principle of the lesser evil, there is no question of doing evil that good may come. <u>Instead, one is not free to do good</u>, but only to choose between evils. And here I think we also do well to remember Elizabeth Anscombe's reflections on circumstances that "in some way…contradict the intention."[109]

The basic idea is the following.[110] If there are already under way causal events that will bring about two awful effects, and one of those two effects is inevitable, if you act to hasten the inevitable effect on the grounds that doing so is a lesser evil than allowing both effects to come to pass, you certainly do intend to bring about that effect, but there is also a sense in which that was not your intention, because after all it was forced on you by the circumstances. To put flesh on this framework, if there are already under way causal events that will bring about the deaths of both mother and child, and no matter what you do, the death of the child is inevitable—that is, whether you let the events unfold, or intervene by performing a placentectomy—it would be a mistake to charge you with murdering the child should you intervene on the grounds that hastening the child's death is a lesser evil than allowing both mother and child to die. Yes, you did intend to kill the child; <u>but</u>, as in the case of jumping from the top of one of the twin towers to escape the fireball, <u>the intention was, as it were, forced on you by the awful circumstances.</u> You were *not* up to no good; you did not bring this intention with you to work, so to speak. So, yes, you certainly intended to kill the child, but in another way that was not *your* intention at all—because you were made to choose between evils, very much against yourself. In brief, the circumstances "in some way…contradict the intention." Accordingly, you are not a murderer—I cannot imagine calling the doctor or the mother or Sister McBride *that*—though it is imaginable that the trauma of the circumstances might well affect you for life.

In the end, I think several lessons can be drawn from the tragedy of the Phoenix case. First, it <u>shows the great need for and importance</u> of casuistry. For some cases will prove perplexing to even the best-formed conscience. The person of good faith and conscience is best honored and served by careful attention to the particularities of the case that perplexes him or her, which is what casuistry at its best does. Second, the Phoenix case suggests that there is reason for the United States Conference of Catholic Bishops to consider the incorporation of the wide form of the principle of the lesser evil into the *Ethical and Religious Directives*. The PDE, which after all is not a doctrine fallen from heaven, is called on far too often to do far too much.[111] For purposes of helping prudence prevail, there is more work to be done than the PDE can do.[112] Third and finally, the Phoenix case indicates that virtue, or moral excellence, is not simply a matter of following all the rules, such as the PDE or, for that matter, the narrow and wide forms of the principle of the lesser evil. The virtuous person, who is "up to good," has insight into the purposes and limitations of the rules of morality. We might even say that he or she *is* the rule and as such discloses to us how to be and act. But here we come again to matters beyond this chapter.

he/she is the = rule

QUESTIONS FOR FURTHER REFLECTION/PAPER QUESTIONS

(1) Imagine that you work for Saint Joseph's Hospital and Medical Center in Phoenix, Arizona. What's more, you're on the hospital's ethics committee. In the aftermath of the 2009 controversy involving Sister Margaret McBride, Bishop Thomas Olmsted revoked Saint Joseph's affiliation with the Catholic Church on the grounds that the hospital was not in compliance with the *Ethical and Religious Directives for Catholic Healthcare Services*. In hopes of reestablishing the hospital's affiliation with the church, the ethics committee has decided to make a case for a change to the *Directives*. In particular, the committee would like to see the *Directives* incorporate the so-called wide form of the principle of choosing the lesser evil.

You've been charged to make the case. Write a letter addressed both to Bishop Olmsted and to the Committee on Doctrine of the United States Conference of Catholic Bishops. Why should the *Directives* incorporate the wide form of the principle of lesser evil? Further, just how should the principle be framed, and where might it appear in the text of the *Directives* (which you must then consult)? Be sure to anticipate and counter objections.

(2) Consider the case, mentioned in passing toward this chapter's beginning, of conjoined twins sharing a heart that can support only one, not two. Would it be morally permissible to separate the two, giving the heart to one by severing and closing off the blood vessels of the other so that the one might live? Use the principle of double effect to evaluate this case. Be sure to distinguish two interpretations of *means*: according to one, every cause of an effect is a means to that effect; according to the other, a means is strictly an intended cause of an intended effect. Also distinguish two interpretations of the *object* of an action: according to one, the object of an action is constituted by the acting person's purpose; according to the other, the object is "constituted *both* by the choice of the acting person *and* by the physical structure of the act"—not just its physical/material component, but also not just the acting person's purpose.[113] How do you come down in this case, and why? Be sure to anticipate and counter objections to your position.

(3) It has been argued that abortions via drugs like RU-486 and Ella may be considered *indirect* abortions.[114] If so, it might further be argued that the use of these drugs should be morally licit at Catholic hospitals when women either have been raped and might then become pregnant or have already become pregnant from rape. Ella prevents the embryo from implanting in the uterus; RU-486 detaches the fetus from the uterus. But can abortions via drugs like RU-486 and Ella really be considered *indirect*? That is, can this argument be made and defended? Speak to this question by bringing to bear the principle of double effect. Be sure to keep in mind the two interpretations of *means* and the two interpretations of the *object* of an action. Also be sure to anticipate and counter objections to your position.

CHAPTER 3

AQUINAS, DOUBLE-EFFECT REASONING, AND THE PAULINE PRINCIPLE

Like all moral philosophy, Catholic moral philosophy is concerned with controversies and cases, as we've seen in the first two chapters. As a long-standing tradition, however, Catholic moral philosophy is also concerned with the interpretation of texts by figures recognized as especially insightful and thus authoritative. Some readers likely will have noticed that Thomas Aquinas has been cited more than a few times so far: in the introduction, in the first chapter, and in the last chapter, nearly a dozen times, again and again and again. In fact, Aquinas appears in every chapter of this book. As authoritative figures in the tradition go, he's unrivaled. And in case there is any confusion whether this book is a work of philosophy rather than theology, let it be noted that Aquinas appears more often here than either Paul, or even Jesus.

The next chapter, on war, reflects some on whether this is at all problematic for a tradition that after all calls itself Catholic and claims to be Christian. But this chapter, much briefer than the last, has a different focus: the interpretation of a key text by Aquinas. This chapter is also quite closely related to the last, so much so that it might be considered an appendix to chapter 2. Readers eager to move on to another controversy might then go directly to chapter 4.

SELF-DEFENSE AND DOUBLE EFFECT, ALL OVER ALL OVER AGAIN

Recall the circumstances of the Phoenix case discussed in the last chapter (or reread the chapter's opening pages). If Saint Joseph's Hospital wanted to try to defend the abortion in this case, one way is to appeal to the ethics of self-defense.[1] By way of example, the philosopher Judith Jarvis Thomson writes in her notorious, celebrated "Defense of Abortion," "It cannot seriously be thought to be murder if the mother performs an abortion on herself to save her life. It cannot seriously be said that she *must* refrain, that she *must* sit passively by and wait for her death."[2] Thomson also writes that, given that the fetus who threatens the mother's life is in the mother's *own* body, third parties (that is, doctors) may rightly act to defend her life, much as third parties (for example, police officers) would be right and even obliged to intervene on behalf of the person to whom an item of property belongs when there is a dispute between that person and another over possession of the item in order to survive.[3] Thomson gives the example of a coat. Admittedly, unlike the person to whom the coat does not belong, the fetus is what is called formally innocent. It has not set its mind, or "formed" its will, on doing any wrong. Arguably, however, the fetus may be seen as what is called a materially unjust aggressor. *What* it's doing—that "matter" at hand—is imperiling its mother's life, and Thomson at least sees the mother as within her rights to defend herself.

In Catholic moral thought, the authority on the ethics of self-defense is, unsurprisingly, Aquinas. The *Catechism* cites and quotes his discussion in his *Summa Theologiae* (II-II, q. 64, a. 7) in order to articulate the church's position (§§2263–2264). Aquinas does not explicitly formulate the principle of double effect (PDE) in his discussion of the ethics of self-defense, but it is easy to read the PDE as we have come to know it into Aquinas's discussion and in particular to understand him as concurring with Paul's dictum—which we know already as the Pauline principle[4]—that evil is not to be done that good may come. If this reading is right, then Bishop Olmsted might have cited Aquinas, too, in his criticism of the hospital, the Catholic status of which he went on to revoke. Further, if this reading is right, my argument drawing from Elizabeth Anscombe at the end of the last chapter would be a little shaken. For while Anscombe is becoming authoritative in some circles, she is no rival to Aquinas, as Anscombe herself would have been the first to say.

To be clear, an argument in philosophy stands or falls on its own merits. Appeal to authority has no place. Accordingly, it's not the case that, if an argument contradicts whatever Aquinas says, that argument must be wrong. There is so much that Aquinas says—on slavery, religious liberty, church-state relations, democracy, the inferiority of women—that the church now ignores, disagrees with, even repudiates. But what Aquinas has to say as a philosopher about the nature of human action is different. A Catholic philosopher who disagreed with him on some central question here would go on being a philosopher, but it's possible she might argue herself out of the church. As one moral theologian has claimed,

> were the Church to put forward ideas incompatible with Aquinas's core insights into the nature of human action, she would be contradicting herself, for magisterial history [that is, the history of official church teaching] is not only replete with statements about the moral character of particular actions that presuppose a Thomistic analysis but also contains endorsements of that method of analysis itself.[5]

At the same time, what have been called the "Thomistic credentials" of double-effect reasoning are hardly to be taken for granted,[6] and there is no little disagreement about just what should be considered Aquinas's "core insights" on human action.[7] As noted in the last chapter, it is widely acknowledged that textbook formulations of the PDE are descended from sixteenth- and seventeenth-century commentaries on Aquinas's theory of action.[8] What has been disputed for some years now is whether Aquinas himself can be counted among the ranks of double-effect thinkers.

More precisely, what is disputed is whether Aquinas in fact holds what, in textbook formulations of the PDE, is typically presented as its third condition: as readers by this point know, that the evil effect of an action with two effects may not be the *means* to the good effect, or (to transpose the terms) that the good effect may not be *produced* by the evil effect.[9] In other words, what is disputed is whether Aquinas does in fact hold the so-called Pauline principle, which the third condition of the PDE is supposed to gloss. In the words of the nineteenth-century French Jesuit Jean-Pierre Gury (1801–86), considered a key figure in the formulation of the PDE as we know it,[10] "It is permitted to posit a good or indifferent cause, from which immediately follows a twofold effect, one good but the other evil, if there is a proportionately serious reason, and the end of the agent is honest, namely, does not intend the bad effect."[11] Elaborating the condition that the good effect must follow "at least equally immediately from the cause," Gury reasons that

> if the cause has a bad effect directly and immediately and the good effect comes only mediately from that bad effect, then good is sought from evil. And it is never lawful to perpetrate evil, however slight, in order to procure any good, for according to the commonly received rule of the Apostle stated in Romans 3:8, *Never are evils to be done, so that goods might come.*[12]

This chapter reconsiders whether Aquinas is rightly read as a double-effect thinker and in particular whether it is right to understand him as concurring with Paul's dictum that evil is not to be done that good may come. The chapter initially covers some well-trodden ground, but then diverges from most of the literature. In the end, I focus my argument, not on the meaning of the Latin term *praeter intentionem* (outside the intention), as recent work has done, but on what to make of Aquinas's position that, though the private citizen may not intend to kill a man in self-defense, those holding public authority, like soldiers and police officers, may rightly do so. In other words, I focus on what bearing this passage should have on our understanding of Aquinas's discussion as a whole. And I argue in the end that, in light of this passage, we *cannot* attribute to Aquinas the third condition of the PDE in its textbook formulation.

WHAT IS UNINTENDED

To turn then to the text, the question that Aquinas poses is whether it is lawful for a person to kill another in self-defense. Aquinas answers,

Nothing prohibits that there be two effects of one action, of which only one would be intended [*in intentione*], but the other unintended [or "outside the intention": *praeter intentionem*]. Morals actions, however, are specified according to that which is intended, not from what is unintended [*praeter intentionem*], since this is incidental [*per accidens*].... Therefore, from the action of someone defending oneself can follow two effects, one indeed the conservation of one's own life, the other however the killing of the attacker. Therefore an action of this kind, from which is intended the conservation of one's own life, does not have the character of being unlawful, since it is natural that one keep oneself in being as far as possible.[13]

Note that what does the justificatory work here is not merely that one's intention is to save oneself, rather than to kill the attacker, but the permissibility under natural law to "keep oneself in being."[14] A more specific question that Aquinas does not explicitly address in the passage that I have quoted, however, is whether it is permissible to *aim* to kill an attacker in the course of defending oneself. There is one way of playing out this question such that the answer appears to be clearly no. If, in the course of defending oneself, one's focus, so to speak, shifts from self-defense to the pursuit of the death of the attacker as an end in itself, then aiming to kill the attacker would appear impermissible. For it is no longer done in the pursuit or toward the end of self-defense, which has dropped away as the end in sight. Instead, one's aim, it appears, is purely and simply murder. In these circumstances, inflicting deadly harm on the attacker would indeed have two effects—the attacker's death and one's self-preservation—but now one's self-preservation is the incidental or secondary effect to one's main aim, the death of the attacker.

But the question can be played out differently. Say one's focus remains on self-defense, but one realizes, with as much certainty as is possible in such circumstances, that the only way to stay alive is to kill the attacker. (Imagine, though I apologize for the image, that the attacker is a lawless militant bent on raping and killing.) May one aim, then, to kill the attacker *as the means* of self-defense?

If we read the textbook formulation of the PDE, in particular its third condition that the evil effect may not be a means to the good effect, back into Aquinas's discussion, then it seems that we must answer no, it is not permissible to aim to kill the attacker as the means of self-defense, even though it is the end of self-defense that is guiding one's actions. Of course, this answer follows only if we interpret *means* in terms of *cause*. On this interpretation, which is Gury's above, every cause of an effect counts as a means to that effect. But readers of chapter 2 will know that there is another interpretation of *means* according to which, while every means is a cause, not every cause is a means. Instead, on this interpretation, a means is an *intended cause* of an intended effect—that is, a cause that figures in what an agent proposes and then chooses to do. Here is the long quotation on this point from John Finnis that we considered in chapter 2:

> What consequences, results, outcomes of one's choosing and doing are to be judged intended and what are to be judged side-effects *praeter intentionem* ["outside the intention"] is not to be determined by considering which consequences…were physically immediate ("directly caused") and which not.…It is settled simply by considering why one is doing what one is doing, counting as within the proposal one has adopted by choice everything which one wants for its own sake or for the sake of what one wants for its own sake.[15]

Readers also know already, from chapter 2, that this account of intentional action is not lacking for critics, including me. I put aside here these criticisms to note simply that, on this account, the killing of the attacker need not be intended. Instead, what is intended may be strictly to do what needs to be done in order to stop the attacker, even if that amounts to killing him or her.

Interestingly, this is just how some older moralists read Aquinas's discussion,[16] and it has been more recently supported by Joseph Boyle's interpretation of what *praeter intentionem* should be taken to mean in this context. Recall that Aquinas writes, "Nothing prohibits that there be two effects of one action, of which only one would be intended [*in intentione*], but the other unintended [*praeter intentionem*], since this is incidental [*per accidens*]." According to Boyle's synthesis of a number of Aquinas's texts, it is not the case that only infrequent or accidental concomitants of an action count as *praeter intentionem*.[17] Instead, while effects that follow always or for the most part from an action cannot be altogether separated from the agent's intention, they need not be per se intended "and thus," Boyle rather quickly concludes, "can be called *praeter intentionem*."[18] The upshot is that an agent may rightly act in such a way that will bring about the attacker's death. The new natural lawyers' position toward fetal craniotomy—as we know, they think it can be permitted under the PDE rightly understood—serves as a striking example.

Boyle's interpretation of *praeter intentionem*, however, is doubtful. In support of his position, Boyle must show that effects joined always or for the most part to an action can count as *praeter intentionem* for Aquinas. But Boyle lacks the textual support to make this move. Aquinas does write in his article on self-defense that what is incidental or *per accidens* to an action is *praeter intentionem*, and in another text, he writes that an evil joined always or for the most part to a good need not be intended per se or "in itself."[19] But he does *not* claim that evil not intended per se is, itself, *per accidens* and thus *praeter intentionem*.[20] In other words, Aquinas does not himself say that effects joined always or for the most part to an action can be *praeter intentionem*. Instead, Boyle constructs this argument himself.

Whatever the ultimate verdict on the new natural law's account of intention, there is a Gury-like reading of Aquinas's text—which is to say, a reading that takes every cause of an effect to be a means to that effect—in support of the position that Aquinas holds it is *not* permissible to aim to kill the attacker as the means of self-defense. On this reading, what Aquinas should be understood to permit is not killing as a means to the end of saving one's life, but only so-called risked homicide: "chancing" the attacker's life in self-defense, or "knowingly and willingly"—in a word, intentionally—exposing him to the risk of death, even very likely death.[21] According to Thomas Cavanaugh, this reading allows us to "discern" in

Aquinas's discussion the "core" of the PDE, including the condition that the agent "does not intend the evil as a means or as an end," where *means* is interpreted, as Gury does, in terms of *cause*.[22]

But Cavanaugh's reasoning seems flawed. Even if we allow that Aquinas holds it is not permissible to aim to kill the attacker as a means of self-defense (which I dispute shortly), if instead we read Aquinas as permitting only exposing the attacker to the *risk* of death, we cannot rightly attribute to him the third condition of the PDE that the evil effect may not be a means to the good effect. For, intentionally exposing someone to the risk of death, say by shooting or stabbing him or her in the chest, is an "evil effect." In chancing the attacker's death by shooting or stabbing him or her, what the agent does is to use this evil effect (the exposure of the attacker to the risk of death by being shot or stabbed) as the means to the good of self-preservation. So, on this reading, while Aquinas may hold that it is not permissible to aim to kill the attacker as a means of self-defense (which, to repeat, I dispute shortly), he cannot be understood to hold the more abstract third condition of the PDE that the evil effect may not be the means to the good effect, where *means* is interpreted in terms of *cause* (that is, where every cause of an effect is thought to count as a means).[23]

WHAT IS INTENDED

As Joseph Mangan observed some years ago, a key difficulty in making sense of Aquinas's discussion lies in knowing whether "'intendere [to intend], when spoken of the will, refers *only* to the ultimate end of action," or whether it refers *also* to the means to the ultimate end.[24] Texts by Aquinas can be cited on both sides of this question,[25] which becomes pressing when we try to understand the long, second-to-last sentence of Aquinas's discussion, where he contrasts the situation of a private citizen with that of a public authority. So let us turn to that passage now.

After having commented that it is not "necessary for salvation that a man omit an action of moderate self-defense in order to avoid killing another, since a man is more obliged to provide for his own life than the life of another,"[26] Aquinas goes on,

But because it is unlawful to kill a man, except by the public authority on account of the common good…, it is unlawful that a man intend to kill a man to defend himself, except for one who has public authority, who, while intending to kill a man for his defense, refers this to the public good, as is clear in a soldier fighting against enemies or an officer of the law fighting against thieves.[27]

This is, to say the least, a difficult sentence. If we take Aquinas to hold that "he who intends the end intends the means"—in other words, if we take *intendere* to refer both to the ultimate end and to the means to that end—then the statement that it is not lawful for a private citizen to intend to kill a man in self-defense prohibits the private citizen's aiming to kill, not only as an end, but also as a means of self-defense. Yet, even on this reading, which Mangan embraces,[28] we still cannot attribute to Aquinas the more abstract third condition of the PDE that the evil effect may not be the means to the good effect—a point that, remarkably, Mangan apparently did not see. For Aquinas allows that someone with public authority, like a soldier or a police officer, may intend to kill in self-defense. Again, *if* we take *intendere* to refer *both* to the ultimate end *and* to the means to that end, then we must take Aquinas's allowing soldiers and police officers to intend to kill in self-defense to mean that a public authority may kill *both* as an end *and* as a means. So, on this reading, there is no general rule against aiming to kill only as a means; instead, there is a rule against a private citizen's aiming to kill only as a means. Just why must strike us as puzzling. To say that the public authority is responsible for the public good is not to say enough. For if it is the case, as advocates of the Pauline principle claim, that to intend to kill as a means is to be guided by evil and as such impermissible, it stands to reason that neither the private citizen nor the public authority should be permitted to intend to kill as a means, whether in self-defense or in defense of the public good.

The other way of reading the passage eliminates this puzzle. If we take *intendere* to refer *only* to the ultimate end, then the statement that it is not lawful for a private citizen to intend to kill in self-defense means that the private citizen, unlike the public authority, may not aim at killing as an end in itself, though he or she is not prohibited from aiming at it only in view of its instrumental value in self-defense (that is, *only* as a means to this end, or *incidental* to this end). By contrast, someone with public authority like a soldier or a police officer, while acting in self-defense, may also lawfully pursue killing the attacker as an end in itself, which is to say independently of its contribution to self-defense, inasmuch as it may contribute to the public good (or, in Aquinas's terms, inasmuch as it may be referred to the public good).

To elaborate the first of Aquinas's examples, think of soldiers in battle, an example that we likewise considered in chapter 2. Assuming that they are fighting for a just cause, and that they are motivated by this just cause and not by malice, they may rightly aim to kill an enemy, not only because doing so may be necessary to the end of self-defense (that is, not only as a means), but as an independent end. The reason is that killing the enemy, even if it is not strictly necessary for self-defense in this or that battle, may serve the wider public interest of winning the war. Here, direct killing—again assuming that one's cause is just, that one is not motivated by malice, and that the enemy is liable to violence—is not murder, but a justifiable act of war. On this reading, taking *intendere* to refer only to the ultimate end, the private citizen and the public authority alike may aim to kill as a means to self-defense. The difference is that the public authority may aim to kill also as an end—that is, he may make killing his goal over and above self-defense—in light of his higher responsibility for the public good.

The upshot is that, on one reading or the other, we cannot attribute to Aquinas the third condition of the PDE, or the PDE itself as we nowadays know it in its textbook formulation, at least when *means* is interpreted in terms of *cause*. Others have argued for this conclusion on different grounds.[29] On what I take to be the stronger reading of his text, we also cannot attribute to Aquinas the position that aiming to kill in self-defense is prohibited where so aiming is the only way to stay alive. Instead, for the private citizen, though not for the public authority, it is aiming to kill as an end in itself, *over and above* the aim of saving one's life, that is prohibited.

WHY IT MATTERS

It might well be asked what relevance my interpretation of Aquinas's text has to the Phoenix case. If my interpretation is correct, then Bishop Olmsted could *not* rightly have cited Aquinas, too, in support of his criticism of the hospital and Sister McBride; but, brilliant as Aquinas was and as important as he is for Catholic moral thought to this day, it is surely not the case that, *unless* Aquinas says that _____ is the case (fill in the blank as you like), _____ cannot be right.[30] Using Aquinas to "proof text" is little better than using Scripture. At the same time, given Aquinas's importance within the Catholic moral tradition, if he says *not-_____* and the allegedly settled moral convictions of the Catholic tradition, such as statements about self-defense and the like appealing precisely to Aquinas, say _____ (the opposite of Aquinas), there is reason to feel a bit unsettled about these moral convictions, or at least to wonder whether they are in fact well-founded.[31]

I have argued that the best reading of Aquinas's text shows that he is open to *some* cases of so-called instrumental intending: doing evil strictly as a means to an end, where the evil is necessary to achieving one's good end. Of course, I am not attributing to Aquinas the jejune position that the end always justifies the means, or for that matter, that one may do whatever it takes (all proportionality to the wind) to save one's life. Even Judith Jarvis Thomson rejects the claim that, in her words,

> people have a right to do anything whatever to save their lives. I think, rather, that there are drastic limits to the right of self-defense. If someone threatens you with death unless you torture someone else to death, I think you have not the right, even to save your life, to do so.[32]

To be clear, what I am claiming is that we cannot attribute to Aquinas the Pauline principle in its widest, "uncabined" interpretation: namely (as Gury put it), that "it is never lawful to perpetrate evil, however slight, in order to procure any good." To my mind, we can only be grateful that Aquinas does not concur with *this* reading of Paul, for the principle in this form is clearly wrong. (By the way, *uncabined* is a legal term used to mean not limited in any way. An uncabined judicial decision is one that is all too open, with implications for all too many cases.)

The obvious difference between killing in war and killing in abortion is that, unlike a soldier liable to violence by virtue of posing a threat of wrongful harm without justification, permission, or excuse—in brief, unlike a *culpable* threat—a fetus is not in the least even *responsible* for the threat of harm that it poses the mother, which arises only because of the fact that the fetus is in the mother's body, what's more through no doing of its own.[33] As the American philosopher Jeff McMahan has noted, the fetus's posing a threat "is just a fact about [its] position in the local causal architecture," and it is difficult to see how this fact could cause the fetus to forfeit its right not to be killed, which is a right that most Catholic thinkers at least would grant it.[34] Now, it has been claimed that a fetus that threatens its mother's life is analogous to a six-year-old child soldier who goes on the attack.[35] But a closer analogy is to an innocent bystander who, by happening to be in the wrong place at the wrong time, poses a threat to one's life for which he or she is entirely nonresponsible. Does this person forfeit his or her right to life? Would it be morally permissible to kill him or her in order to save oneself?[36] Imagine that the innocent bystander is obstructing one's means of escape from someone who is in fact a culpable threat.[37] Against Thomson, the fact that the *place* in question may be one's *own*—for example, one's house or one's land—surely does not give one permission to kill the innocent bystander in order to escape the culpable threat to one's life, and third parties would also do wrong if they killed the innocent bystander on one's behalf. (They ought to focus on the culpable threat.) The claim that, when the place in question is one's own body, one *does* have permission to kill an entirely nonresponsible fetus must be argued out on its own terms, without recourse to dubious analogies.[38]

In the end, as we saw in chapter 2, one question raised by the Phoenix case is whether there could be a lesser evil justification for some cases of abortion, namely, when the fetus poses a threat to its mother's life. This question is not unknown to the Catholic moral tradition, or somehow unthinkable within it. In fact, from the mid-fifteenth century to nearly the end of the nineteenth, moral philosophers and theologians in the tradition generally gave greater weight to the mother's interests in cases of vital conflict,[39] now and then on the basis of a lesser evil argument that, if an abortion were *not* performed, both mother and child would die.[40] As the historian and jurist John Noonan has remarked, "As the balance was once struck in favor of the mother whenever her life was endangered, it could be so struck again."[41] Drawing from the Jewish sages, and in particular Maimonides, Alan Donagan claims along these lines that a child owes a debt of gratitude to its mother for its very life, and that "bystanders are called upon, unless she directs otherwise, to save her life by removing from her body the child that is killing her"—for example, by aggravating a condition that she already has, like pulmonary hypertension—"treating [the child] as an involuntary pursuer."[42] I do not pretend here to evaluate these claims. But, in the Phoenix case, surely it did not count for nothing that the mother had four children at home. Anyone who does not see the tragedy here does not have eyes to see. In order to come to terms with the question at hand, we also need to see beyond the Pauline principle in its widest, misleading form. Enshrined in the PDE, it only distorts our vision.

QUESTIONS FOR FURTHER REFLECTION/PAPER QUESTIONS

(1) There is reason to be wary of recourse to analogies in considering the ethics of abortion. At the same time, analogies can provoke our thinking. Consider the analogy between an unborn child in a pregnancy gone tragically wrong and an innocent bystander who, by happening to be in the wrong place at the wrong time, poses a threat to your life for which he or she is entirely nonresponsible. Would it be morally permissible to kill him or her in order to save yourself? Why or why not? First flesh out the circumstances of the case in question; then draw from Aquinas, among others, to develop your position. Finally, consider what bearing, if any, this analogy has on the ethics of abortion in a

pregnancy gone tragically wrong. Does the analogy suggest any insights, or do the differences between it and the case of a pregnancy gone tragically wrong matter for purposes of moral evaluation?

(2) Does it make sense to hold, as this chapter notes in closing figures in the Jewish tradition have, that a child owes a debt of gratitude to its mother for its very life such that "bystanders are called upon, unless she directs otherwise, to save her life by removing from her body the child that is killing her"? In other words, can the argument indicated by Alan Donagan be made and defended? It might be countered, after all, that a child does not ask to be brought into being. Does a child have, then, a debt of gratitude to its mother for its life? What's more, even granting the child does have such a debt, what is its extent? Does it extend to owing his or her life in cases of vital conflict? Identify, elaborate, and assess the claims here.

(3) Two prominent critics of the principle of double effect, the philosophers Judith Jarvis Thomson and T. M. Scanlon, have used variations of the following thought experiment to cast doubt on double-effect reasoning. You are the prime minister of this or that country. You are at war with another country; your cause is just, namely, self-defense against baseless acts of aggression. The commander of your country's air force comes to you with a plan to destroy a munitions factory. The air raid would also more than likely kill a significant number of innocent civilians and probably have the further effect of undermining public support for the war in the country you're fighting. The commander asks you whether it's morally permissible to carry out the raid. Both Thomson and Scanlon claim that you would *not* answer, "Well, it all depends on what your intentions would be in dropping the bombs."[43] If you (speaking still to the commander) would be intending to destroy the munitions factory as a step toward winning the war, merely foreseeing, though not intending, the deaths of the civilians, then yes, you may drop the bombs. But if you would be

intending to destroy the munitions factory *and* intending the deaths of the civilians *and* intending to terrorize the enemy population in order to bring a quicker end to the war, then no, you may not drop the bombs, because your intentions would be bad....

Thomson and Scanlon think you would not reply in this way because what is decisive for whether the action in question is morally permissible is *not*, at bottom, the intention with which it would be carried out, but such considerations as whether the bombing of the munitions factory really would make a difference in the war and whether the civilian deaths would be disproportionate to the effect of destroying the factory. For Scanlon, intention does matter, but not for questions of the moral permissibility of actions; instead, we consider intention when we assess the *character* of agents.[44]

Imagine that you are the prime minister in question. How would you reply to the commander of the air force? You are also a Roman Catholic. Draw from Aquinas's account of the ethics of self-defense for your answer. (See also chapter 2, note 88.)

CHAPTER 4

JUST WARRIORS, UNJUST WARS?

The Evolution of Just War Theory

A beloved teacher of mine used to scoff at the idea that philosophy could make progress in discovering truth. Progress in discovering truth belonged to the natural sciences; philosophy was about diagnosing and dissolving deep confusions generated by misuse and misunderstandings of language. My teacher's attitude and understanding of philosophy had been shaped by the later writings of the great Austrian philosopher Ludwig Wittgenstein (1889–1951). In response to a claim that philosophy had not advanced beyond Plato (ca. 428/427–ca. 348/347 BCE) in its understanding of reality, Wittgenstein famously retorted, "What a peculiar situation. How extraordinary that Plato was then able to get even as far as he did! Or that we could get no further afterwards! Was it because Plato was *so* clever?"[1] The tone of this remark suggests that we are not supposed to answer *yes*.

The contemporary American philosopher Jeff McMahan opens his extraordinary book *Killing in War*, published in 2009, with a story about Wittgenstein, who McMahan notes "is generally regarded as the greatest philosopher, and certainly the greatest philosophical iconoclast, of the twentieth century."[2] But this great philosophical mind and iconoclast did not question whether it was right for him to enlist in the Austrian ranks as a soldier in World War I. His country had declared war, and he believed himself not only morally permitted to fight, but morally obligated to do so. Remarkably, he believed the same for Englishmen (Wittgenstein had studied at Cambridge from 1911 to 1913) and disagreed with the decision of his friend and former teacher, Bertrand Russell (1872–1970), to oppose the war, for which Russell lost his teaching position and was imprisoned.

Note that Wittgenstein believed it morally permitted and even obligatory for Austrians like himself and Englishmen like Russell to fight without regard to the question of which side, if either, had just cause to go to war. For Wittgenstein, considerations of what is called *jus ad bellum*—the principles governing the resort to war—were apparently independent of considerations of what is called *jus in bello*—the principles governing the conduct of war. Though one's country could *be* in the wrong in resorting to war, say by lacking just cause or right intention, one would not *do* wrong in fighting on its behalf, so long as one both discriminated between civilians and combatants and did not use violence excessive to one's ends (that is, so long as one observed the principles of *jus in bello*). Readers of literature might recall Shakespeare's *Henry V*. If the king's cause be wrong, a soldier says, "our obedience to the King wipes the crime of it out of us." All that soldiers need know or worry themselves over is that "we are the King's subjects."[3] If the soldier had cared for biblical support for his position, he might have cited the Letter to the Romans, where Paul calls the ruler "God's servant for your good" (13:4).

McMahan is a former student of the influential Oxford philosopher Derek Parfit. According to a fascinating profile of Parfit published a few years ago in the *New Yorker*, he has lived his adult life nearly singularly devoted to progress in philosophy. He eats, drinks, and sleeps philosophy: he gobbles his food, passes on the brandies, desserts, and cigars that the other fellows at All Souls College enjoy, and has great trouble lulling his racing mind at night.[4] Like Parfit, McMahan clearly believes in progress in philosophy, in particular moral philosophy, and to the point for present purposes, he also believes that philosophers have, to date, done a bad job in securing and transmitting what he calls "moral knowledge about war."[5] McMahan's work, in *Killing in War* and a great many articles, is representative of what has come to be known as the *revisionist* account of the just war, to which a number of other philosophers have likewise contributed.[6] A main claim of the revisionists, of whom McMahan is the most prominent, is that "the theory of just war in its received form…is not a reliable source of guidance."[7] Accordingly, they seek to undo the hold that the traditional theory of the last several centuries has on our thinking yet today (I also call it, in the following, the *orthodox theory*) and to replace it with an account that, as they see it, demands much more of the individual soldier. This chapter's title, "Just Warriors, Unjust Wars?" points to the questions that the revisionist account has brought to the fore: When may soldiers rightly fight? And when, if ever, should they refuse?

THE JUST WAR TRADITION IN THE CATHOLIC TRADITION

Catholics have special reason to care about the revisionist account and the debate that it has stimulated over the last decade or so. The just war tradition was outlined by Aquinas in his *Summa Theologiae* and systematically developed by later Scholastic thinkers like Francisco de Vitoria (ca. 1490–1546) and Francisco Suárez (1548–1617).[8] The just war tradition cannot be considered simply Catholic: it has also seen development in the hands of both Protestants from Hugo Grotius (1583–1645) to Paul Ramsey (1913–88) and secular thinkers like the political philosopher Michael Walzer, whose excellent 1977 book, *Just and Unjust Wars*, has for decades been the text of reference on this topic. Catholic popes and bishops, however, have arguably been key in keeping the tradition present in the deliberations of presidents and other policymakers.[9] As opposed to the Christian pacifism associated with various Protestant denominations, the public doctrine of the Roman Catholic Church has been that war sometimes *can be* justified, and this doctrine has been heard if not always heeded in spirit or to the letter in political circles.

In any event, as the scholar of religion James Turner Johnson has been at pains to emphasize, the concept of a just war has as its framework Augustine's political theory, according to which the sovereign authority has responsibility for order, justice, and peace: the responsibility to secure what Augustine called the *tranquillitas ordinis*.[10] A pacifist in this Augustinian tradition is not someone who abjures war, but one who works for the peace or tranquility *of just order*, which may sometimes call for the use of violence by duly authorized persons. This is war properly

91

speaking. From this point of view, "war is not the only, or the worst, evil."[11] Worse evils can justify, and even morally require, the sovereign authority's decision to open the iron gates of war despite what fury and bloodlust lie howling behind, in the ancient Roman poet Virgil's searing image from the *Aeneid*.[12] (Virgil lived 70 to 19 BCE.)

Another, more contemporary reason that Catholics have to care about the new debate over the morality of war is that, arguably, the just war tradition to which Catholics have contributed over the centuries has facilitated the recourse to war in two crucial ways: by disguising its reality—fury and bloodlust, as the ancient Romans at least acknowledged—with a veneer of theological and philosophical respectability, and by providing presidents and policymakers with a set of criteria that can be easily manipulated and abused. Whether these charges are finally fair or not, it is certainly remarkable that they can be plausibly leveled at self-proclaimed followers of Jesus, with his radical rejection of violence. The key text here is Matthew 5:38–39, including the injunction not to resist an evildoer; the key example may be Jesus' submission to his arrest and crucifixion. In contrast to this rejection, the principles of *jus ad bellum* and *jus in bello* suggest that war can be governed by clear heads and minds, tamed and defanged by the stipulation of limits not to be crossed. The historical record, however, can make this suggestion seem like all too wishful thinking. Writing in the aftermath of the invasion of Iraq under the George W. Bush administration, and in view of the carnage and havoc the Iraq war wreaked, the moral theologian Daniel Maguire mordantly suggested renaming just war theory, in the interests of honesty, the "justifiable slaughter theory."[13] Maguire also charged that, too often, justifications for war function as but "shady rationalizations for the failure to build peace."[14]

Maguire's is not a lone voice crying in the wilderness. Scandalized by the uses to which just war theory has been put by the perpetrators of war, others have decried the "desperate maneuvers [of modern Augustinians] to preserve the doctrine of the just war from the museum or the junk pile."[15] Less colorfully but no less critically, pacifist thinkers like the Mennonite theologian John Howard Yoder have questioned whether the churches, like the Roman Catholic Church, that teach that war sometimes *can be* justified have done nearly enough to educate and prepare believers for the possibility that the answer in a given case could be *no, this war isn't*—such that they should, if they psychologically even could, resist the decision to go to war and be willing to pay the price for this resistance.[16] Another critical question is whether these churches have reckoned seriously with the possibility that the answer no is more than likely to fall on deaf ears in a given case—the culture of the United States, for example, being what it now is, or for that matter human nature being what it long has been.[17]

In this regard, it is one thing to issue statements against a particular war, as the United States Conference of Catholic Bishops presciently did in 2002 against the impending invasion of Iraq.[18] It is quite another thing to face squarely the realities of squalor and sin and to consider in that context not only the prospects of such statements, but the likely fate of the very teaching that war sometimes *can be* justified, which has the understated implication that sometimes, if not most times, it cannot. As the Anglican theologian Oliver O'Donovan has trenchantly observed, "When self-defense, of state, community, or individual, has the last word"—that is, when the fact that one is threatened is taken to warrant a no-holds barred response—"paganism is restored,"[19] and just war theory is speaking into the wind.

Finally, it is only right to recall that, in the aftermath of the 9/11 attacks and in the build-up to the Iraq war, there was, in the words of the philosopher and theologian Paul Griffiths, an "intense debate" in Catholic circles "about the meaning, history, and contemporary applicability of just war theory."[20] As Griffiths went on to note, much of that debate was conducted in the magazine *First Things*. A central figure in this debate was the Washington-based Catholic public intellectual George Weigel. In a series of articles and exchanges from 2002 through 2007, Weigel sought to recover what he termed "the classic Catholic just war tradition" over and against the distortions that, to his mind, it had suffered the last several decades at the hands of religious leaders, including none other than the United States Conference of Catholic Bishops. In particular, Weigel accused his opponents of "forgetting" the framework of just war theory, namely, what he called "classic Catholic international relations theory," which with Augustine "starts with a 'presumption for justice,' not a 'presumption against violence.'"[21] In other words, Weigel emphasized that the first responsibility of the sovereign, according to the Augustinian tradition, is to secure the tranquility *of just order*, which may sometimes call for the use of violence. Drawing from the work of James Turner Johnson, Weigel inveighed against the view that "the use of even proportionate and discriminate armed force is, at the outset of the moral analysis, presumptively deplorable."[22] This view, he claimed, smuggles into the tradition a pacifist premise that is foreign to the Augustinian understanding of the responsibility of the sovereign to secure the tranquility of just order—not merely to keep the peace until all else has been tried. Weigel, as this argument suggests, supported the Bush administration's decision to invade Iraq.

One other plank of Weigel's argument is worth noting. After disputing that the classic or authentic just war tradition includes a presumption against war, Weigel claimed, in his January 2003 article "Moral Clarity in a Time of War," that "what we might call the 'charism of responsibility'" to judge whether resort to war is justified lies, not with religious leaders and public intellectuals, but with "duly constituted public authorities."[23] (A charism is a gift of the Holy Spirit for the building up of the kingdom of God.) Such authorities, Weigel went on, enjoy "a charism of political discernment that is unique to the vocation of public service."[24] As religious leaders and public intellectuals lack this charism, they must exercise "a measure of political modesty" in presuming to judge whether the principles of *jus ad bellum* have been satisfied in a given case.[25] Recall the soldier in Shakespeare's *Henry V* who says, "We know enough if we know that we are the King's subjects."

It is interesting to note that no Catholic bishops joined the debate in *First Things*. Instead, the then Archbishop of Canterbury, Rowan Williams, replied at length to Weigel's argument, both questioning whether his defense of preemptive action could be accommodated within the just war tradition and retorting that "there is no charism that goes automatically with political leadership."[26] But the drums of war were already beating too loudly to be stilled.

The revisionist account of the just war likewise challenges the claim that only political leaders have the competence to make judgments about *jus ad bellum.* The revisionists would have us go further, however, and question Shakespeare's soldier's claim that, "if [the King's] cause be wrong, our obedience to the King wipes the crime of it out of us." In other words, the revisionists challenge the very separation of the principles of *jus ad bellum* from the principles of *jus in bello*—an orthodoxy that Weigel does not even think to defend. The position that moral responsibility for the decision to go to war falls to rulers and frees soldiers to participate whether the war be just or unjust again traces back to Augustine: to quote from book 1 of *The City of God*, he who is commanded to kill "is like a sword which is the instrument of its user" and as such does not incur the guilt of murder.[27] The present chapter elaborates and examines the revisionist challenge to this position. I claim, in the end, that the revisionist account of the just war represents progress in moral philosophy—in brief, that it brings us closer to truth—though it, too, needs yet further development.

JUS AD BELLUM, JUS IN BELLO

Outlines of the principles of *jus ad bellum*—the criteria that need to be satisfied before going to war can be considered morally permissible—normally note at least six, explicated in various ways and different orders: (1) the war must be fought for a just cause; (2) it must be declared by a legitimate authority; (3) it must be fought with right intention (so ultimately for the sake of the peace of a just order, and not out of malice); (4) it must be necessary, which is to say resorted to because the just cause it serves cannot be achieved by less violent means; (5) there must be well-founded hope of success; and (6) the destructiveness it is sure to cause must not be out of proportion to the value of the just cause it serves.[28] The principles of *jus in bello*—the criteria concerning conduct in war—normally number three: (1) attacks must discriminate between people who are and who are not liable to attack; (2) attacks must be necessary, which is to say not in excess to what is needed for the end in question; and (3) any evils that an attack wreaks on either innocent persons or infrastructure needed for life—so-called collateral damage—must not be out of proportion to the good sought.

Even this simple outline suggests the difficulty of altogether separating these two sets of principles, which historically derive from quite different traditions.[29] Imagine that a state's cause is unjust. In this case, can any attack its soldiers undertake satisfy the third principle of *jus in bello*, namely, that the evil it wreaks not be out of proportion to the good sought? It certainly seems not, for how can military advantage be considered a "good" if the cause that a military is fighting for is unjust, which is to say wrong or even evil? But let's consider the matter more deliberately.

Toward the beginning of *Just and Unjust Wars*, Michael Walzer writes, "The moral reality of war is divided into two parts": *jus ad bellum* (the justice of going to war) and *jus in bello* (justice in war).[30] This "dualism," he allows, is "puzzling," for how can a soldier fight rightly when the war that he is fighting is not itself right?[31] Walzer does not challenge, however, what he calls the "dualism of our moral perceptions."[32] Instead, he seeks to understand how a state could be in the wrong in going to war, but a soldier of that state nonetheless within his or her rights to seek to kill enemy soldiers whose cause is just while that soldier's is not.

Walzer's principal answer is to ground what he calls the moral equality of soldiers in "shared servitude."[33] "The enemy soldier, though his war may well be criminal, is nevertheless as blameless as oneself," he writes.[34] For "war isn't a relation between persons but between political entities" that have turned human beings into mere instruments[35]—"food for powder, food for powder," Shakespeare's Falstaff says in *Henry IV*.[36] As such, soldiers are not responsible for the war they now have to fight. But they are also not innocent in the technical sense of *not harming*. It is civilians who are innocent in this sense: they do not pose a threat of harm. Instead, soldiers in arms do threaten one another, and so, Walzer claims, they may rightly attack one another, like the gladiators of old. But they are innocent of the evil of the war. For this, it is the political leaders of the state in the wrong who bear the guilt.[37]

A simple way to explain the revisionist challenge to the current orthodoxy of just war theory is to say that it rejects as incoherent the dualism that Walzer seeks to understand. To begin with, it can be agreed that the enemy soldier is blameless, and not criminal, for fighting an unjust war; but as McMahan notes, blamelessness need imply "nothing more than that an unjust combatant is excused," not that he or she is justified in fighting. The so-called unjust combatant may act impermissibly, yet not culpably and so not criminally.[38] Duress, limitations in knowledge, and diminished responsibility—think of child soldiers—often exculpate soldiers, so that even though one's cause be wrong, "the crime of it" falls on one's leaders. Yet these excuses are not always available, and McMahan argues that what's needed is an authoritative, international court that could limit or even eliminate the excuses available to soldiers by publicly judging—in advance—a state's cause for war. He also rejects the "counsels of despair" that would dismiss such a court as forever unrealistic.[39]

The analogy of war to gladiatorial combat fares no better in the revisionists' hands. McMahan acknowledges that "a war in which both sides deploy brutalized child soldiers" might be comparable, but important differences between war and gladiatorial combat include the following: (1) "gladiators fought only for self-preservation" and not in service of an unjust cause threatening ill to many; (2) while gladiators who refused to fight would be killed, nowadays soldiers or conscripts in states like ours who refuse to fight do not have death to fear; and (3) while all gladiators were expendable and so it was of no use for all to refuse to fight, no state can kill all its soldiers.[40] And even if we assume that a state might well execute soldiers who refuse to fight—as the Nazis executed the Austrian peasant Franz Jägerstätter, whose story deserves to be remembered[41]—do we want to say that Jägerstätter would have been *justified* in fighting for the Nazi cause, which is to say within his rights to kill in its service? McMahan notes that Jägerstätter's fellow Catholics, including the bishop of Linz, "all offered him the familiar forms of advice that still constitute the received wisdom on these issues: that he lacked the competence to judge the war unjust, that as a citizen he had no responsibility for the acts of the government and could therefore participate in the war with a clear conscience."[42] Perhaps Jägerstätter would have been *excused* in joining the fight, for how many of us would have the courage to say as he did that "I cannot turn over the responsibility [for my actions] to the Führer" and suffer beheading as a consequence?[43] But he surely would have been materially cooperating with evil had he fought, and it is hard to see how we could hold that he would have acted rightly (in the sense warranting commendation) so long only as he observed the principles of *jus in bello* and thus did not directly attack civilians, use excessive force, and the like.

Finally, Walzer's account of why soldiers may rightly attack one another also does not bear scrutiny. Threatening harm, as soldiers in arms do to one another once a war is under way, does not appear to make one liable to attack, such that soldiers could then permissibly kill one another no matter which side, if either, had justice in its cause. (To be clear, a person is liable to attack when "he would not be *wronged* by being attacked, and would have no justifiable complaint about being attacked."[44]) For example, the police threaten harm to criminals—say, terrorists like those who bombed the Boston Marathon in 2013—and a person acting in self-defense threatens harm to his or her assailant. But it is *not* the case that, because the police and the person acting in self-defense threaten harm, they may then be rightly attacked. Criminals who attack the police commit a further crime, and there is no right of self-defense against a person acting in self-defense. McMahan puts the point succinctly: "One does not make oneself morally liable to attack by posing a threat if one is morally justified in posing that threat."[45] Instead, one is liable to attack by virtue of one's moral responsibility for an *unjustified* threat. So, should attack be necessary to the end of preventing harm, terrorists and assailants are liable to attack, as are soldiers bearing some measure of responsibility for an unjustified threat. (Child soldiers make for a difficult case here.) But soldiers serving a just cause, through just means, are not liable to attack— they are like the police or the person acting in self-defense—with the upshot that a soldier like Jägerstätter would have acted wrongly, though perhaps not culpably, had he fought for the Nazi cause.

Other implications of this argument may be more unsettling. As McMahan notes, the traditional doctrine of absolute civilian immunity from attack holds that "if posing a threat is the criterion of liability to attack in war, then combatants are liable but noncombatants are not."[46] But, as we have seen, revisionists like McMahan reject the notion that merely threatening harm suffices to make one liable to attack. If, instead, what matters is moral responsibility for an objectively unjustified threat, then not only are just combatants *not* liable to attack, but—conversely— civilians responsible for unjust wars and unjust acts of war *could be* liable.

In other words, attacks on some civilians could be justifiable, if those attacks would contribute to the achievement of a just cause.[47]

This argument seems to open the way to attacks not only on munitions workers (which orthodox just war theory has been tinkered with to allow anyway),[48] but on professors of physics, chemistry, and computer science, and anyone else doing research that will lead to more destructive bombs, more deadly chemical weapons, viruses, and so on. Arguably, however, this implication does not in fact follow. Liability to harm is sensitive to causal proximity: that is, to how close or remote a person's action is to an unjustified threat. And as another representative of the revisionist account of the just war has observed, normally "contributions made by noncombatants to threats posed by their states will be far down the causal chain" and so insufficient to ground liability.[49] In any event, whereas for orthodox just war theory, *innocent* has the technical sense of not posing an immediate threat of harm, for the revisionists, the innocent are those *not morally responsible* for a wrong and as such immune to direct attack. By contrast, with responsibility comes liability.

Interestingly, in rejecting "the idea that in war both liability and immunity are *collective*," simply a matter of membership in a group, McMahan notes that we find the idea of collective liability not only in orthodox just war theory, according to which simply being a soldier makes one liable to attack, but also "at the heart of alleged justifications for terrorism,"[50] according to which simply being a citizen of the United States or some other nation makes one liable. The revisionists reject collective liability as pernicious in both instances.

THE CONSCIENCE OF THE SOLDIER

A clear difference between the revisionist account of the just war and Weigel's account of what he considers "the classic Catholic just war tradition" is that the revisionist account is addressed to soldiers and conscripts, whereas Weigel apparently takes for granted the separation of *jus ad bellum* from *jus in bello* and reserves considerations of *jus ad bellum* to "duly constituted public authorities." The revisionists' practical aim in undermining "the idea that no one does wrong, or acts impermissibly, merely by fighting in a war that turns out to be unjust" is to make it more difficult for states to fight unjust wars by articulating for soldiers moral reasons to resist going along.[51] In McMahan's words, "We must stop reassuring soldiers that they act permissibly when they fight in an unjust war, provided that they conduct themselves honorably on the battlefield by fighting in accordance with the rules of engagement."[52] His idea is that, once what he calls the doctrine of the permissibility of participation has been discredited, "an important resource for the prevention of unjust wars" will become available that, to date, has been set aside by the separation of *jus ad bellum* from *jus in bello*: "the moral conscience of individuals."[53]

Readers of literature might consider in this regard the novelist Tim O'Brien's *The Things They Carried*, where the narrator struggles in his conscience with whether "to fight a war I hated," namely, the American war in Vietnam.[54] What difference would it make for such a man if it were *not* a prevalent belief in our political culture that a soldier does no wrong in fighting honorably for his country, right or wrong? And how much more responsible and transparent would our political leaders have to be in making the case for war?

However we answer these questions, which I examine more closely below, the revisionist account gives support to positions staked out the last several decades by the United States Conference of Catholic Bishops. In landmark letters issued in 1983 and 1993, the bishops affirmed both that a "citizen may not casually disregard his country's conscientious decision to call its citizens to acts of 'legitimate defense'" and that, "at the same time, no state may demand blind obedience."[55] This attention to "the relationship of the authority of the state and the conscience of the individual on matters of war and peace" (quoting from the 1993 document) was a relatively new development, though with deep historical roots.[56] It came as a response, the bishops explained, to the vastly "destructive nature of modern war,"[57] which had likewise disturbed the world's bishops at the Second Vatican Council, leading to the striking claim, in the 1965 document *Gaudium et Spes*, that there was a need to reexamine war in an entirely new spirit.[58] The affirmation "No state may demand blind obedience" led the U.S. bishops to go on to support both "conscientious objection in general and...selective conscientious objection to participation in a particular war, either because of the ends being pursued or the means being used."[59] The bishops presented so-called selective conscientious objection—that is, the refusal to participate in a particular war on grounds that it is unjust—as "a moral conclusion which can be validly derived from the classical teaching of just-war principles."[60] They also called for the provision of legal protection for selective conscientious objectors, just as there is legal protection for persons who refuse to participate in all wars.

Legal protection for selective conscientious objection is likewise what the revisionists want.[61] To date, however, no such legislation has been passed in the United States, and the United States Supreme Court, in the fascinating 1971 case *Gillette v. United States*, rejected a challenge to the constitutionality of limiting legal protection to so-called general objectors while excluding selective objectors from the same protection.[62] Selective conscientious objectors to the U.S. war in Vietnam had seen the Nuremberg trials in Germany after World War II as providing precedent for refusing to participate in an unjust war. As John Howard Yoder has observed, the Nuremberg trials "provided institutional demonstration for the claim that it is morally and legally incumbent on persons other than sovereigns to refuse to obey an unjust order."[63] Selective conscientious objectors asked, How, then, could it not also be morally incumbent on persons to refuse to fight an unjust war? And why, then, should it not be legally incumbent on the state to protect persons objecting on such grounds?

The lack of legal protection for selective conscientious objection is a major problem for the revisionists and the United States bishops. The problem is twofold.[64] First, since after all, the law is a teacher, this lack of legal protection might be understood as communicating that whether a war is just or unjust is none of a citizen's business. In other words, to recall once more the language of Shakespeare's *Henry V*, it might be thought that all that soldiers or would-be soldiers need know or worry themselves over is that "we are the King's subjects." Such a position might be understandable against the background of the belief that a ruler is divinely appointed—the doctrine of the divine right of kings—but it seems to have little to recommend it in an era of democratic institutions.[65] Second and closely related, this lack of legal protection appears to pull whatever teeth just war theory might have as a constraint on the immoral use of force.[66] If it is legally obligatory for soldiers and conscripts to fight once the state's rulers declare war, and if the state's courts reject moral challenges to the law as ill-founded, what do unscrupulous rulers really have to fear from just war theory? If it is generally believed that, though the king's cause be wrong, "our obedience to the King wipes the crime of it out of us," then the iron gates of war will be easy to open. The unscrupulous ruler will be able to count on soldiers to do as they're commanded.

OBJECTIONS AND REPLIES

The revisionist account must answer, however, a number of objections. To begin with, it could be objected—as McMahan anticipates—that "if the Permissibility of Participation were widely repudiated, soldiers would be more likely to disobey when ordered to fight in a war that was just."[67] In a word, they would *malinger*: find some or other excuse to escape duty.[68] Whether this would really happen is an empirical question that only experience could answer for sure, but there seem to be good grounds to think it would be unlikely to occur when the war is either one of national defense or a humanitarian intervention to stop, say, a genocide. McMahan allows that extending provisions for selective conscientious objection to active duty soldiers could well impair the ability of a state to fight an unjust war or a war of dubious justifiability, but his counter here is a question in turn: How could this be an objection? His worry is rather that the recent and accelerating development of robots for military uses will allow a state to "reduce its reliance on soldiers with consciences."[69]

A more challenging objection concerns just what is the moral duty of the conscientious soldier. Does the soldier have a moral duty and so a right to refuse to fight if he or she plausibly believes a war is unjust, or does the soldier have a duty to fight—and no right to refuse—so long as his or her legitimate leaders plausibly believe the war is just?[70] Another way to put this question is to ask whether a soldier has a "role-based duty to defer to the judgments of…civilian and military commanders when those judgments are not clearly erroneous," which is to say when the war is not patently or manifestly unjust.[71] The same question needs to be asked for the able-bodied citizen drafted into military service; recall here the narrator of Tim O'Brien's *The Things They Carried*, struggling in his conscience with whether "to fight a war I hated." Does the conscript have a moral duty and so a right to refuse to fight when he or she plausibly believes a war is unjust, or does the conscript have a duty to fight—and no right to refuse—so long as his or her legitimate leaders plausibly believe the war is just, that is, so long as it is *not* the case that the war is patently or manifestly unjust? Interestingly, American soldiers have a legal duty and right to refuse to obey only *manifestly* unjust orders in war; and the medieval theorist Francisco de Vitoria, oft-invoked by the revisionists, claimed that soldiers had a moral duty to refuse to fight only in wars they believed to be *patently* unjust.

A yet further question along the same lines is what duty, if any, soldiers and conscripts have to investigate for themselves the justifiability of a war.[72] Here, too, do they have role-based duties to defer to legitimate leaders, who after all may well have information and expertise common soldiers and citizens lack? The distinction between unjust wars and dumb or unnecessary wars is relevant to this question.[73] A dumb or unnecessary war—like, perhaps, the war in Vietnam, or the George W. Bush administration's war in Iraq—may not be manifestly or patently unjust either at its beginning or in the midst of the so-called fog of war. McMahan claims at one point, "No government's moral judgments about its own resort to war can be expected to be more reliable than those of a well-informed, impartial, and morally scrupulous individual."[74] This may be so, but how difficult it is to be well-informed, forget about impartial and morally scrupulous! Interestingly again, in an article published in 2013 assessing "The Moral Case for Military Strikes against Syria," McMahan himself wrote, "I lack the information and expertise necessary to be confident that limited strikes against Syria could be effective in deterring or preventing further massacres of civilians."[75] Imagine that a soldier or a conscript were to come to this same realization. Shouldn't she then defer to the judgment of her legitimate leaders? Wouldn't that be the morally right decision?

These questions suggest that the conscientious soldier or conscript would rarely have moral grounds to exercise a legal right to selective conscientious objection. In other words, in most cases, the soldier or conscript should defer to her legitimate leaders and concern herself with the actions that pertain to her role, which is to say actions taken *in* war, governed by the principles of *jus in bello*.[76] I don't think, however, that these questions undercut the case for selective conscientious objection altogether; they don't show it can never be justified or never is a moral duty. In other words, there is more to say.

A critic of the revisionist account has observed that "in the criminal justice system, executioners are not expected to pass independent judgment on death penalty cases; indeed it is inappropriate for [executioners] to do so" lest they undermine the rule of law.[77] Analogously, it might be claimed that it is wrong for soldiers or conscripts to pass independent judgment on the justifiability of going to war lest they undermine civilian control of the military. Extending this point, yet another critic notes, "History has given us too many examples of the disastrous effects of a politicized military," with the upshot that "the wisdom of…decisions [about war] ought to be decided in ballot boxes, legislatures, and courtrooms, *not* in barracks."[78]

The analogy between executioners and soldiers, however, can be turned to cut against the critic of the revisionist account. "Suppose an executioner worked within a system which is radically flawed": it sentences all too many innocent persons to death.[79] Shouldn't that executioner quit? Shouldn't he or she refuse to do his or her job? Isn't it the executioner's moral duty, precisely because the rule of law has been corrupted, no longer to participate in this system? And wouldn't the executioner have blood on her hands—wouldn't the executioner be a *murderer*, or at least complicit to murder—if she did *not* refuse to go along? Analogous claims might be made about the soldier or conscript faced with, at least, a patently or manifestly unjust war. Remember Franz Jägerstätter, the Austrian peasant who would not fight for Hitler! What's more, history has surely given us too many examples of the disastrous effects of war-mongering leaders, democratically elected or not, with the upshot that it would be *unwise* for the soldier or conscript to sign his or her conscience away. The moral risk, that is, the risk of doing great wrong, is too great.

FROM THEORY TO PRACTICE

Two last objections of the form, "That makes sense in theory, but what about in practice?" have to be anticipated. First, it could be wondered whether providing legal protection for selective conscientious objectors would not prove unworkable. To quote from the majority decision in *Gillette v. United States*, "Ours is a Nation of enormous heterogeneity in respect of political views, moral codes, and religious persuasions."[80] How, then, are the courts to adjudicate fairly among grounds for objection that warrant respect and grounds that don't? Or do all claims of conscience suffice to free the soldier or conscript from the war to which he or she objects?[81] One way or the other, must courts somehow pry into the hearts of claimants to determine if they are sincere rather than simply malingering? In a case dating from 1953, *Burns v. Wilson*, the United States Supreme Court stated, "The rights of men in the armed forces must perforce be conditioned to meet certain overriding demands of discipline and duty":[82] like it or not, the rights of soldiers must bend to what the Court later called, in its 1981 decision *Haig v. Agee*, the "'obvious and unarguable'" governmental interest in "the security of the Nation."[83] To restate this objection: yes, a right to selective conscientious objection appears well-founded in theory, but trying to accommodate this right would both entangle our courts in logistical thickets and put at risk national security, which is of such overriding importance that even rights must bend before it.[84]

The second objection is of a quite different spirit and brings us back to the beginning of this chapter. Yes, pacifists like John Howard Yoder might say, a right to selective conscientious objection appears well-founded in theory—otherwise put, the so-called doctrine of the permissibility of participation appears false—but doesn't the resistance to legally protecting this right speak volumes about our culture and polity? Is it really the case that no workable legal remedies could be devised, or is there purportedly no way only because, in fact, there is little to no will? After all, it is not as if no attention has been given to solving the practical problems in question![85]

Arguably, the opposition to selective conscientious objection points to a deeper opposition to just war theory in *both* its orthodox and revisionist forms: in particular, opposition to the real possibility that, sometimes, going to war or using this or that means in war is *not* justifiable because there are limits to what can rightly be done in the name of national security. In other words, arguably, the opposition to selective conscientious objection reflects a deeper hardheartedness and is evidence that, while the language of just war theory may be on our political leaders' lips, it is not in our leaders' hearts, no doubt because they represent *us*, the American people—and public sentiment is not open to sacrifice of safety for the sake of morality. Honesty compels noting that it is a sad and ugly fact that the language quoted above from the 1981 decision *Haig v. Agee*—namely, "It is 'obvious and unarguable' that no governmental interest is more compelling than the security of the Nation"[86]—figures prominently in the first of the so-called *Torture Papers*: Deputy Assistant Attorney General John C. Yoo's September 25, 2001 memorandum concerning "the scope of the President's authority to take military action in response to the terrorist attacks on the United States on September 11, 2001."[87] This memo concludes by rejecting "any limits on the President's determinations as to any terrorist threat, the amount of military force to be used in response, or the method, timing, and nature of the response."[88] The theologian Oliver O'Donovan's trenchant observation, quoted earlier in this chapter, is relevant here again: "When self-defense, of state, community, or individual, has the last word, paganism is restored,"[89] and just war theory is speaking into the wind.

These two last objections that we have just considered, though of the same form—That makes sense in theory, but what about in practice?—clearly work against one another. The first worries that selective conscientious objection will become rampant. Taking as its evidence none other than the first objection, that is, the *worry* that resort to war might become more difficult, the second objection worries that arguments for selective conscientious objection—more generally, arguments that take just war theory seriously—have no legs in our culture and polity. The second objection is more fundamental. I think the answer to it is to acknowledge that just war theory cannot stand on its own. Instead, it grows out of, and takes its life from, what a respondent to John Howard Yoder's criticism has called a broad and more basic "set of ethical commitments, virtues, and dispositions" such as love of neighbor, generosity of spirit, willingness to forgive, and ingenuity.[90] These and many others need to be in place for just war theory to be more than words, words, words.

When all is said and done, the revisionist account of the just war certainly looks like progress in moral philosophy to me. But is it more than words, words, words? That is, can it realistically pass into deed? Can it vie against the drums of war? Or is it more likely to fall on deaf ears? Another advantage of the revisionist account over the traditional or orthodox theory of the last several centuries is that it invites us to an examination of conscience: Is our first commitment to the peace of a just order, or to safety at whatever the costs?

QUESTIONS FOR FURTHER REFLECTION/PAPER QUESTIONS

(1) Read the majority and dissenting opinions in *Gillette v. United States* from 1971. The U.S. Supreme Court has recently agreed to hear a new case challenging this decades-old precedent—call this new case *McMahan v. United States*. Imagine that you are either the lead attorney for the defendant, or the United States Solicitor General representing the federal government. Either argue against *Gillette* in favor of provision for selective conscientious objection, or argue for *Gillette* against provision for selective conscientious objection. One way or the other, discuss McMahan's challenge to orthodox just war theory; also be sure to anticipate and counter objections.

(2) Not all of Franz Jägerstätter's fellow villagers in Sankt Radegund, Austria, saw him as a hero or saint for refusing to fight for the Nazi cause. Some, like the priests who counseled him, thought he had neither the facts nor the competence to judge the justice of the war; some thought it was clear that his primary obligations were to his wife, three daughters, and mother, who would suffer because of his obstinacy; and some thought he was simply deranged, a religious fanatic no longer in his right mind. Write either a

series of letters or a dialogue between Jägerstätter and these critics. What should he have done? What was the right course of action—either in the sense that it was the best course available in the situation, or in the sense that it was morally commendable?

(3) Toward this chapter's end, the question was asked whether the soldier or conscript has a role-based duty to defer to legitimate leaders and military commanders when a war is *not* manifestly or patently unjust. The sixteenth-century Spanish Dominican Francisco de Vitoria argued for the policy, "In case of doubt, fight."[91] In other words, doubt should be resolved in favor of the authorities. Critically assess this position. What's there to say for it, what's there to say against it, and how do you come down in the end and why?

(4) Against McMahan's revisionist just war theory, Michael Walzer has observed that, on McMahan's own account, "there are typically a variety of excusing or mitigating conditions when combatants fight in unjust wars," including coercion, uncertainty, and ignorance, among others.[92] The upshot is that, again on McMahan's own account, soldiers very often are not to blame even when they are fighting for an unjust cause. What Walzer disagrees with is that we should say such soldiers are then *excused*. For the so-called excusing conditions of coercion, uncertainty, and ignorance are not exceptional circumstances in time of war; instead, in Walzer's words, they simply are "the reality of war."[93] According to him, "Conventional just war theory is nothing more than the adaptation of everyday moral rules to that reality."[94] From this point of view, soldiers are more than merely excused when they fight for an unjust case; they have every right to do so because of the typical circumstances of war.

You work for the U.S. Department of Defense, which takes a keen interest in just war theory. None other than the secretary of defense has charged you with evaluating the latest in the philosophical literature. Begin by clarifying and elaborating Walzer's rejoinder to McMahan's revisionist theory; then consider how you think McMahan would reply in turn. Conclude the memo by adjudicating between the two. Be sure to anticipate and counter objections.

CHAPTER 5

ANIMALS AND US

From very early in church history, abstaining from meat was met with suspicion. The Greek church father Origen (184/185–253/254) distanced "our ascetics" from the Pythagoreans, who abstained from meat "on account of the fable about transmigration of souls";[1] Augustine praised "perfect Christians" who abstained from meat in order to gain mastery over bodily desires and passions, but attacked the Manichaean elect who abstained as a matter of doctrine.[2] And it goes on. Augustine argues in *The City of God* that the commandment "Thou shalt not kill" does not apply to animals, since "these do not share the use of reason with us." Instead, "by the most just ordinance of [the] Creator, both their life and death are subject to our needs."[3] The text in question here is Genesis 9:3, where after the flood, God gives Noah and his family "every moving thing that lives for food." Lest there be any doubt, Aquinas affirmed the justness of God's ordinance many centuries later in his *Summa contra Gentiles*. Aquinas reasoned that since man is the end toward whose generation all of nature is directed, "it is no wrong for man to make use of [dumb animals], either by killing or in any other way whatever."[4] In the words of Psalm 8, quoted by Aquinas, everything has been put at our feet.

Or so it was once thought. But should we here and now, many centuries later, believe it still today? The growing ranks of vegetarians and vegans have answered no, and it appears that many others don't know quite what to think.[5] The remarkable number of discussions in our newspapers and magazines about what we eat and how we raise our food, and the popularity of "free-range," "cage-free," "grass-fed," and "organic-pastured," suggest that change is afoot. And that makes sense. The question of meat eating has long been bound up with the question of human beings' place in nature. As the historian Tristram Stuart observes in his book *The Bloodless Revolution*, there is a deep connection between "the ancient question of man's nature" and "the equally ancient question of man's natural food."[6] Against the background of major changes in our conception of nature, the question itself becomes natural: What ought we to think about meat eating today? Is killing animals for food morally permissible? If so, what animals? Yes to fish, but no to whales? Yes to cows and pigs and turkeys, but no to horses and dogs and chimpanzees? Why or why not? And what about pets?[7]

As these questions indicate, the main subject of this chapter is what to make of our use of animals for food. The chapter also discusses, however, subjects that readers not already familiar with the literature on meat eating might find surprising if not shocking in this context. Cannibalism makes an appearance, and the question of the moral standing of human beings with severe cognitive impairments figures prominently. But these are not distractions. As the chapter's title, "Animals and Us," is meant to suggest, thinking about animals inevitably involves thinking about ourselves: human beings, persons, or however we want to name, and draw boundaries around, who or what "we" are. After all, we are also animals. What then makes us different from other animals? And, to the point for present purposes, what is the difference between us and animals that makes a moral difference—that makes it all right, if it is all right, to eat an animal, but not all right to eat one of ourselves?

Truth to tell, I find this topic really quite difficult to feel sure about. My hope for this chapter is that it will help readers both to understand what's so difficult here and to get clearer on what they hold and why, or at least on what they need to think through further in order to be morally responsible. My thesis is that, in principle, meat eating can pass moral muster; in fact, however, there's much about our treatment of animals that's just abominable.

AFTER DARWIN

The Christian tradition isn't of one mind on the question of meat eating. For example, the Latin church father Jerome (ca. 347–420) considered

God's giving Noah the animals to eat a "grudging concession" to our fallen nature.[8] In Genesis 1, God gives humankind as food "every plant yielding seed…and every tree with seed in its fruit" (1:29); it's only after learning that "the inclination of the human heart is evil from youth" that God relaxes the rules (Gen 8:21). In *Against Jovinianus*, Jerome went so far as to argue that "by fasting we can return to paradise, whence…we have been expelled."[9] The church responded, however, not by prohibiting meat altogether, but by institutionalizing periodic fasting, as in Lent. Even Saint Francis (1181/1182–1226), who preached to the birds, as legend has it, did not preach vegetarianism. The problem wasn't only that beggars can't be choosers (Jesus instructs his disciples in Luke 10:8 to "eat what is set before you"); it was also that by rejecting meat, one risked being associated with the heretical Manichaeans and Cathars—which in the Middle Ages meant a date with the Inquisition. Seventeenth-century religious radicals like the Diggers in England echoed Jerome's call to renounce meat and argued for extending the Golden Rule to animals; but, according to Stuart, "'vegetarianism' as a separate religious position did not take hold as much in Catholic countries as it did in Protestant regions after the Reformation."[10] Ironically, Catholic fast laws also institutionalized the eating of meat—that is, on those days it wasn't prohibited.

In recent times, the most forceful challenge to meat eating may be *Created from Animals: The Moral Implications of Darwinism*, by the late American philosopher James Rachels (1941–2003).[11] Catholics have reason to dissent from Rachels's anthropology,[12] but his argument must be engaged. Rachels begins by claiming that, "after Darwin, we can no longer think of ourselves as occupying a special place in creation—instead, we must realize that we are the products of the same evolutionary forces, working blindly and without purpose, that shaped the rest of the animal kingdom."[13] Darwinism "poses a problem for traditional morality," according to Rachels, because traditional morality, like traditional religion, "assumes that man is 'a great work'" and "grants humans a moral status superior to that of any other creatures on earth."[14] But what happens to this belief, Rachels asks, "if man is but a modified ape?"[15] His answer is simple: "Human life will no longer be regarded with the kind of superstitious awe which it is accorded in traditional thought, and the lives of nonhumans will no longer be a matter of indifference."[16]

Both these conclusions need examination, but for now, what's important is to understand Rachels's argument. It turns on an analysis of the "core idea" of human dignity and the grounds for our belief in this idea. Rachels identifies two parts to this idea:

> The first part is that human life is regarded as sacred, or at least as having a special importance; and so, it is said, the central concern of our morality must be the protection and care of human beings. The second part says that nonhuman life does not have the same degree of protection. Indeed, on some traditional ways of thinking, nonhuman animals have no moral standing at all. Therefore we may use them as we see fit.[17]

If traditional morality is founded on the idea of human dignity, Rachels argues, and if this idea founders once we take evolutionary theory to heart, then traditional morality also founders and we can no longer hold that human life enjoys nearly absolute protection and nonhuman life enjoys none, or next to none. In Rachels's words again, "Darwinism provides reasons for doubting the truth of the considerations" supporting the idea of human dignity, namely, "that humans are morally special *because* they are made in the image of God, or because they are uniquely rational beings," essentially different (say in terms of soul) from all other animals.[18] That we evolved from animals means that we, too, are animals, different only in degree, not in kind, from the rest of the animal kingdom. This is the burden of Charles Darwin's argument in *The Descent of Man*.[19]

It may well follow from Rachels's argument, if we take it to heart, that "human life will no longer be regarded with the kind of superstitious awe which it is accorded in traditional thought"[20]—though we shouldn't deceive ourselves that all human beings, like the severely cognitively impaired, always have been accorded respect rather than neglected and even tormented. It's noteworthy that a collection of writings by Rachels's fellow animal liberationist, the Australian philosopher Peter Singer, is frankly titled *Unsanctifying Human Life*. And it's also noteworthy that

Rachels was the author of a very clever and frequently anthologized article in favor of voluntary active euthanasia.[21] But does "unsanctifying human life" threaten to liberate much more, and much worse, than Rachels hoped for? As Stuart documents in *The Bloodless Revolution*, "Vegetarianism was in fact as prominent [in the early twentieth century] in the Fascist Right as it was on the Left." There were a variety of reasons, from attraction to "the vegetarian rhetoric of purification" to "antipathy to Judeo-Christian anthropocentrism."[22] But what ought to give us pause is that the Nazis' recalibration of the moral worth of animals "did nothing to encourage sensitivity to the suffering" of those whom the Nazis deemed human nonpersons and instead appears to have helped anaesthetize the consciences of physicians who experimented on these human beings with abandon.[23] It might well be asked, then, whether it would be wiser to increase our estimation of some other animals—for example, those capable of what the British philosopher Mary Midgley has called "emotional fellowship"—rather than lower our estimation of humanity.[24]

We might wonder, too, whether undercutting human dignity necessarily means bringing liberation to nonhuman life—or, as Rachels puts it, making nonhuman life "no longer…a matter of indifference." Rachels never considers whether there is a connection between belief in human dignity and commitment to the moral life. He seems to take for granted that people will always care about morality and even consider it of utmost importance. But it could be that denying human dignity risks jeopardizing our sense of responsibility to the natural world and might thereby lead to precisely the indifference that Rachels seeks to vanquish. This worry is speculative—there's no evidence to prove it—but that's not to say it's baseless. If humans have no "special importance," no vocation or calling that other animals don't have, why would we feel any special responsibility to be the natural world's steward?[25] As the American philosopher Cora Diamond has claimed (somewhat gnomically, as is her style), "It is not members of one among species of animals that have moral obligations to anything. The moral expectations of other human beings demand something of me as other than an animal."[26] No other animal, after all, shows pity for other animals. No other animal can be accused of being *inhuman*, and no other animal can be enjoined to be *humane*.

114

So long as we do care about morality, however, the case for vegetarianism cannot be easily dismissed. After Darwin, there is no disputing our kinship with the rest of the animal kingdom, and so Rachels's central claim stands: Darwinism presents a challenge to traditional morality's double standard for human and nonhuman life. What's more, though Catholics and others might want to rebut Rachels's attack on human dignity, the conviction that humans are made in God's image hardly supports a denial of God's bounty elsewhere in Creation. To cite just a couple examples, it's worth recalling that, at the end of the Book of Job, God goes on and on about his care for animals (including lions and asses and ostriches), apparently reproving Job for his self-centeredness. Likewise, the Creation story in Genesis 1 attests to the goodness of all of Creation, not only the work of the afternoon of the sixth day.

THE ARGUMENT FROM MARGINAL CASES, OR MORAL INDIVIDUALISM REDUX

In positing a baseline equality between human and nonhuman life, supposed to be different only in degree, not in kind, Rachels is on common ground with many other philosophers. Peter Singer, for one, has urged "that we extend to other species the basic principle of equality that most of us recognize should be extended to all members of our own species": like consideration for like interests.[27] By contrast, the most tried and true way to distinguish humans from animals is to observe that, as Augustine put it, "these do not share the use of reason with us." Lacking reason, animals lack the necessary condition for having duties and obligations. Therefore, it is claimed, they do not belong to the moral community. Yet, against these observations, it can be countered that not all human beings share the use of reason at every point of life, notably the beginning and the end; and some, such as the severely cognitively impaired, do not even have the potential to do so. What's more, the fact that a human being does not or even cannot have obligations implies neither that she cannot be the beneficiary of obligations, nor that others have no obligations toward her. Think of children, to whom we owe more rather than less when they are very young, or the very elderly, to whom family members—and I would want to argue society as a whole—owe duties of care. In sum, the fact that animals "do not share the use of reason with us" cannot be the reason why we hold that they can be eaten. Otherwise, horribly, we would have to agree that it is licit to eat many human beings as well.

This line of thought is often called—though offensively, I think—the argument from marginal cases. It takes a human being who is lacking or severely impaired in rationality and independence (the so-called marginal human being in question) and argues that, if such a human being is nonetheless inviolable in various ways—for example, neither fit for food nor a subject for nonvoluntary medical experimentation—animals with comparable or even more formidable capacities must likewise be inviolable. Think, for example, of marine mammals, great apes, and elephants to begin with, but perhaps many other animals as well if the class of human beings whom we hold to be inviolable includes children like the American philosopher Hilde Lindemann Nelson's sister Carla, who was afflicted with a neural tube disorder depriving her of self-awareness, rationality, and various other capacities which philosophers over the years have proposed as necessary for moral standing.[28]

The argument from marginal cases conceives of moral standing—in brief, what one has when one warrants moral consideration[29]—as turning on the possession of this or that set of properties, normally identified as psychological in nature and termed *capacities*. Possession of the relevant properties is sufficient for moral standing: as Rachels nicely writes, it means that "your interests constitute morally good reasons why you may, or may not, be treated in this or that way."[30] In technical terms, _____'s possession (fill in the blank) of the relevant properties gives rise to *agent-neutral* moral reasons to respect him or her, which is to say reasons that *all* agents have to do so, regardless of how they are related to _____, so whether they are strangers, friends, family, or whatever. The kicker is that, as Jeff McMahan has observed, "whatever we take to be the range of psychological capacities that differentiate us morally from animals, there are some human beings whose psychological capacities are

116

no more advanced than those of certain animals."[31] So whatever animals these are must be brought into the moral fold—so long as we hold that severely cognitively impaired human beings likewise belong.[32]

This argument is intended to break any link between moral standing and species membership. To quote McMahan again—an important revisionist on animals as he is on war—"Whatever the exact criterion for membership in the human species is, it will be a purely biological criterion. As such, it is difficult to see how it could have any intrinsic moral significance."[33] If species membership does not matter morally, then to invoke it as the justification for treating a member of another species in ways that one would not treat a member of one's own species—for example, killing it for food or subjecting it to medical experiments—is to be guilty of unjust discrimination, in a word *speciesism*, much as invoking race or gender in similar ways would make one guilty of racism or sexism.

Recall here, from chapter 4, McMahan's rejection of the relevance of group membership for liability to attack in war. As we saw then, according to him, what matters morally is not whether one is a civilian or a combatant, but whether one bears moral responsibility for an objectively unjustified threat, whatever group one belongs to. In the present case as well, McMahan is committed to what Rachels before him dubbed *moral individualism*, which is "a thesis about the justification of judgments concerning how individuals may be treated."[34] As Rachels explains it,

> The basic idea is that how an individual may be treated is to be determined, not by considering his group memberships, but by considering his own particular characteristics. If A is to be treated differently from B, the justification must be in terms of A's individual characteristics and B's individual characteristics. Treating them differently cannot be justified by pointing out that one or the other is a member of some preferred group, not even the "group" of human beings.[35]

But let's complicate matters. Tristram Stuart tells the tale of Richard Brothers, an eighteenth-century British religious radical (1757–1824) who sought to revive the prelapsarian diet of fruit and vegetables and who, for various reasons, suffered the fate of many other radicals of his day: he was thrown in jail. There, Stuart writes, "The jailers' masterstroke was giving these prisoners a choice: eat beef or starve."[36] Brothers ate beef, and who could blame him? It is difficult to imagine that there could be much to say for the claim that he failed morally—though surely he would have failed had he agreed to eat, say, newborn human babies, or the severely cognitively impaired, whether young or old.

Philosophers like Rachels, Singer, and McMahan agree with the position that Brothers did no wrong in eating beef rather than starving to death. They further agree with the position that, had he needed to kill a cow in order to live, this too would have been morally permissible for him to do. Singer puts the reason simply in an imaginative dialogue with his daughter Naomi, who says to him that when she was little, she used "to wonder who you would save if the house caught fire," her or the family dog Max.[37] Singer replies,

> I'm your father, of course I would have saved my lovely baby daughter. But [beyond the fact that you're my daughter], normal humans have capacities that far exceed those of nonhuman animals, and some of these capacities are morally significant in particular contexts. Look at you....Your whole life is future-oriented to a degree that is inconceivable for Max. That gives you much more to lose, and gives an objective reason for anyone—not just your father—to save you rather than Max if the house catches fire.[38]

More technically, McMahan contrasts what he calls the *time-relative interests* of animals with those of persons, by which he means "individuals who are self-conscious, irrespective of species."[39] What it means to have an *interest* in something is for one's well-being to depend on it in some or other way.[40] So human beings and animals have, all other things being equal, a basic interest in staying alive, without which we would not *be* at all, at least in our present state. What it means for an interest to be *time relative* is that it can be greater or lesser depending on one's present investment in it: in other words, though a bit roughly put, depending on whether or not it is a matter of egoistic concern for one here and now. As McMahan quotes the British novelist Aldous Huxley (1894–1963), because "the dumb creation

118

lives a life made up of discreet and mutually irrelevant episodes," an animal's time-relative interest in living into the future is much weaker than that of a normal, adult human being, the paradigm of a person on McMahan's account.[41] In brief, you, a human person, have much more to lose than an animal, because you, like Naomi, are greatly interested in your future, to an extent that an animal like a cow or a dog just cannot be.[42]

THE MORALITY OF SPECIAL RELATIONS

So far, we might say, so good: Naomi lives instead of Max, Brothers instead of the cow—but what about an elderly person suffering from severe dementia who has but a few weeks to live? Can we say that he is greatly interested in his future, to an extent that an animal just cannot be? It's instructive to consider in this regard how offensive and disgusting it would be to *name* the human being whom—we recoil even at the thought—Brothers might have eaten in place of the cow he did eat. Why do we recoil at the thought of Brothers's eating _____, so-and-so's son or daughter or sister or brother?

Here is one possible answer, in dispassionate philosophical terms. Though possession of this or that set of intrinsic properties is *sufficient* for moral standing (it suffices, meaning it's enough for one to qualify), possession of the relevant properties may not be *necessary* for moral standing, which is to say one may warrant moral consideration nonetheless, even without the intrinsic properties in question. Instead, some so-called *relational properties*—the fact that one is related to someone else in some significant way—may likewise suffice to make one morally considerable. So, for example, a mouse or even a rat may warrant moral consideration because it is someone's pet. While to kill a mouse or rat in one's house might normally be morally permissible, to kill the pet mouse or rat, simply because it is in one's house, would be to do the pet owner a wrong. The mouse or rat warrants some measure of moral consideration because it is someone's pet and that person cares for it. Considerations like this fall under what is called the morality of special relations.

This answer to the question of why we recoil at the thought of Brothers's eating _____ can be developed by turning to McMahan,

119

though it's suggested as well by Singer's dialogue with his daughter, a morally significant special relation if there is one. According to McMahan, while "many—perhaps most—of the moral reasons we have to act or not to act in certain ways derive from a consideration of the intrinsic properties of other beings who might be affected by our action," the so-called *agent-neutral* moral reasons we thereby have "may be supplemented, strengthened, or reinforced by reasons deriving from one's relations to others," that is, by so-called *agent-relative* moral reasons.[43] These are moral reasons that some but not all people have because they stand in morally significant special relations with others: for example, Singer with his daughter Naomi. But—and here's the important point for present purposes—all persons have agent-neutral reasons to respect other persons' agent-relative reasons. By way of explanation, think of the pet owner again: that he cares for his pet gives all of us reason not to harm it. Bluntly put, then, Brothers had moral reason not to eat _____ because she was someone's sister or daughter, which is to say related to persons who had special reasons to protect and care for her because of the morally significant special relationships in which they stood to her. Brothers's moral reason not to eat _____ was then indirect or derivative.[44] Technically put again, it was an agent-neutral moral reason (a moral reason all agents have) to respect the agent-relative moral reasons (the reasons only people with special relations to _____ had) not to harm her, if she was alive, or to desecrate her, if she was not.

It's not hard to imagine someone's objecting at this point that, had _____ been dead already, eating her, whether she was once severely cognitively impaired or not, would have been morally permissible, or if not permissible ("nothing stands in its way") then at least excusable given the extreme circumstances. Readers might recall, toward the end of Dante's *Inferno*, the tale of Count Ugolino, who, imprisoned with his four sons, succumbed in the end—or so Dante's Italian allows and the context suggests—to eating his sons' flesh after they had died at his feet.[45] Perhaps this was morally permissible or at least excusable, but keep in mind that we hear this story in…hell. Whether it was damnable or not for Ugolino to have eaten his dead sons, he tortures himself for it. And who, in nearly his right mind, would not? What Ugolino's jailers did to him, I think, was to dehumanize him. They pushed him, with the connivance of his own hunger, beyond the bounds of the human, well past any point of return.[46] And so his life became hell.

Brothers's jailers, though dastardly, were not nearly so diabolical. But imagine, only a little while longer, that they were. Imagine that Brothers had to kill his food: _____, who recall is severely cognitively impaired, or a cow, or a pig (often compared in the literature to dogs for intelligence). Imagine also that _____ had no living relations, so apparently no relational properties giving rise to moral reasons to respect her apart from whatever intrinsic properties she possessed.[47] Incredibly, or at least incredibly to me, McMahan appears committed to holding that, had Brothers killed a pig instead of _____, he would have been guilty of speciesism, unjust discrimination.[48] For here we have the case of an animal with, it seems, more advanced psychological capacities, and so presumably a stronger time-relative interest in living into the future, than a human being. Singer leaves little doubt that this would be his position:

> Normally…if we have to choose between the life of a human being and the life of another animal, we should choose to save the life of the human; but there may be special cases in which the reverse holds true, because the human being in question does not have the capacities of a normal human being.[49]

The reason why McMahan appears committed to the position that it would be *speciesist* to kill the pig instead of _____ is in fact twofold: (1) not only does the pig seem to have more advanced psychological capacities and so presumably a stronger time-relative interest in living into the future; but (2) McMahan also rejects that bare comembership in the human species counts as a morally significant special relation. As he notes, there are two ways that special relations might be significant. First, a special relation might be *instrumentally* significant because it contributes other goods—that is, it is instrumental to other goods—that otherwise might not be enjoyed. The example McMahan gives here is membership in a nation: being in the relation of conational or fellow citizen to others contributes to people's sense of security and self-esteem.[50] (For example, it is *something* to be a Spaniard or an American or an

Aussie.) Second, a special relation might be *intrinsically* significant "if it generates moral reasons for action that are independent of or irreducible to the contribution that the relation might make to any other good," or in other words, if it figures as "a fundamental or nonderivative source of moral reasons."[51] To explain by way of example, take the parent-child relationship. The reason why Singer ought to give preferential treatment to his daughter Naomi is that she is his daughter, full stop, and not because giving preferential treatment to her contributes to other goods in his life (say it makes him profoundly happy), though it might do that as well.

But here is the trouble for the case we are imagining. According to McMahan, comembership in the human species

> is not, like the parent-child relation, a close or personal relation. Nor is it, like cultural membership, a relation that is constituted by shared values; for radically cognitively impaired human beings do not and cannot share our values any more than animals do. Mere co-membership in the human species is instead like co-membership in a racial group in being a purely biological relation: a matter of genealogy, genetics....It is hard to see how this could be intrinsically significant.[52]

As he sees it, the upshot is that "what has been called 'speciesism'—giving preference to members of one's own species—turns out to be remarkably like racism after all."[53] For, to reiterate and then some,

> bare co-membership in the human species, which is what we share with the cognitively impaired, does not involve personal ties, mutual sympathy, shared values, a common commitment to a certain way of life, social cooperation, or any of the other features that are more readily recognized as legitimate bases for partiality.[54]

Bare comembership in the human species involves just biology. Other things being equal, since invoking biology does not justify discrimination between persons of different races, how then could invoking biology justify discrimination between living beings of different species?

If comembership in the human species isn't an *intrinsically* significant special relation, however, it might still be an *instrumentally* significant special relation: one that contributes goods that otherwise might not be enjoyed. And this McMahan allows: according to him, it could be that "loyalty and partiality within the human species" elicit "special solicitude for the weaker and more vulnerable members of our species, particularly the radically cognitively impaired," who thereby have better lives than they otherwise would.[55] But trouble arises again. A special relation that has instrumental significance—that brings goods—might also bring evils. If it brings greater evils than goods, we would have reason to repudiate it. Nationalism is McMahan's example here. "While nationalist sentiment may have beneficial effects within the nation," it can also be mobilized to dehumanize members of other nations—think of Aryan anti-Semitism— and thus lead the way to brutality and atrocity.[56] One last quotation makes McMahan's position clear:

> I believe that our treatment of the severely retarded and our treatment of animals follow a similar pattern. While our sense of kinship with the severely retarded moves us to treat them with great solicitude, our perception of animals as radically "other" numbs our sensitivity to them, allowing us to abuse them in various ways with an untroubled conscience....When one compares the relatively small number of severely retarded human beings who benefit from our solicitude with the vast number of animals who suffer at our hands, it is impossible to avoid the conclusion that the good effects of our species-based partiality are greatly outweighed by the bad.[57]

NAMING THE NAMELESS

As chapter 4 showed, McMahan is a creative, rigorous philosopher to be reckoned with; but the preceding quotation does not show him at his best. What is his evidence for such a provocative claim? On what grounds does he believe that the good elicited by partiality to our fellow human beings has, as its obverse, evil to animals? The American philosopher Eva

Feder Kittay, who is the mother of a child named Sesha "diagnosed as severely to profoundly retarded,"[58] has aptly replied that she "was inclined to think that it was general greed and insensitivity that was responsible for the massive abuse of animals"—but that it was "the same greed and insensitivity that refused funds to educate and treat with decency...mentally retarded individuals" and that, for so long, allowed "mentally retarded adults to languish and die from neglect."[59]

If Kittay is right, McMahan is mistaken in his calculation of the instrumental significance of comembership in the human species. Contrary to his account, there is no basis for holding that partiality to our fellow human beings, however gifted or disabled, brings more evil than good; what's to be blamed is greed and insensitivity, which we see not only in our treatment of animals, but in our treatment of the vulnerable among us and in the general day-to-day crumminess that seems endemic to human beings. Perhaps, accordingly, McMahan would not hold in the end that it would be wrong for Brothers to kill a pig over _____ that it would be speciesist to do so. Perhaps, instead, he would allow that solicitude for our fellow human beings generates overall good. But the problem with his argument lies, I think, deeper than a miscalculation of goods and evils.

It is a remarkable fact that, while arguments over animals and meat eating sometimes do change people's minds and behavior, in my experience, they often don't. Instead, they fail to engage, or at least to convince people fully. What makes this remarkable is that these arguments, as we have just seen, are both sophisticated and well-developed.

Some acknowledge the force of arguments against eating meat (which, it is assumed, is the status quo in need of defense), but don't feel compelled to stop—and wonder whether the lesson here is that morality does not trump all other commitments, such as to the comforts of tradition (think of the Thanksgiving turkey) or the spice of culture (think of ethnic and regional cuisines). I wonder whether the reasons for indifference and resistance do not lie deeper. Here is one suggestion: Could it be that we are so accustomed to eating meat—to its pleasure and convenience—that we just do not want, even *cannot* want to take seriously arguments against it? *Without* assimilating the industrial production of meat to the American system of chattel slavery or to the Nazis' slaughter of the Jews and other peoples—deliberately provocative points of comparison found in the literature—these remind us that people can be unable to see evil even when it is plain as day. Even slaves can fail to see the evil of slavery, instead seeing themselves as only slaves, not persons, unfit for freedom, unworthy of respect.[60] The problems in this case lie deeper than argumentation can reach. They are problems of moral imagination and vision, which philosophical argumentation rarely supplies and normally has to take for granted. Arguably, a similar failure of moral imagination and vision may be at work in the present case: many of us do not want, perhaps even *cannot* want, to envision the "conditions of production" that bring our food to us; we prefer to look away. If so, however, we are looking away from a matter that, as we glimpse but do not care to see, calls uncomfortably for our attention.[61]

I think this suggestion is correct so far as it goes, but how far it goes isn't clear to me. For here is another, rather different suggestion: arguments against meat eating often fail to engage because they are badly framed. More fully, many of these arguments operate with a distorted understanding of the moral life, more precisely the basis of our concern for our fellow human beings, and so not only do they *not* click with some of our basic moral commitments, they clash with and to some extent threaten these commitments. The upshot is that, even when they impress us, these arguments do not move us—or at least a good many of us—to change. Instead, we go away with a vague feeling that there is some problem somewhere, maybe even a deep and serious problem, though whether it's with us or with the arguments we can't say.

McMahan's argument certainly clashes with and threatens commitment to the vulnerable among us, like Hilde Lindemann Nelson's sister Clara and Eva Feder Kittay's daughter Sesha. There is some urgency, then, to understanding where his argument goes wrong. Recall my observation, some pages ago, that it is instructive to consider how offensive and disgusting it would be to *name* the human being whom Brothers might have eaten in place of the cow he did eat: _____, so-and-so's daughter or sister or brother. We did not tarry to consider this, but looked instead at possible answers to why it would be wrong to eat such a human being, named or not. These answers all focused on the human being's properties.

125

Did she have any *intrinsic properties* warranting respect? Did she have any *relational properties* warranting respect? If not, it seemed that she warranted less respect than a pig, in the extreme case where such a man as Brothers had to choose between the life of the two. But recall also my brief discussion of the torture of Count Ugolino. What Ugolino's jailers did to him, I claimed, was to dehumanize him. Would not Brothers, too, have dehumanized himself by killing and eating _____? Would not this have been inhuman? Would it not have pushed him beyond the pale of the human?

It is a peculiar feature of much contemporary moral philosophy that it does not recognize any significance to being human. What counts, instead, is being a *person*, which it is claimed some human beings fail to be, if they lack self-awareness, rationality, or whatever other property (normally a psychological capacity) is supposed to be necessary to make the cut. McMahan's thinking is exemplary here. But such philosophies fail us. For, to paraphrase Hamlet, there are more things on earth than they are able to account for. What sense can they make of the fact that it would be dehumanizing, inhuman, beyond the pale to kill and eat _____? They seem unable even to account for what would be dehumanizing about feeding on one's dead children. Granted, they could reject these claims as question begging: as assuming precisely what needs to be established, namely, that it's dehumanizing to eat another human being. But it's not tough-minded to hold that Brothers ought to kill and eat _____ over a pig.[62] It's not insightful to see no violation in Ugolino's repast. Instead, it is deeply blind to the fact that the concept *human being* is not merely descriptive, useful for classifying living things as this rather than that, but itself a moral notion.[63] Cora Diamond again puts the point gnomically but well: "Life with the concept *human being* is very different from life with the concept *member of the species Homo Sapiens*."[64] To have the concept of human being is to belong to a much richer, morally significant world.

Consider as an example, finally, naming. Diamond asks a striking question: "Are human beings—most or all of them—such as to *merit or justify* being named not numbered? Or is the giving of names, the treating of naming and of names, significant as a part of the having of that

notion of the human that is ours?"[65] Take _____, the severely cognitively impaired human being we have not yet named. Does she *warrant*
a name, as opposed to a number or no name or number at all? We might
ask, Does she have intrinsic or relational properties that would make
naming her not only appropriate, but called for? Or are these considerations simply confused, out of touch with the practice of giving names,
which is not justified or warranted by the properties of the human being
in question, but is one of the practices that *goes into* what it is to live as
human beings? In support of this last suggestion, would it not be shocking to refuse to name _____, but only to assign her a number—as
we know the Nazis did the Jews? Would this not be inhuman?

A further observation of Diamond's is to the point: "Doing [a child]
out of a name is not like doing her out of an inheritance to which she has
a right and in which she has an interest."[66] What's different is profound.
To quote Diamond at length:

> It is not out of respect for the interests of beings of the class to
> which we belong that we give names to each other, or that we
> treat human sexuality and birth or death as we do, marking
> them—in their various ways—as significant or serious.
> And…it is not respect for our interests which is involved in
> our not eating each other. These are all things that go to deter-
> mine what sort of concept 'human being' is. Similarly with
> duties to human beings. This is not a consequence of what
> human beings are, it is not justified by what human beings
> are: it is one of the things which go to build our notion of
> human beings.[67]

I think we can now answer the question of why it would it be offensive and disgusting to name the severely cognitively impaired human
being whom Brothers might have eaten: naming her acknowledges her
humanity, thereby changing her from being an abstract philosophical
example to being "of woman born." And we do not eat our fellow human
beings. To anticipate an objection, yes, the historical record shows that
some human societies have practiced cannibalism, in particular under
conditions of famine, as part of funeral customs, and as a special ritual

after war or to appease the gods;[68] but no society has looked upon all its members, as a matter of course, as potential food. How otherwise could it have become a society? In any event, such a form of life is deeply foreign to us with our concept of human being.[69] It does not occur to us that so-and-so might be tasty or at least nutritious, and we do not have to silence this thought. Only the deeply ill and estranged would have to put such thoughts out of mind.

The philosopher, however, might persist. What justifies our form of life? he might ask. On what grounds do we not eat each other? Why shouldn't we? Surely it is, if it is at all, because of our properties and interests! But, to reply, is that why we give names to our children?[70] Is that why we solemnize birth, marriage, and death? Are justifications in place for these practices, or are they instead *sources* of moral life, which is to say partly constitutive of the framework in which properties and interests matter at all? After all, why care about, for example, self-awareness and rationality? Why should we be impressed by these? That an argument like McMahan's, which takes properties as basic, would apparently lead to the noxious conclusion that Brothers should kill and eat _____ indicates that taking properties as basic is a mistake.

IF A LION COULD SPEAK

The many questions in the last several paragraphs point beyond what an introductory work of moral philosophy can investigate. More positively put, they represent invitations to enter more deeply into the practice of moral philosophy. In order, however, to link back to the matter of our treatment of animals, which after all is what sent us down this path, we have to consider a different question. Why is it that we have moral concern for the severely cognitively impaired, when in fact we do? If it is not because of "properties" these human beings possess, what is the reason?

I think the reason is that, so long as we have some measure of moral imagination and sympathy, we human beings who are, for example, capable of reading books like this one cannot help but see ourselves in human beings who are not so capable or even nearly so. We recognize that we share the same vulnerability of human flesh and are subject to a common weal and woe; we acknowledge that "there but for the grace of God go I."[71] And therein lies the basis of our concern for one another. Human dignity, which I discuss at greater length in the following chapter, appears to be based not on properties some human beings exhibit, but on being of woman born, being a member of the human family. Accordingly, Kittay rejects as both "otiose and odious"—beside the point and offensive—comparing what her daughter Sesha can and cannot do with what a dog can and cannot do. Kittay goes on, however, to observe that the things "Sesha can do she does as a human being would do them, though frequently imperfectly, but…humanly imperfect, not canine perfect." Sesha exhibits "a discordant set of abilities and disabilities," quite different from those of any dog, pig, or other animal.[72] Anyone who has eyes to see can see him or herself in Sesha, can recognize the deep commonality of our condition, and can acknowledge the appropriateness, indeed the imperative of extending moral concern to her. To do otherwise would be inhuman.

Now we can turn back to animals. The Austrian philosopher Ludwig Wittgenstein, whom we met at the beginning of chapter 4, notoriously remarks in his masterpiece *Philosophical Investigations*, "If a lion could speak, we could not understand him."[73] This remark has been puzzled over and disputed; but here is some sense that we can make of it for present purposes. As I noted above, it does not occur to us that so-and-so might be tasty or at least nutritious. Only the deeply ill and estranged would have to put such thoughts out of mind. It is part of the concept of human being—and it is normative for our interactions with one another and care of ourselves—that a human being is neither food for other human beings, nor a pet, nor a collection of parts available for perusal and purchase (relevant to the next chapter on markets in human kidneys). Our attitude toward one another is categorically different from our attitude toward food, pets, and prosthetics. But how would a lion see us? What would be its attitude toward us and the world more generally?

Given that animals cannot talk, or more precisely, that they do not have language like ours, it is difficult to imagine what it is like to be an animal. So much of what we're conscious of—for example, that today's date is _____ (fill in the date of your reading this sentence), or that Christmas is coming, or the end of the school year—animals cannot be, inasmuch as what we're conscious of cannot be represented without language.[74] And how to describe what a lion sees when it sees what we call an antelope running across the savanna? It is not even precise to say that the lion sees prey in motion, for a lion does not have any of these concepts.[75]

If Wittgenstein's lion *could* speak, however, why could we *not* understand it? I think the suggestion is that the lion's form of life is so alien to us that, although we could understand its words, we could not understand—perhaps better: we could not see likewise for ourselves—its way of conceiving the world. In brief, we still could not see human beings as food; this bearing toward one another is one that we can't put on without beginning to lose hold of our humanity. (Just try it, though not for long.) We're repulsed, because the lion's attitude toward the world is not only alien to us, but self-alienating should we put it on ourselves. Here's how I imagine replying to the lion: No, I just can't see the world like that. No, I just can't understand you, or how you could see things as you do. (For example, if the lion's a he, I'm not with you in killing off and eating male cubs you didn't sire.) I mean, I understand what you're saying, but I just can't understand things the way you do—I'm just not like that. How you see things is incomprehensible to me, and I'm glad of it![76]

Yet, so long as we have some measure of imagination and sympathy, the lives of animals—even rats, chickens, snakes, frogs, and birds—are not entirely foreign to us, not entirely beyond our ken. Animals, too, suffer the afflictions of the flesh; like us, they are subject to the imperatives of sexuality and death. As the American philosopher Elizabeth Anderson has observed, "It is always rational to sympathize with a sentient being who is suffering"; this response always makes sense and is appropriate.[77] What's more, anyone who has eyes to see can see that some animals, among others chimpanzees and dogs, have distinctive "personalities," so to speak, which is to say individualized *takes* on the world that lay claim on our respectful attention.[78] Finally, some animals, like whales and orcas and eagles and sea otters, lay claim on our admiration for the beauty, intelligence, athleticism, and other excellences they exhibit.[79] In all these cases, we can see once more the appropriateness of extending some measure of moral concern. We can see, that is, that there are claims of value here that we have reason to heed.

THEOLOGICAL-PHILOSOPHICAL ANIMADVERSIONS

What, then, are we to do? More precisely, how, then, are we to eat?

Some years ago, in response to a relatively brief article on vegetarianism that I published in the magazine *Commonweal*, the British Anglican theologian Andrew Linzey sent me an email taking me to task for making the mistake of almost all Catholic moralists who write on this topic: focusing on the modern secular, philosophical literature on animals and ignoring modern theological discussions. Shortly thereafter, Linzey published the book *Why Animal Suffering Matters*. As I found then, at his best, Linzey is an impressively creative theologian. He brings fresh eyes to the tradition, discovers in it unexpected resources, and breathes new life into doctrines that had come to seem antiquated, such as the fallenness of the whole of Creation and not only humankind. (He rightly makes much of Romans 8:22: "We know that the whole of creation has been groaning in labor pains until now.") Think of him as our apostle for the animals. Whereas Paul wrote, "You foolish Galatians!" (Gal 3:1), Linzey has similar words for contemporary men and women most everywhere. Also like Paul, however, Linzey is an apostle for good. So let us, to begin to close this chapter, come to terms with him.

Why Animal Suffering Matters, which is as much philosophical as theological, focuses on making "the rational case for extending moral solicitude to animals."[80] Its key claim is that "the very rational considerations" that ground moral concern for young children should likewise "ground solicitude to animals."[81] Because Peter Singer is associated with this claim, Linzey goes out of his way to contrast his own thinking with Singer's. As we have seen, for Singer, some animals—a pig, for example— have a greater claim to moral consideration than do some human beings: a severely disabled infant, for example, or an elderly person suffering from severe dementia with but a few weeks to live. According to Linzey, Singer is guilty of *adultism*: that is, of granting people and animals moral standing only "insofar as they get closer to being mature, human adults" who have the capacities that Singer thinks warrant respect and so serve as his yardstick for all other living beings.[82] A further problem with Singer's approach, from Linzey's point of view, is that "it gives the impression that the cause of sentient animals can be advanced by minimizing our obligations to sentient humans" and thereby "confirms the worst slander on animal advocates—that our cause represents not an expansion but a narrowing of human sympathy."[83]

As we have also seen, justifications for exploiting animals typically turn on some alleged difference between human beings and animals. The question to consider is whether this or that difference is morally significant, which is to say whether it is the sort of difference that could justify, for example, our eating animals but not other human beings. Linzey focuses on three alleged differences. One is that animals lack language. Another is that, because it does not make sense to hold animals morally responsible for this or that action, they are not moral agents. And a third, which is theological in nature, is that according to Genesis (1:26–27), only human beings are made in the divine image.

In response to each of these claims, Linzey says not only "So what?" but, more originally, "So much the better for animals!" For if they do not share language with us, they obviously cannot consent to being sacrificed for research, butchered for food, caged for spectacle, and so forth. The twentieth century saw the development—and eventually the triumph—of the principle of informed consent, which in a medical context requires healthcare providers to obtain express permission for this or that intervention from any patient who is capable of giving it. According to Linzey, because animals are incapable of giving informed consent, we human beings have a special obligation to make sure that animals' interests are taken into account and respected. This is what the strong owe the vulnerable—and what most of us think adults owe children who are incapable of informed consent: not less consideration but more.[84]

As for the claim that animals are not moral agents, what follows from this, according to Linzey, is not that they may be treated with moral indifference but that they are "morally innocent or blameless" and therefore never deserve to be made to suffer.[85] Again, a parallel may be drawn with young children. They, too, are not moral agents. What follows, however, is not that we adults may treat them however we want, but instead that it would be a moral outrage to inflict suffering on a colicky baby, for example, as if the baby were morally responsible for being so thoughtlessly noisy.

Finally, the conclusion that Linzey draws from the claim that only human beings bear the *imago Dei* is that it then falls to human beings to be like God, who in the incarnation identifies with all creatures of flesh and blood and is revealed by Jesus to have special regard for the weak and powerless. In other words, "the divine image only warrants a more careful, diffident, and conscientious stewardship of creation"—children and animals in particular.[86] Such is the good news that Linzey proclaims.

Linzey's animal gospel, to use his own term, has been proclaimed by others as well. For example, the American Catholic theologian John Sniegocki cites "the Christian call to mercy, compassion, and the proper stewardship of the world's resources" as supporting vegetarianism in our day and age.[87] "This compassion," he explains, "is both for the innocent suffering of animals and for the suffering of humans that a meat-based diet contributes to," from ill effects on human health,[88] to the waste of foodstuffs that could otherwise feed the world's poor,[89] to the ecological devastation now threatening us all.[90] Others, however, have found reason to dissent. Robert Heaney, a professor of medicine who focuses on osteoporosis and has contributed as well to research on nutrition more generally, has claimed that, while "clearly we should avoid cruelty in our use of animals"—for example: fur farming and commercial sealing—"equally clearly, we need to eat animals…because they provide what is essential for our health."[91] According to Heaney, "There are many nutrients essential for human health that are found only in animal foods, particularly meat," among others vitamin B12 and the branched chain amino acids essential for insulin sensitivity.[92] Admittedly, artificial supplements can be taken, but, again in Heaney's words, "the book of nutrition is not yet fully written,"[93] and there is a case to be made that "for nutrient after nutrient, plant sources come up short when solely relied upon for human nutrition."[94]

In brief, then, one possible argument for eating meat is that we are constituted to benefit from it, especially before birth and during pregnancy, and that there are cumulative risks to abstaining. Here, against Linzey, the interests of children and the interests of animals appear to split apart—though only *appear*, because the science is ardently disputed,[95] so

133

much so that I have sometimes wondered whether there is an account of the biological facts that does not already reflect a position on the ethics of meat eating. Moreover, there's a case to be made that, for the great, great majority of people, becoming completely vegetarian would be healthier than any alternative they are likely to choose.[96]

In an earlier book titled *Animal Theology*, Linzey takes up the question of what to make of the fact that nature really is "red in tooth and claw." He does not claim that we ought to prevent carnivores from eating the meat that they need to survive, but he does claim that, with modern technology and science, we human beings both can and ought to approximate the peaceable kingdom envisioned in Isaiah 11:6–9—the wolf living with the lamb, the leopard lying down with the kid, the lion eating straw. On Linzey's reading, Jesus' so-called nature miracles are signs that in him "is a birth of new possibilities for all creation."[97] Moreover, according to Linzey, one of those new possibilities has been realized in our own time: we can live healthily as vegetarians, as the first human beings were enjoined to do before the flood (see Gen 1:29–30 and 9:1–4).[98]

One question here is whether the fact that there are alternatives to eating meat obliges us to take those alternatives. Normally, adult human beings don't need meat in order to survive and thrive,[99] and there are vegetarian options that are nutritious and tasty themselves. Another question is this: What should our position be toward the natural order? And yet another: Just what is our own nature? Like Linzey, most philosophers hold that the suffering caused by predators who need meat in order to survive is justifiable.[100] In the words of the American philosopher David DeGrazia, "Nature really seems to be 'red in tooth and claw' when it comes to carnivores"—which is all right, as he sees things, since predators have as much a right to live as prey do.[101] What is not all right, DeGrazia claims, is for us humans to try to justify our hunger for meat by claiming that we need it when we don't. But it might well be asked why eating meat is justifiable for carnivores but not for omnivores when we, too, eat meat to live, not only because we like it, if we do. Although adult human beings normally don't need meat to survive, eating meat comes naturally to us by way of our evolutionary history; recall Heaney's observation that "there are many nutrients essential for human health that are found only in animal foods, particularly meat." Recall also Tristram Stuart's observation, quoted some while ago, that there is a deep connection between "the ancient question of man's nature" and "the equally ancient question of man's natural food." For philosophers like DeGrazia and theologians like Linzey, eating meat is justifiable for carnivores because they have no choice, but humanity's reason requires us to correct our nature in this regard. In other words, our nature *as rational beings* leads us to see that the alleged facts of human biology do not justify what is otherwise unjustifiable: the needless suffering of sentient beings.

From one perspective—that of Augustine—there is a hint of heresy here, a worrying suggestion that nature, or at least our nature, fundamentally needs correction. From another—that of Jerome—there is a truth: nature needs correcting because it is fallen. (To recall Paul's words in Romans 8:22, "The whole creation has been groaning in labor pains until now.") Ultimately, it may be that the question of what to think about meat eating comes down to how we understand nature and our place in it. Is the natural order good? Is it good that there are human beings? Does our natural constitution give us a *natural right* to eat animals, supposing that an ideally health diet would include some meat? In terms of theology, we might well ask why God has allowed Creation to unfold according to the principle of natural selection. What does natural selection suggest about God? Is it to be understood as a consequence of Creation's fallenness? Is the way Creation currently works to be lamented and resisted, or is it a mystery, which might make us uneasy but must be acknowledged and lived with, even in our own diets?[102] After all, life lives from life....

BACK TO THE FACTORY FARM

These are rather big questions. It's no wonder, then, that so many people today don't know quite what to think about eating meat, and I hope it's clear by now why I find this topic difficult to feel sure about. For myself, after a period of vegetarianism in my twenties, I'm no longer a vegetarian, at least for now, as I tend to think that eating meat, though only occasionally and in modest quantities, might be justifiable on the grounds (1) that we are naturally constituted to benefit from it and (2) that our interests in this regard normally take precedence over those of so-called dumb creation (quoting McMahan quoting Huxley, above). Also, as this chapter has explained, I'm not impressed by the charge of speciesism, which I think is based on a misunderstanding of the basis of our moral concern for one another. That someone is of woman born—a member of the human family—suffices to give him or her a claim to our respect.

This doesn't mean, though, that I think we may treat all other animals however we please—or that all animals should be considered dumb and so candidates for our diet![103] If eating meat is justified because it is natural for us and may help us to flourish, consistency requires that we respect in turn the natures of the animals we eat: chickens, pigs, cows, fish, sheep, turkeys, and many others. Today's methods of industrial farming—agribusiness—notoriously do not show this respect. The conditions of life down on the factory farm have now been amply documented; see the Web site of People for the Ethical Treatment of Animals (PETA) for more than you probably want to know, but that you should before you decide to go on eating meat or not.[104] As one oft-quoted exposé puts it, "Cruelty is acknowledged only where profitability ceases."[105] In Singer's concise summary, "Animals are treated like machines that convert low-priced fodder into higher-priced flesh, and any innovation that results in a cheaper 'conversion-ratio' is liable to be adopted" without regard for the animals' natural impulses and needs.[106] Even antivegetarians like the food writer Nina Planck agree. According to her, "factory farms wreck the natural order," abusing animals, degrading the environment, and spoiling the quality of the meat we eat, with noxious consequences for our health.[107] Vegetarianism and veganism represent one response to this disturbing reality; the local-food movement represents another.[108]

Consistency with my proposed justifications for eating meat—that we are naturally constituted to benefit from it and our interests in this regard normally take precedence over those of so-called dumb creation—also requires one positive injunction. While the conditions of life on factory farms are not natural and ought to be resisted, the extension of our powers of sympathy beyond our own human species is natural and ought to be encouraged. I made this point earlier, in reflecting on chimpanzees and dogs and whales and orcas and eagles and sea otters…and the list could go on and on. One consequence of this injunction is that cruelty should not be an afterthought, "acknowledged only where profitability ceases." As Proverbs puts it, "The righteous know the needs of their animals, / but the mercy of the wicked is cruel" (12:10). Another consequence is that our appetite for meat should by no means be unrestricted. For example, animals that exhibit what Mary Midgley calls "social and emotional complexity of the kind which is expressed by the formation of deep, subtle and lasting relationships"—animals like the great apes, elephants, and dolphins—naturally elicit our sympathy and lay claims on us for respect, irrespective of what other intellectual capacities they have.[109]

It's easy, however, to profess respect for great apes, elephants, dolphins, and the like. Much harder—though really only because it's *inconvenient*—is to take a pass on meat that was "produced" through methods that, if only we did not look away, would disgust and appall us as both inhumane toward animals and irresponsible with respect to the environment and human health.[110] In criticizing McMahan, this chapter demonstrated what I take to be the problem with many arguments against meat eating: in brief, in the same terms used earlier, these arguments operate with a distorted understanding of the moral life, more precisely the basis of our concern for our fellow human beings. But there are also, I think, some problems with us.

I'm imagining that it's difficult to feel there is much objectionable about eating, say, a fast-food burger. Perhaps grass-fed would be better, but who, it might be countered, has the cash for that? Further, would that we all lived next to a family farm raising pigs and beef cattle, so that we all could be sure the animals we eat had good lives and we all could know what price they paid in nourishing us,[111] but how many of us do live in such a setting and so can eat such food? Instead, for most of us, our food comes to us the same way that nearly all of our other consumer goods do: from far away, and in a form that conceals the conditions of the good's production. This is the phenomenon known as *commodity distancing*, which unpacked means that as consumers, our relationship is first and foremost to the goods we buy,[112] while normally we have no knowledge of the people who made these goods and the conditions under which they worked—or the conditions of the lives of the animals that, killed and processed, we eat.[113] As one commentator has remarked in this regard, "It is easy to eat anonymous pigs or even factory-bred pigs purchased at the supermarket—it is very easy to forget about the cost to the pig. In fact, there is no need to *forget* it, for one was never aware of it in the first place."[114]

With awareness, however, should come action—so long as we can overcome what has been called the spiritual disease of speed, tempting us always to give priority to convenience.[115] Here is one reason to be wary of convenience with respect to our food. In the end, responsibly raised, even grass-fed beef in fact costs much, much less than the apparently cheap factory-bred products to be had at fast-food chains or the supermarket. When we take into account the so-called externalities of a fast-food burger—the costs passed down the line, or as economists say *externalized*, not reflected in what the buyer pays the seller—the conclusion follows that "industrial food has manipulated cheap prices for excess profit at excess cost to everyone," most evident in pollution, environmental degradation, and chronic disease.[116] The conclusion follows, in other words, that our diet is a mess, not least morally.

QUESTIONS FOR FURTHER REFLECTION/PAPER QUESTIONS

(1) Does the analogy between speciesism and racism hold up or collapse under scrutiny? Relevant to this question, is *human being* in fact a moral notion, not merely a biological classification? (Recall Cora Diamond's remark that "life with the concept *human being* is very different from life with the concept *member of the species Homo Sapiens*."[117]) Finally, which account of the basis of our moral concern for one another has more going for it, that of Singer and McMahan or that developed in this chapter? First explain what's at stake, then present your own position. Be sure to anticipate and counter objections.

(2) Look a bit further into the science of whether eating meat is at all good for us human beings. Consider the case that it is—that we are naturally constituted to benefit from it, and that there are cumulative risks to abstaining. If this case is credible, can it be claimed that we have, then, a *natural right* to eat at least some animals, namely, those with only minimal time-relative interests and without emotionally complex relationships? Or is a claim to having a natural right to eat such animals dependent on a now-discredited understanding of the natural world according to which the purpose of the lower is to serve the higher? (Recall Aquinas's argument cited at the very beginning of this chapter and James Rachels's argument concerning the implications of Darwin's theory of evolution.) In any event, if it is claimed we have a natural right to eat such animals, what would be its basis? Make the best case for this claim that you can, and then critically evaluate whether it is well-grounded or not. Be sure to anticipate and counter objections.

(3) You work for an animal liberation/animal rights think tank dedicated to protecting and advancing nonhuman animals' interests. For some years, the main thinker on which your organization has drawn for intellectual support has been Peter Singer, the founding figure of the contemporary animal liberation movement. More recently, Jeff McMahan has also been important to you. But you have just read this chapter subjecting Singer's and McMahan's arguments to criticism, while claiming to be sympathetic to animals' plight. Your job is to write a memo on whether your think tank and the animal liberation movement more generally should criticize this chapter in turn, or instead seek to draw from it in order to advance your cause. Title your memo "Friend or Foe?"

(4) Read Mark Bittman's blog post "Some Animals Are More Equal Than Others," published online by the *New York Times* on March 15, 2011 (http://opinionator.blogs.ny times.com/2011/03/15/some-animals-are-more-equal-than-others/?_r=0). Bittman draws attention to the double

standard in the way we treat pets, on the one hand, and animals raised for food, on the other. Write, for publication by the *Times*, a reflection on Bittman's argument, summed up in his statement "There's no rationality to be found here." Do you agree with him? One way or the other, which is to say however you come down, draw from this chapter's reflections on the morality of special relations. Lay out Bittman's argument toward the beginning of your response.

CHAPTER 6

KIDNEYS AND DIGNITY

On the Moral Limits of Markets

The subject of this chapter is no mere thought experiment: a movement to legalize the sale of human organs, in particular, kidneys, has gone mainstream.[1] What's more, this movement has unfolded against the background of a booming underground market for kidneys. According to the World Health Organization, "As many as 10 percent of the sixty thousand plus kidney transplants carried out each year involve payment to a non-related donor."[2] But what should we think of this movement? Just war theory has undergone development. Our attitudes toward animals appear to be in flux. Should we open our minds to new markets in human body parts?

If Aquinas is the key figure for Catholic moral philosophy, the great German philosopher Immanuel Kant (1724–1804) may be the key figure for modern moral philosophy more generally. Textbooks typically oppose Kant's deontological moral theory—his account of duty or of what is obligatory, which is the rough etymology of the word *deontology*—with the utilitarianism of the British philosophers Jeremy Bentham (1748–1832) and John Stuart Mill (1806–73). And so let us do here, though it should be noted that utilitarianism has become considerably more complex and refined since the nineteenth century. The so-called *utility* of an action is its power to produce good or bad consequences: more precisely for Bentham and Mill, pleasure (good) or pain (bad)—the consequences that Bentham and Mill take to matter for moral evaluation of an action.[3] Simply put, for Bentham and Mill, the better the consequences of an action in this regard, the better the action. Vice versa, the worse the consequences of an action in this regard, the worse the action. Utilitarianism is thus a species of the more general moral theory called *consequentialism*, which focuses, as the name suggests, on the consequences of actions.

By contrast, Kant is an arch anticonsequentialist. For him, too, the consequences of an action cannot help but matter for moral evaluation—after all, there is a sense in which an action is exactly identical with "the causing of each and every consequence to which the doer's agency in doing it extends"[4]—but the critical difference is that the rightness or wrongness of an action does not turn simply on the consequences: for example, what comes of a lie, or whether torture produces intelligence, or whether firebombing a city brings a quicker end to a war. Instead, Kant famously holds, a human being is never to be used merely as a means, but must always be respected as an end.[5] To explain in brief for now, when a human being figures in a so-called action plan as but another thing to do things with, we can be sure that he or she is not being accorded proper respect, whatever the consequences.[6] Sex trafficking is a heartrending, flabbergasting example. The offense against human dignity is patent.

Kant's own wording of the principle in question is as follows: "So act that you use humanity, whether in your own person or in the person of any others, always at the same time as an end, never merely as a means."[7] Such a principle is at the heart of modern liberal theory: each and every person is worthy of being *free* from domination; each and every person has a claim to *autonomy*, which is to say to direct his or her own life, rather than serve merely as an instrument to others' ends. According to Kant, actions are morally permissible or impermissible depending on whether the maxim or policy they reflect jibes with or flouts this principle. The maxim or policy of ours that an action reflects might be considered the "meaning" of the action inasmuch as it's what we mean to do in pursuing this or that end. An action plan includes not only the end of the action and the intended means to this end, but the maxim or policy. Policies of ours—from "always be kind" to "never fail to press your own advantage" and a thousand others—may be more or less explicit and also more or less available to scrutiny.

But here is a question: If, exercising your autonomy, you choose to use your own body for profit—say by selling it in sex, or by selling an organ like a kidney—would you run afoul of Kant's principle? In other words, would you be using "your own person…merely as a means"? And another question in turn: If so, would your action be wrong, or is what's wrong the principle that would prohibit it? Along these lines, is it not your body in question? Do we not *own* our bodies, and should you not then be free to do with your body as you will, so long as no one else is thereby injured? Following a tradition that is inspired more by John Stuart Mill than by Kant, the *libertarian* liberal theorist might claim that respect for autonomy requires respect for a person's unfettered voluntary choices and that only the prospect of harm to others suffices to justify constraint.[8]

THE EXPANDING MARKET

Twenty years ago, the American philosopher Elizabeth Anderson—cited in passing in chapter 5—remarked in her outstanding book *Value in Ethics and Economics*, "Liberal theory has not yet come to grips with the full implications for human freedom of [the] most expansionary institution of the modern world," namely, the market.[9] It has been some 120 years now that Catholic social thought has been explicitly wrestling with the implications of the market for human dignity. In the aftermath of the dissolution of "the ancient workingmen's guilds," Pope Leo XIII remarked in his groundbreaking encyclical *Rerum Novarum* (*Of New Things* or *Of Revolution*), "It has come to pass that working men have been surrendered, isolated and helpless, to the hardheartedness of employers and the greed of unchecked competition."[10] The pope went on to discuss, among other pressing matters of the day (1891), whether it is right to hold that wages are "regulated by free consent."[11] In other words, does a worker's agreement to a wage suffice to make it just, or is this agreement only a necessary and not a sufficient condition to satisfy the demands of economic justice? Pope Leo famously argued, from consideration of the nature of labor, that "wages ought not to be insufficient to support a frugal and well-behaved wage-earner"—in our terms today, that a wage is not just if it is not a *living wage*, adequate for a dignified human life.[12] Leo accordingly affirmed the development of labor unions as a means of humanizing, we might say, the labor market, lest its expansion come at the expense of workers' human dignity.[13]

As passing acquaintance with today's news would make clear, the struggle to protect workers from "the hardheartedness of employers and the greed of unchecked competition" is by no means over and won. In the United States, we know, income inequality has skyrocketed over the last several decades, while labor unions have sharply declined.[14] Further, the national minimum wage is more inadequate than ever to support a family.[15] What has changed as well is that, whereas forty years ago, "there was no expectation that fast-food or discount-retail jobs would provide a living wage, because these were not jobs that, in the main, adult heads of household did," the great loss of middle-class jobs over these same decades has pushed older and better educated workers into low-wage labor, which is where the market has been growing.[16] Meanwhile, the April 2013 collapse of an eight-story factory near Dhaka, the capital of Bangladesh, killing more than 1,100 people, serves as notice of the deplorable working conditions endured by the world's poorest of the poor—conditions seen in the United States in the nineteenth century, giving rise to the labor movement here and figuring in the background of Pope Leo's encyclical.[17] Reacting to news reports that the people who died in the factory in Bangladesh made the equivalent of thirty-eight euros per month, Pope Francis remarked, "This is called slave labor. Today in the world, this slavery is being committed against something beautiful that God has given us—the capacity to create, to work, to have dignity. How many brothers and sisters find themselves in this situation!"[18]

Despite these abuses and worrisome trends, enthusiasm for market institutions appears unabated. To quote another American philosopher, Debra Satz, even after the Great Recession that began in 2008, market institutions figure in our political discourse as "an all-purpose remedy for the defects of the cumbersome government bureaucracies of the Western world, the poverty of the Southern world, and the coercive state control of the planned economies."[19] There are, of course, good reasons to value markets, which Satz succinctly defines as "institutions in which exchanges take place between parties who voluntarily undertake them."[20] To begin with, markets are efficient mechanisms for the satisfaction of wants or desires, or in other words, for the maximization of utility. If you have tickets to a game or show but really want money, and I have money but want the tickets, a market in scalped tickets will be an efficient mechanism for you to satisfy your wants and for me to satisfy mine. As this example suggests, markets also serve freedom. Ideally at least, markets place people into horizontal, egalitarian, and anonymous relationships with one another.[21] If we don't like a price, for tickets or for our labor, we can take it or leave it—we can, in any event in principle, *exit* the relationship, which was not open in principle or in fact to retainers, servants, and peasants under the system of feudalism, which capitalism overcame.[22]

Two recent books with the same subtitle attest, however, that the expansion of the market into goods once thought off limits to buying and selling—more precisely, goods that people never considered buying or selling—makes even friends of the market uneasy. Should organs like kidneys be for sale? Should gametes (that is, eggs and sperm)? Should permits to pollute? Should women's reproductive labor? And what is wrong, if it is wrong, with selling sex? Debra Satz's 2010 *Why Some Things Should Not Be for Sale: The Moral Limits of Markets* and Michael Sandel's 2012 *What Money Can't Buy: The Moral Limits of Markets* focus on just these questions.[23]

CONSEQUENCES AND CONVICTIONS

This chapter focuses on but one of the controversial markets considered by Satz and Sandel: a market in human kidneys. I have chosen to focus on a market in human kidneys for a handful of reasons. First, though nearly all countries currently prohibit the sale of organs—Iran is a notable exception[24]—this ban is under growing pressure, as I noted at this chapter's very beginning. Second, the argument against legalizing a market in human kidneys is hardly open and shut. Consequentialist considerations—first and foremost, the fact that a ban on a market means that more people likely will suffer and die than otherwise would—point strongly in favor of changing the status quo. More than 100,000 persons in the United States now need a kidney; donations from living and deceased donors number between 16,500 and 17,000 annually. The upshot is that, as one advocate of changing the law has written, "Between now and this time tomorrow, 14 people will die, many after languishing on dialysis for 5 to 10 years."[25] These consequentialist considerations are often underwritten by libertarian convictions. So long as others are not thereby injured, the libertarian argument goes, a person ought to be free or "at liberty" to do what he wills with his or her body, or in any event, with his or her alienable body parts.[26]

The third reason to focus on a market in human kidneys is that we have two papal documents commenting explicitly and forcefully, if briefly, on the sale of organs and tissues: a 1991 address by Pope John Paul II and a 2008 address by Pope Benedict XVI. Rejecting the consequentialist and libertarian cases alike, both popes take stands against organ sales. In Pope Benedict's words, "The body can never be considered a mere object; otherwise the logic of the market would gain the upper hand."[27]

Finally, there are instructive differences among theorists who argue against a market in kidneys. Reflection on these differences, I claim, suggests that liberal theory's interest in protecting and promoting human *freedom* must involve it in questions of how to protect and promote human *dignity*—the longstanding interest of Catholic social thought. In other words, here liberal theory and Catholic social thought have interests in common. Kant, we might say, meets Aquinas.

DONATE, YES; SELL, NO?

Roman Catholic thought on organ and tissue donation and transplantation unfolds against the background of what has come to be called the principle of totality, derived, as we might expect, from none other than Aquinas.[28] Responding to the question of whether it is ever lawful to maim anyone, Aquinas writes,

> Since a member is only part of the whole human body, it is for the sake of the whole, as the imperfect is for the sake of perfect. Hence a member of the human body is to be disposed of according to what is advantageous for the whole. However, a member of the human body is of itself useful for the good of

the whole body, yet accidentally it may happen that it be hurtful, as when an infected member is a source of corruption to the whole body. If therefore the member is healthy and is in keeping with its natural disposition, it cannot be cut off without detriment to the whole man[29]

—but it may be cut off if doing so is necessary for the good of the whole human body to which it belongs.

We can see this principle in §29 of the *Ethical and Religious Directives for Catholic Health Care Services* promulgated by the United States Conference of Catholic Bishops:

> All persons served by Catholic health care have the right and duty to protect and preserve their bodily and functional integrity.[30]

The next sentence, however, qualifies this "right and duty":

> The functional integrity of the person may be sacrificed to maintain the health or life of the person when no other morally permissible means is available.[31]

A note explains further that "functional integrity" is not to be equated with "biological integrity":

> While the donation of a kidney represents loss of biological integrity, such a donation does not compromise functional integrity since human beings are capable of functioning with only one kidney.[32]

So the principle of totality is interpreted in such a way that makes room for some kinds of organ and tissue donation.

The *Directives* immediately specifies just what kinds in §30:

> The transplantation of organs from living donors is morally permissible when such a donation will not sacrifice or seriously

impair any essential bodily function and the anticipated benefit to the recipient is proportionate to the harm done to the donor. Furthermore, the freedom of the prospective donor must be respected, and economic advantages should not accrue to the donor.[33]

The interpretation of bodily integrity in terms of functional integrity comes as expected: what has to be preserved is the functioning of the person as a whole and not, in all cases, his or her whole body. What might puzzle us is why "economic advantages should not accrue to the donor," which the text does not explain. Having satisfied both the proportionality condition that the value gained is at least equal to the value sacrificed,[34] and the requirement of the principle of totality that the donation "will not sacrifice or seriously impair any essential bodily function," why should donors *not* be free to benefit financially from relinquishing, for example, a kidney?

Here is Pope John Paul II on this question:

> The [human] body cannot be treated as a merely physical or biological entity, nor can its organs and tissues ever be used as items for sale or exchange. Such a reductive materialist conception would lead to a merely instrumental use of the body, and therefore of the person. In such a perspective, organ transplantation and the grafting of tissue would no longer correspond to an act of donation but would amount to the dispossession or plundering of a body.[35]

The basic claim seems clear—though it should be noted to forestall any confusion that, unlike some contemporary philosophers such as Singer and McMahan, the pope does not contrast human beings and persons. (And so I sometimes speak in the following of "human persons" and use the terms *human being* and *person* interchangeably, as Kant too appears to do.[36]) According to John Paul, should we think of the human body as merely physical or biological and, as such, a natural resource at our disposal for sale or exchange, human persons would be valued improperly, merely for our usefulness. Instead, according both to the Catholic tradition and to his own elaboration of it, the pope holds that, as free beings capable of precisely such acts as organ and tissue donation—a near-paradigmatic example of spending of ourselves on others without demand for recompense—we show ourselves to be more valuable than any object could be.[37]

Admittedly, it is possible to understand the pope as merely suggesting a slippery-slope argument along the following lines: should we think of the human body as merely physical or biological and, as such, a natural resource at our disposal, we risk the consequence that at least some human persons will be used merely as means, or in other words, dispossessed and plundered. But I take it that John Paul is opposed not only to conceiving of and using others as mere means, but to one's conceiving of one's own self in this way, whether one would then be dispossessed and plundered or not. From his perspective, the human person, including one's own, is demeaned when we think of the body as merely physical or biological—in other words, as stuff at our disposal. Arguably, popular culture's depiction of sexuality as a plaything to be used and exploited at will provides a case in point.[38]

Michael Sandel's argument in *What Money Can't Buy* can help clarify these claims, lest we think the pope is simply restating Kant. Sandel comes at the question, "Are there some things that money should not be able to buy?" indirectly by means of the question, "Are there some things that money cannot buy?"[39] The answer to the latter question is yes, obviously. Money cannot buy friendship, for example, though it can buy what look like acts of friendship. The reason money cannot buy genuine friendship is that a friend who is motivated by financial gain would not really be a friend. Instead, friendship is constituted by such motivations as shared interests and interest in the other's well-being for his or her own sake. Someone whose initial motivation in becoming a "friend" to another was financial gain could become a genuine friend if that motivation were eliminated and these others took its place, but it seems at least as likely that these other motivations would be crowded out and never gain a foothold. In such circumstances, "the monetary exchange spoils the good being bought."[40]

The obvious difference between goods that money cannot buy, like friendship, and goods like sex and kidneys, the buying and selling of which generates controversy, is that goods in the latter category indisputably survive selling. Whereas a friend for the money is a false friend, sex for sale is sex nonetheless, and a kidney gotten through cash may function just as well as a kidney gotten through donation. Yet Sandel suggests that there is a connection between these two categories of goods: according to him, markets in goods like sex and kidneys may likewise *spoil*, not these goods themselves, but social attitudes and norms that we have reason to value—what he also calls "moral and civic goods."[41] By way of example, it might be argued that "prostitution is a form of corruption that demeans women and promotes bad attitudes to sex," which then would make selling sex objectionable "even in a society without poverty, even in cases of upscale prostitutes who liked the work and freely chose it."[42] Further, it might be argued that markets in human kidneys "promote a degrading, objectifying view of the human person, as a collection of spare parts," which then would make selling kidneys objectionable even when, however unrealistically, the seller is not compelled by financial desperation.[43] What is spoiled in these cases, if these arguments could be carried through, is not the goods themselves (sex and kidneys), but our regard for human persons, which conditions both our interactions with one another and our care of ourselves.

MARKETS AND CHOICES

Whether such an argument against a market in human kidneys could in fact be carried through, however, is by no means evident, and unfortunately neither Pope John Paul II nor Sandel gives us much more to work with. They thereby leave themselves vulnerable to predictable objections. For example, the libertarian political journalist Matt Welch retorts against Sandel, though the charge could be aimed at John Paul as well, that "people are dying right now because we have let our revulsion at markets create serial prohibitions of consensual behavior, whether it's buying and selling marijuana, sex, or kidneys."[44] The choice of the word *revulsion* suggests that prohibition of markets in these goods is at bottom irrational, founded on emotional reactions that do not withstand scrutiny. Welch writes further, "We know that maintaining prohibition [of the buying and selling of kidneys]…will certainly increase the body count," given the great disproportion between persons in need of a kidney transplant and the kidneys available through donation.[45] He also claims, "We know [both] that boosting the number of kidney donors from the living is the only real way to whittle the waiting list down" and that "legalizing monetary rewards is a guaranteed method for expanding the pool of living donors," a claim that he supports by pointing to markets in human eggs.[46] So, to him, the moral conclusion is clear: "The burden of argumentative proof on the legality of kidney sales should fall squarely on those who back the lethal status quo."[47] Consequentialist considerations, Welch implies, support legalizing a market. Libertarian convictions second his conclusion.

Debra Satz's argument against a market in human kidneys differs from John Paul's and Sandel's in rejecting the relevance of concerns about corruption. By contrast, her focus falls on "inequality, not the corruption of value."[48] Welch writes, in the course of criticizing Sandel, "People who live in market-averse societies [that is, societies leery of markets]…invariably have fewer choices."[49] What is central to Satz's argument is that she disagrees with this claim. She does not deny that having markets for goods typically increases choice, for of course it does; what she denies is that it always does. Instead, in some cases, "the set of choices that an agent faces is *endogenous*," which is to say "affected by the choices of others" within his or her society.[50]

Child labor presents a clear example. Say that a poor parent in a developing society does not want to put his children to work. Instead, he wants to support his family through his own labor, and he wants his children to go to school. But imagine that child labor is permissible within his society, or at least that the prohibition of it is unenforced. In other words, there is a market for "kids." Imagine further that a good number of other parents choose to put their children to work with the idea of increasing family income. Tragically, the upshot is that wages for adult laborers will be depressed, and the poor parent who did not want to put his children to work will have no better choice but to put his children to work after all, if he wants his family to have food. As Satz observes, "The institution of child labor restrains the set of alternatives available to poor families."[51] A market in kids does not increase choices. Instead, effectively prohibiting such a market would enable a parent to choose both to support his family himself and to send his children to school.

What concerns Satz about a market in human kidneys is that, similarly, "it may reduce or change the available choices open to others, and those others will be worse off."[52] As she notes, citing anthropological research, in areas of India with widespread sales of kidneys, operable women have become collateral for loans.[53] A peasant who wants credit has to choose whether to "put down" his own kidney, or the kidney of a wife or perhaps daughter. The thought of such a choice might repel us, but if human kidneys may be bought and sold like other commodities—like, for example, houses and cars—why should a peasant who wants a loan *not* have to put down a spare kidney when that is all he has of value? (Putting down another person's kidney is objectionable on different grounds.) Likewise, if human kidneys may be bought and sold like other commodities, why should a family who wants financial aid for college for a child *not* have to sell, not only the family's second home, but the parents' and child's spare kidneys? In other words, why should these kidneys *not* be counted with the family's other assets?

The suggestion that human kidneys be counted as assets like other commodities such as houses and cars seems likely not only to repel us, but to strike us as ridiculous. Just why, however, is a difficult question for anyone who, like Welch, favors legalizing kidney sales. One answer that comes quickly to mind is that the extraction of a kidney is risky to a person's health and even life in a way that the alienation of a house or car is not. Not only might the surgery go wrong; one's remaining kidney might fail in the future. But this worry has been unfounded for some years. As a 2001 *New York Times Magazine* article reported, "Of the half-dozen studies performed on donors, including a 20-year follow-up, none have revealed any increased mortality." Tellingly, "health-insurance companies do not raise their rates for kidney donors."[54]

It is true, however, that removal surgery can be painful,[55] and so this is another possible answer to the question of why kidneys should not be counted as assets like other commodities. Yet this answer, too, seems wrong. To begin with, some people suffer emotionally after having to sell a house—people can become profoundly depressed. Further, and more to the point, it does not seem to be the *painfulness* of having to part with a kidney that explains the intuition that, in Satz's words, one "should not have to pay a cost for refusing to part with body parts."[56] Similarly, it is not the painfulness of having to part with one's purse that explains our conviction that it is wrong to have to choose between one's money and one's life. And it's not considerations of the *pain* of childbirth, or even the emotional pain of having to part with a child whom one has carried and labored into being, that underlie critics' objections to commercial surrogacy. In both cases, the demands of respect and consideration for persons do the work.[57] Putting these two other cases aside, *what if* the removal surgery could be done with minimal pain, as we might imagine given the oft-invoked progress of medicine (and as laparoscopic surgery is working toward)? Would it then be unobjectionable to have to put down a kidney as collateral for a loan, or to have to sell a kidney as a condition of qualifying for financial aid? Would there then be no good reason to resist the expansion of the market to include all body parts of ours that we could live without? Indeed, on libertarian grounds, why stop there?[58]

THE COSTS OF BUSINESS

Invoking Kant's injunction that human beings must never be treated merely as means, Satz proposes that "the strongest argument against [a market in human kidneys] must ultimately rest on our judgment that a person's relationship with [his or her] body (and its parts, or at least most of its parts) is so important" that it warrants protection.[59] Her account of the importance of this relationship, however, is all too cursory.[60] What makes our relationship to our bodies and body parts "so important," Satz writes, is that it "is so closely bound up with our ability to control what happens to us [and to] what we can be and do."[61] In other words, it seems, my relationship with my body is so important because I exist and act as embodied. Loss of control of my body then comes close to, if it does not in every instance amount to, loss of control of myself and domination by someone else. Accordingly, as Satz suggests in a footnote, "perhaps one way to understand a ban on organ sales is as an extension of our revulsion with slavery."[62] From this perspective, what is objectionable about having to put down a kidney for collateral, or having to sell a kidney as a condition of qualifying for financial aid, is that it commodifies not only my body, but *me*, reduced to the status of an object fit for market regulation, which is no way to regard and treat persons. As an example of market regulation, think of being compelled, under threat of legal penalty, to carry through on the terms of an agreement you entered. In this case, the agreement is to undergo a nephrectomy.

But there is a problem with this argument. Satz does not claim that selling one's kidney is itself wrong or objectionable. As an egalitarian, concerned with inequality rather than corruption, she wants to argue against the practice of selling kidneys because of its potential effects on third parties to such transactions (that is, because of its so-called externalities) should a market in human kidneys take hold.[63] In these circumstances, a person who does not want to have to part with or risk parting with her kidney might have no choice but to do so if she really wants or needs a loan. One way or the other, there is a high price to pay here: your kidney, or your money, which might be crucial for a person's life plan.

But does selling a kidney wrongly reduce one to the status of an object, or not? If a willing seller is not wrongly reduced by selling his or her kidney, why should we think that reluctant sellers would be? More precisely, if selling human kidneys is not in itself wrong or objectionable, what grounds does a person who does not want to have to sell or put down her kidney have to resist? Why should she *not* have to do so, other than that she does not want to do so?—which is not a good enough reason, note, should we be talking about houses or cars that she likewise might not want to part with. In brief, what reasons are there to think that she should *not* have to sell or put down her kidney, whether she wants to do so or not?

Consider the matter from this different angle. In keeping with the liberal tradition that she represents, Satz wants to protect human *autonomy*, which we can understand in this context as self-governance by principles and according to values that one affirms under conditions of freedom.[64] (By *freedom*, understand in this context access to an array of principles and values, as opposed to being locked into some quite limited way of assessing things and persons.[65]) But no one would argue that autonomy is violated when a person has to decide whether or not to part with a second house or car in order to raise enough money to enjoy some other good that he or she desires. What reason is there to think that autonomy is violated when a person has to decide whether or not to part with a spare body part toward the same end? Satz answers that a person's relationship with his or her body is different (from a relationship to a house or car), because exerting control over one's body is exerting control over oneself. But here the argument runs into the same problem: if it is not wrong for you willingly to sell body parts that you can do without, why is it wrong for someone to require you to sell those parts *if* you want some other good, which after all you are free to take or leave? Granted, it would be wrong to take your kidney by force—this clearly would be exerting control over you wrongly—but if kidneys can be rightly bought and sold on the market, that is, if there is nothing objectionable to commodifying the human body in this way, what is objectionable about making it a condition of doing business with you that you bring to the table, so to speak, all the assets at your disposal?

Recall Satz's rejection of Sandel's concerns about corruption and her claim that inequality is more relevant. I suggest that this contrast is overdrawn. When we push Satz's argument to its end, we find two things. The first is a strength of her argument: we find that there is reason to shift some measure of "the burden of argumentative proof" (Welch's words) back to proponents of kidney sales, lest persons be pushed into selling body parts as an externality of a market, which I think clearly would be bad. In other words, we find reason to be leery of legalizing a market in human kidneys. But the second thing we find is a weakness of her argument. In brief, Satz cannot defend human *autonomy*, as she wants to do, without also invoking human *dignity*, which is to say the sorts of considerations that Sandel and Pope John Paul II have in mind. More concretely, in order to protect the poor person who does not want to have to sell or put down her kidney and thereby be reduced to the status of an object fit for market regulation, Satz must argue that the buying and selling of kidneys is itself morally objectionable—not only because of the effects that a market might have on unwilling others, but because the buying and selling of kidneys debases human beings. Otherwise, as I have sought to show, she cuts the ground out from under her feet.[66]

DIGNITY AND RESPECT

It is a deeply entrenched principle—though not simply to be taken for granted,[67] and certainly contested in its application[68]—that a human being ought not to be valued merely for his or her usefulness, which is to say purely instrumentally, toward ends to which he or she is subordinate. Recall, again, the flabbergasting example of sex trafficking. This principle, which was formulated by Kant but finds more ancient expression in the biblical doctrine of the creation of human beings in the image of God, underlies Satz's resistance to the market's conscription of the bodies of unwilling sellers. But it is less clear why a person should not be free to sell a body part if that is in fact what he or she wants to do, or for that matter sell his or her body in sex. Here a person uses her own body instrumentally, but she is not subordinated to an end of someone else's choosing. So it might well appear that autonomy is respected, not violated, by permitting such sales. And if autonomy is respected, how is dignity violated? Yes, we might worry, like Satz, that the autonomy of others will be imperiled if parting with a body part becomes a condition of access to some other good that persons want; but then, the counter could be, these persons need to decide whether they really want this other good or not. If not, they are free, after all, to exit the market.

I think a way out of this apparent impasse is to attend a little more closely to the meaning of the terms *dignity* and *respect*. *Dignity* has gotten a lot of attention in bioethics the last decade since the publication of a controversial article titled, helpfully enough, "Dignity Is a Useless Concept." According to this article, *dignity* reduces to "respect for persons or their autonomy" and so "can be eliminated without any loss of content."[69] Ironically, however, according to another article published but a year later, *respect* has likewise been largely emptied of content in bioethical discourse, reduced to noninterference with autonomy.[70] In other words, respect for persons has come to mean no more than respect for autonomy, which more concretely means no more than, first, letting others do what they will so long as no one else is thereby injured and, second, securing consent before acting in other-affecting ways. After all, why interfere with the acts of consenting adults? More to the point for the present chapter, how to justify interfering with the acts of consenting capitalist adults, so-called hard paternalism?[71]

This line of thought, however, goes nowhere fast. To begin with, consent does not always make right. More fully, simply because a person consents to have this or that done to him or her does not always make it morally permissible to do so and does not mean one has no grounds to intervene.[72] A lurid case in Germany, once more from a decade ago, may serve as an example: to quote the title of a newspaper article reporting on it, "Victim of Cannibal Agreed to Be Eaten."[73] This case suggests that respect for persons cannot rightly be reduced to respect for autonomy. Let us stipulate that the victim in question voluntarily agreed to this self-harming conduct.[74] Though the cannibal secured his victim's consent and fulfilled his will, it seems preposterous to say that he showed his victim respect.

There are a number of reasons why we might respect persons' autonomy. For example, maybe exercising it contributes to happiness or leads to self-development and independent mindedness. Or maybe exercising it is itself a good, whether it leads to other goods or not. Here's an argument, however, that respect for persons cannot rightly be reduced to respect for autonomy. In the end, it is imperative to value someone's autonomy—to care to protect and promote it—only if it is imperative to value that person in him- or herself. If a person did not warrant respect, why would his or her autonomy?[75] It's not as if autonomy were a free-floating good! Instead, it's good because it's in the interests of a being whose interests count *because that being counts*. The upshot is twofold: first, respect for persons and respect for autonomy cannot be collapsed into one another without losing the reason why persons' autonomy must be respected; second, we cannot do without the concept of dignity after all, since we need an answer to the question of why persons warrant respect.[76]

Why we cannot do without the concept of dignity needs explaining, of course. Kant's argument for his principle that our humanity puts limits not only on what we may rightly do to others, but on what we may rightly do to ourselves, is notoriously complex.[77] The basic claim, however, is that if it is imperative to value human beings' interests—as Kant holds we experience it is—then human beings must be valuable in themselves. For it is imperative to value the interests of someone only if that someone is valuable in him- or herself. Otherwise put, if it is imperative to value other human beings' interests and our own—as Kant holds we experience it is—then human beings must have a value that is different in kind from goods that are valued merely *because* they are of interest to human beings, that is, because human well-being depends on these goods.[78] (Recall the definition, from chapter 5, of what it means to have an interest in something: for one's well-being to depend on it in some or other way.)

Take the goods of autonomy, thriving, or dying a dignified death. These are valuable to human beings: human well-being depends on these goods. A good like these, however, derives whatever value it has from the fact that it is valuable *to* a being whose value is itself nonderivative: a being *for whose sake* the good in question is worth valuing, a being who is an "end." If human beings were not valuable in themselves, what value would these goods have? What would they be worth? And, finally, what sense would there be even in saying that autonomy, or thriving, or dying a dignified death is a good? These are goods only if they are good *for* a being who is worth valuing in him- or herself! The word for the value that a human being has in him- or herself, which is to say his or her so-called intrinsic value *that makes his or her interests worth valuing*, is precisely dignity.

An example from literature might prove helpful. If, as we have seen Satz suggest, "one way to understand a ban on organ sales is as an extension of our revulsion with slavery,"[79] let's look briefly at a depiction of a slave: Jim, in Samuel Clemens's great *Adventures of Huckleberry Finn* from 1885. (Clemens, aka Mark Twain, lived 1835 to 1901.)

There are two relevant moments. The first comes at the end of chapter 8, just after Jim and Huck, both on the run (though for different reasons), meet on Jackson Island in the Mississippi River. To close a conversation about money, Jim says to Huck, "Yes—en I's rich now, come to look at it. I owns myself, en I's wuth eight hund'd dollars. I wisht I had de money, I wouldn' want no mo.'"[80] There is a pathos to the comedy here. While, as the British political theorist Anne Phillips has observed, "there is a long tradition of radical thinking that sees the assertion of property rights in one's self and one's body as the central challenge to slavery and a crucial part of establishing women as the equals of men,"[81] Jim speaks of himself not as a human being with a dignity that puts him beyond all price, but as his slaveholding society assesses him: *chattel*, a man with a market price, a fungible good that can be bought, sold, and stolen—as later in the story, some ways down the river, Huck worries he has done.[82] The joke is that, if Jim got the money that his slaveholding society sees him as worth, he wouldn't possess himself any longer, or for that matter the money itself for long, since he would once more be a slave.

The second relevant moment comes at the end of chapter 15. After being lost for a night in an enveloping fog, Huck at last finds Jim and the raft. Huck comments,

> When I got to it Jim was setting there with his head down between his knees, asleep, with his right arm hanging over the steering oar. The other oar was smashed off, and the raft was littered up with leaves and branches and dirt. So she'd had a rough time.[83]

Shamefully, Huck does not take notice that *Jim* had had a rough time: Huck finds Jim in a posture of mourning and defeat, "his head down between his knees." We soon learn, after Huck tricks Jim into thinking the night in the fog was all a dream, that Jim was in fact in mourning, for what he took to be the loss of Huck. Jim says to Huck about all the trash in the raft,

> "What do dey stan' for? I'se gwyne to tell you. When I got all wore out wid work, en wid de callin' for you, en went to sleep, my heart wuz mos' broke bekase you wuz los', en I didn' k'yer no mo' what become er me en de raf'. En when I wake up en fine you back agin, all safe en soun', de tears come en I could a got down on my knees en kiss' yo' foot I's so thankful. En all you wuz thinkin 'bout wuz how you could make a fool uv ole

Jim wid a lie. Dat truck dah is *trash*; en trash is what people is
dat puts dirt on de head er dey fren's en makes 'em ashamed."[84]

Jim then draws himself up and walks slowly away from Huck and goes
into the wigwam on the raft. *This*, and not when he comes into money,
is the moment in the story when we see that Jim owns himself, so to
speak. His dignity—what other word?—is unmistakable, plain to see, in
need of no proof, such that even Huck acknowledges it: "But that was
enough," Huck says—*enough*. "It made me feel so mean I could almost
kissed *his* foot to get him to take it back."[85]

What is this dignity that we see Jim has and that even Huck—who
struggles throughout the novel to escape the hold of the slaveholding society that reared him—has to acknowledge and feels himself bound to
respect? The American bioethicist and physician Daniel Sulmasy has distinguished three senses of dignity. There is, to begin with, what he calls
attributed dignity, which is a worth or value that we ascribe to people
whom we consider important in some way or other—in a word, digni-
taries. By contrast, *intrinsic dignity* is the worth or value "human beings
have simply by virtue of the fact that they are human beings"—apart from
social standing, talents, or powers. Finally, so-called *inflorescent dignity* is
the worth or value that blossoms or flowers forth when someone acts in
some particularly admirable way.[86]

In chapter 15 of *Adventures of Huckleberry Finn*, Jim's dignity is
inflorescent: it blossoms or flowers forth for Huck, and readers, to admire.
But, as Sulmasy notes, inflorescent dignity is related to intrinsic dignity.
Inflorescent dignity is *revelatory* of the intrinsic dignity that a human
being possesses by virtue of being human. In other words, inflorescent
dignity shows the dignity that was already there but needed expressing.
When Jim draws himself up and walks slowly away from Huck and goes
into the wigwam on the raft, it is Jim's dignity as a human being that is
revealed. Huck sees that Jim, too, is a human being who suffers, who
mourns, who celebrates; and this is enough to upend Huck's attitude
toward him. Accordingly, Jim's dignity is not lost when, in the notorious
last third of the novel (chapters 34 and following), he reverts to becoming the plaything of Tom Sawyer.[87] Becoming the plaything of Tom

Sawyer is an insult to Jim's intrinsic dignity, which the novel earlier revealed once and for all. During the novel's long and difficult ending, readers and Huck alike know that there is something fundamental about Jim that commands respect. This something fundamental is his humanity, which is the ground of his dignity, and which his slaveholding society would keep buried. Importantly, the respect that is commanded by Jim's intrinsic, human dignity is not merely noninterference, but much more richly a summons to protection, service, and care.[88] Jim's interests matter to Huck because, he has seen, Jim matters as a human being. He has intrinsic dignity, worth beyond any price. Tellingly, Huck never loses this respect for Jim, even when his dignity is lost from sight.

BACK TO INEQUALITY

When Jim's intrinsic dignity as a human being is revealed, what is also revealed about him, at one and the same time, is his *equality* with all other human beings. Like Huck, Jim suffers, mourns, and celebrates; he is subject like all other human beings (to recall language from chapter 5) to a common weal and woe. As a human being with intrinsic dignity, however, Jim could not but be the equal of every other human being. For Jim's having dignity puts him beyond price: it means, in other words, that it would be wrong to value him merely in terms of what goods or benefits he could bring to others—the way that a slave is assessed; it would be wrong to put a price on his head, whether low or high, for he is the kind of being for whose sake things have value. In brief, he is an "end," not a mere means, and no being who is an end is any more or less valuable than another.

Recall also Satz's concern that legalizing the buying and selling of kidneys would undermine equality by subjecting some persons, unwilling sellers, to dominant others, creditors and the like. I have argued in the present chapter that Satz's case against a market in human kidneys does not suffice as she leaves it. More fully, I have argued that, in order to protect unwilling sellers, it must be shown that the buying and selling of kidneys is itself morally objectionable—not only because of the effects that a market might have on third parties, but because the buying and selling of kidneys debases human beings, or in other words, somehow offends human dignity. I can now begin to make this case.

A concrete way in which human beings are equal to one another is that we all not only have bodies, but are bodies—and so share the same vulnerability of human flesh. Focus firmly on the first-personal experience of the body. Talk of *having* a body makes sense in light of my body's responsiveness to my will, its manipulability (so to speak), and the alienability of some of its parts and elements: not only organs like kidneys, but bone marrow, blood, hair, and so on—up to the point that we would pass away ourselves. All other things being equal, putting on the body, as the British novelist Virginia Woolf (1882–1941) put it, comes as easily to us as washing and dressing in the morning.[89] Yet not everything, we know, is always so simple. By way of example, "we need only demand of our body some unaccustomed activity to find ourselves faced again with problems like those of a child learning to walk,"[90] or for that matter to talk.[91] Sexuality, too, presents noteworthy complications, as does pregnancy. In Woolf's words, "Who shall measure the heat and violence of the poet's heart when caught and tangled in a woman's body?"[92] And then think of illness, in which the brokenness of human bodily existence can become overwhelming. It is in the light of such experiences that talk of *being* a body likewise makes sense.

No question, my body is profoundly, irreducibly my own—after all, it cannot be alienated in full while I live—but sometimes it is just as undeniable that my body owns me, so to speak: I am responsive to it, it bends my will, it claims me as its own. Accordingly, the Catholic tradition speaks of the human being as a "unity in duality, a reality in which spirit and matter compenetrate."[93] Otherwise put, we exist at once *as* bodies and *in* bodies. These two orders of experience impose themselves upon us ineluctably. My body is at once "the absolute focal reference of all things" in my environment *and* one thing among others in which I am mysteriously located, while yet standing in consciousness over and against it.[94] To put it in an image, human bodily existence is *eccentric*: we live from a center that we also hold, or at least strive to hold, at a precarious length.[95]

The way to argue against a market in human kidneys *isn't*, however, to claim that the body is sacrosanct and so should be protected from commodification. Satz gestures this direction with her cursory account of the importance of "a person's relationship with [his or her] body (and its parts, or at least most of its parts)."[96] The British political theorist Anne Phillips, cited in passing earlier in this chapter, puts the problem with such a claim simply: "Since we take the body with us in everything we do"—since after all we not only have bodies, but are bodies—"we cannot simply say 'the body is special' and leave it at that."[97] More fully, "the fact that we uncontroversially send our bodies to market every time we agree to work makes it harder to locate a moral meaning in 'the body' that could differentiate between problematic markets in intimate bodily services and unproblematic markets in anything else."[98] What's more, some work that human beings do is arguably rougher on human bodies than selling a kidney would be; take working in a coal mine, or playing professional football. In sum, we can't object to a market in human kidneys either on the grounds that it intimately involves the body whereas other forms of labor don't, or on the grounds that it exacts a toll beyond what's normally permitted.

That we "send our bodies to market every time we agree to work" suggests, however, an objection to a market in kidneys that we *can* make. One last question can help us understand: Why shouldn't human beings be allowed to make themselves servile?—more concretely, to work for so-called slave wages, or for that matter really to enslave themselves, say through bonded labor? Otherwise put, what's the justification for prohibiting human beings from selling themselves into slavery, or (positively put) for minimum wage laws, the eight-hour work day, and health and safety regulations in the workplace, all of which "set a floor…below which workers cannot bid against one another for employment"?[99]

Imagine yourself into the question. Let's say you agree to work for slave wages or even to sell yourself into slavery, which presumably no one would do in any other than desperate circumstances. Clearly, your value in such an exchange would be merely that of a *thing* to do things with, worth however much or little the market happens to bear; you would not be considered as a being valuable in yourself, an "end" whose interests are worth valuing because you have value of an altogether different kind from goods that are valuable merely *because* they serve human interests. The upshot is that, while it could be rational for you to work for slave wages or to sell yourself into slavery if there were no other means to feed yourself and your family, you still could only sell yourself short and do your humanity an injustice—though the blame here should go to both your exploiter and the social system that has manifestly failed you.

The reason you could only sell yourself short is that you are not properly valued when your worth is assessed in terms of what *use* you can be in serving people's interests. As a being with intrinsic dignity, you should instead command respect—protection, service, and care. In this light, prohibiting human beings from selling themselves into slavery, minimum wage laws, the eight-hour work day, and health and safety regulations in the workplace all represent attempts to safeguard human dignity, which it is important to see is everyone's affair.[100] It is false and pernicious to regard enslavement as "just another cost that a person should be allowed to risk in pursuit of his interests."[101] All human beings have reason to reject enslavement as an affront to human dignity. The debasement of one human being is an insult to every human being, including the perpetrator of the offense.

When we send our bodies to market and the market is in human kidneys, I think a similar story must be told. Yes, it's imaginable that someone well-to-do might decide to sell his or her kidney; perhaps more cash is always welcome. This is not, however, either likely or realistic. Instead, as Phillips has remarked, the only realistic explanation for why some of us become positioned here as sellers and others as buyers lies in *inequality*—which, as we saw, Satz was likewise onto. In Phillips' words, "In the decision to become a vendor rather than a purchaser of organs…, neither taste nor talent can conceivably be involved."[102] For who, at least in his or her right mind, would aspire to sell a kidney? Perhaps a person could aspire to be a high-end sex worker when he or she grows up—though this, too, seems neither likely nor realistic—but it is imaginable only in a world deeply unlike our own that a person could aspire to make a living by selling his or her spare parts.[103] The question, What do you want to be when you grow up? does not admit the answer, I want to be a physical resource for other people (or, more provocatively, I want to be a body bag for the rich). Accordingly, we have to acknowledge that "markets in human organs rely on a systematic inequality between recipients and vendors."[104]

What's problematic here should be clear by now: the seller is valued merely as a means; he or she figures in the action plan in question not as a human being who is valuable in him- or herself, but merely as a thing to do things with—frankly, a valuable piece of meat, valuable as a source of living meat for others. The seller is not, of course, eaten, but his or her body—and so he or she—is treated merely as a consumer item. The offense against human dignity is again patent, regardless of whether the seller is unwilling or has gotten into this business autonomously, that is, of his or her own volition, for lack of better choices. And so it is also clear that there are solid grounds to object to a market in human kidneys. For, to reiterate, safeguarding human dignity is everyone's affair. The debasement of one human being is an insult to every human being. Our common humanity is denigrated when any one of us is, willingly or not.[105]

FREEDOM AND DIGNITY

Quite early in this chapter, I claimed that, in order to protect human freedom, it was also necessary to protect human dignity. If we understand freedom, as I defined it in this chapter, as access to an array of principles and values, as opposed to being locked into some quite limited way of assessing things and persons,[106] we can understand why.

The philosopher Elizabeth Anderson, likewise cited quite early in this chapter, is insightful here. As she has observed, "Different spheres of social life, such as the market, the family, and the state, are structured by norms that express fundamentally different ways of valuing people and things," which she calls modes of valuation.[107] Anderson calls the mode of valuation proper to commodities *use*, which contrasts with other modes of valuation, like respect, consideration, appreciation, and love, corresponding to other spheres of social life.[108] I hope it is uncontroversial to claim that we have good reason to value the diversity of modes of valuation. We also have good reason to resist the reduction of value to use-value. Human life is made rich by the fact that it includes experience of a multitude of things the value of which cannot be accounted for merely in terms of those things' *usefulness* toward satisfying our wants. Think, only to begin with, of a child, a painting, or a friend!

What is dangerous about a market in human kidneys is that it threatens to crowd out and displace norms and attitudes that relate us to others and ourselves in terms categorically different from the logic of the market. Satz is correct, I think, to fear the effects for third parties of a market in human kidneys. But it is not only the autonomy of third parties that might be imperiled by the establishment of such a market. Both human freedom and human dignity likewise would be imperiled if use-value were to crowd out and displace other norms, attitudes, and ways of valuing things and persons—an echo of Sandel's point that markets in goods like sex and kidneys may spoil, not these goods themselves, but social attitudes and norms that we have reason to value.

QUESTIONS FOR FURTHER REFLECTION/PAPER QUESTIONS

(1) The underground market in human kidneys is booming for a reason: as the statistics cited early in this chapter show beyond a doubt, there is great and even desperate need. The current system of kidney donation in the United States, as in many other countries, clearly is inadequate. What, then, should be done?[109]

You are a powerful member of the United States Congress. After many years of wasting its time on political games, Congress has decided to try to redeem itself by taking on, at last, whether to permit a regulated market in human kidneys, or whether to take measures to crack down on the underground market that has slowly established itself. You have read several discussions of this question, not least this chapter. You are also aware of the possibility of moving from an *opt-in* system of organ donation, as states in this country now have, to an *opt-out* system: in other words, of implementing "a well-advertised and regulated system of presumed consent" after death.[110] Research indicates, however, that this would not be a cure-all: other measures, including public education and employing dedicated physicians at each and every hospital trained to screen for and talk with potential donors, would have to accompany this change to make it effective.[111] Finally, you understand that rejecting a legal market in kidneys—and cracking down on the underground market—need not rule out introducing other innovative incentives to donate, as well as eliminating disincentives like unreimbursed costs and the lack of guaranteed medical follow-up should complications arise after the fact.[112] By way of example, a tax credit to a donor's estate might sway someone who is wavering over whether to opt in under our current system or to opt out under a system of presumed consent.[113]

Write a memo to your fellow Congresspersons outlining your thinking and the legislation that you would be prepared to support. Are you for or against legalizing a market in human kidneys? Are you for or against moving from an opt-in system of organ donation to an opt-out system? And so forth. Be sure to anticipate and counter objections to your position.

(2) You are editor-in-chief of the *Daily Times*, your town's newspaper of record, and in this role, it is your responsibility to write the paper's editorials. A strange thing has recently come to pass in your town. The owners of Liberty Tax Inc. have taken to paying people, men and women alike, five thousand dollars to have the words "Ask Me about Liberty Tax Inc." permanently, prominently tattooed on their foreheads. You find this campaign, well, both weird and wrong—an affront to human dignity. Whether there should be a law against it is one question; law or not, whether public opinion should be strongly against it, even outraged by it, is another. Drawing from your undergraduate education—in particular chapter 6 of the book *Catholic Moral Philosophy in Practice and Theory*—write an editorial opposing Liberty Tax's new campaign. Why should public opinion be outraged by it? Why is it wrong? And what

should be done? Be sure to anticipate and counter objections to your position.

Alternatively, defend the campaign against the outrage it has generated. What's the crime here? Should not individual liberty be respected against moralistically motivated legislation? Where's the harm? What's to be feared, instead, is living in a society given to legal paternalism on that grounds that persons are not being respected or respecting themselves as "ends." Again, be sure to anticipate and counter objections.

(3) It has just recently become legal to buy and sell human kidneys in the United States. At the behest of the board of trustees, your college's associate vice president for enrollment management and chief financial officer have produced a study on the question of whether your college, following the lead of several peer institutions, should require students to part with one functioning kidney (only of course if the students have two healthy kidneys) as a condition of enjoying financial aid. In other words, students would have to bring to the table, so to speak, all the assets at their disposal before asking the college for more. Write that study. (That is, be the associate vice president for enrollment management and the chief financial officer.) Design it as a memo addressed to the president of your college. Lay out both sides of the question—for and against—and present a final recommendation. Be sure to draw from chapter 6 of this book. Should paired organs be viewed and treated as resources people have, analogous to money or housing or apples? Why or why not?

(4) Markets in human kidneys might seem like a boon to the world's rich. But are they a blessing or a curse to the world's poor? Consider the arguments for and against legalizing markets in human kidneys. You are Pope Francis, who stated shortly after his election to the papacy, "How I long for a church...for the poor!" Write an evaluation of these arguments *from the perspective of the world's poor*. Frame your evaluation in the form of a letter addressed to all

people of good will. What would someone with the poor's best interest in mind think about the idea of legalizing markets in human kidneys? Be sure to consider both sides of the question and to anticipate and counter objections to your position.

CHAPTER 7

FROM PRACTICE TO THEORY

Learning from Conscience

Imagine circumstances in which the question, "Have you no conscience?" might be asked. The question implies, on the one hand, that the person to whom it's put is gravely deficient in some or other way. He or she has no moral knowledge, or has it but has failed to apply it, or has no compunction, no scruples, no shame. On the other hand, the question implies that the person is better than all that. It aims precisely to shame him, to shake him out of moral obtuseness or malice, to make him take mind of what he already knows or at least should acknowledge. In other words, the question appeals to just what it also calls into question: namely, the person's conscience.

It is an old, much-discussed question whether a person's conscience can ever be extinguished. This question clearly can't be answered, however, without an account of what conscience is. This question, too, is old and much-discussed.[1] Further, with what authority does conscience "speak"? What reason is there to heed its "voice"? The question, "Have you no conscience?" suggests that, if one did, one ought to follow it. But can't people disagree in good conscience, so to speak? What work, then, does appeal to conscience do for us? Why bother with invoking it at all?

An especially attentive reader might have noticed that this book has invoked conscience multiple times. For example, I noted in the introduction that Saint Paul appears to claim that there is a natural knowledge of the moral law or, in other words, a natural law, knowable in some way through conscience. I also noted the debate over whether Catholics must submit to all papal teachings or must respect all papal teachings. The latter position allows for the possibility of dissent from at least some teachings after the rigorous examination of conscience. Chapter 2 concerned none other than cases of conscience. As I wrote, sometimes even a person with a well-formed conscience—who knows quite well that adultery, stealing, and murder are wrong and can never be done rightly—might really not know what to feel, think, or do in a given case. Some cases will prove perplexing to even the best-formed conscience. Much of chapter 4 had to do with the conscience of the soldier. Revisionist accounts of the just war aim to mobilize, I wrote quoting Jeff McMahan, "an important resource for the prevention of unjust wars": the moral conscience of individual soldiers. The chapter also twice referred to the novelist Tim O'Brien's *The Things They Carried*, where the narrator struggles in his conscience with whether "to fight a war I hated," the American war in Vietnam. Finally, I noted in chapter 5 that the Nazis' recalibration of the moral worth of animals apparently contributed toward anaesthetizing the consciences of physicians who experimented on human beings with abandon. I also quoted McMahan's claim that "our perception of animals as radically 'other' numbs our sensitivity to them, allowing us to abuse them in various ways with an untroubled conscience."

Recent Roman Catholic thinking about conscience has unfolded against the backdrop of two great documents from the Second Vatican Council: *Dignitatis Humanae* (*Of the Dignity of the Human Person*, 1965), concerning religious liberty,[2] and all the more *Gaudium et Spes* (*Joy and Hope*, 1965), concerning the church in the modern world.[3] This chapter begins by reflecting some on the teaching in *Gaudium et Spes*. But here's my interest: to move thereby from discussion of controversies, the focus of this book so far, to consideration of what more general moral theory could support the various arguments I've put forth, the focus of this concluding chapter.

The word *theory* is derived from the Greek word for spectator: someone who has a good view, for example of a play. Speaking roughly, what we want from a moral theory is a vision of how our well-considered moral convictions hang together. That is, we want to see how they're connected and coherent both with one another and with other convictions we hold, say about human beings, about the nature of being, and about

God. We also want reason to believe that our way of seeing things is not distorted, but has well-founded credibility. In other words, we want to see that there is something to say for our way of seeing!—which suggests the problem with aspiring to "ground" a theory beyond all possibility of doubt. (How can we see that there is something to say for our way of seeing without looking into things in the way that we do?) Finally, what's helpful about having a theory is that it allows us to develop views on controversies that had confounded us. A more general moral theory gives us a framework within which we can hope to extend our vision, or maybe even see some of our convictions anew, from an angle that leads us to think twice.

What I propose here is that thinking about conscience is one way into moral theory. Not only do different conceptions of conscience correspond to different moral theories; what's more, the phenomena of conscience—the experiences we call by that name—put pressure on moral theories and so can help us clarify which theories really do promise to sharpen and extend our vision. In brief, as this chapter's subtitle suggests, conscience has lessons to teach.

TEXT AND CONTEXT

The teaching on conscience in *Gaudium et Spes* comes early in the document: the sixth article of part 1, §16 of the document as a whole. Part 1 concerns "The Church and Man's Calling"; its opening chapter concerns "The Dignity of the Human Person." Importantly, *Gaudium et Spes* is addressed to "the whole of humanity" in the diversity of our modern world (GS §2). In the words of the document's preface, "nothing genuinely human fails to raise an echo in [the] hearts" of the followers of Christ (GS §1)—alluding, appropriately enough, to the dramatic words of a pre-Christian author, the comic playwright Terence.[4] The reason "nothing genuinely human fails to raise an echo," the document goes on, is that the followers of Christ themselves consist of "a community composed of men," though they believe they are led by the Spirit. The opening article of part 1 likewise emphasizes the church's "supremely human character" (GS §11). It is because the church is composed of men, though nowadays we would say as well of women, that "the People of God and the human race in whose midst it lives" may "render service to each other" (GS §11)—service like clarifying the aspirations of women, or the fundamental stirrings of the heart.

The opening chapter of part 1 extends this gesture toward common ground, in particular through what it has to say about conscience. This teaching is couched in theological language, but conscience is presented as a birthright of all human beings, followers of Christ or not. Here is §16 in full:

> In the depths of his conscience, man detects a law which he does not impose upon himself, but which holds him to obedience. Always summoning him to love good and avoid evil, the voice of conscience when necessary speaks to his heart: do this, shun that. For man has in his heart a law written by God; to obey it is the very dignity of man; according to it he will be judged. Conscience is the most secret core and sanctuary of a man. There he is alone with God, Whose voice echoes in his depths. In a wonderful manner conscience reveals that law which is fulfilled by love of God and neighbor. In fidelity to conscience, Christians are joined with the rest of men in the search for truth, and for the genuine solution to the numerous problems which arise in the life of individuals from social relationships. Hence the more right conscience holds sway, the more persons and groups turn aside from blind choice and strive to be guided by the objective norms of morality. Conscience frequently errs from invincible ignorance without losing its dignity. The same cannot be said for a man who cares but little for truth and goodness, or for a conscience which by degrees grows practically sightless as a result of habitual sin.

The teaching on conscience in *Gaudium et Spes* has its critics. Before he became Pope Benedict XVI, Joseph Ratzinger viewed §16 as raising "many unsolved questions about how conscience can err and about the right to follow an erroneous conscience"[5]—questions that came to the fore in the aftermath of Pope Paul VI's 1968 *Humanae Vitae* (*Of Human*

173

Life), concerning contraception, which deeply polarized the church.[6] This criticism, however, is more about what the document does not say (that is, its lack of answers to subsequent pressing questions) than about what it does say, which generally is quite traditional. Despite its diversity on various points, the Catholic tradition agrees that conscience names our deeply personal experience of a law which we do not give ourselves, but which we find holds us to obedience (sentence 1). It agrees that conscience names our experience of being summoned to love good and avoid evil, and further our experience, on occasion, of being called, in an intimate yet insistent way (hence the image of the voice), to "do this, shun that" (sentence 2). And it agrees that the law that we encounter in experiences of conscience is the *lex indita non scripta*—the law inscribed on our hearts rather than written on tablets, scrolls, paper, or screens—which, Paul proclaims in his Letter to the Romans (2:14–15), the Gentiles show they have when they do instinctively what the law requires, which gives us the dignity of being a law unto ourselves when we heed it, and by which we will be judged (sentence 3).

Here, though, is another criticism of the teaching on conscience in *Gaudium et Spes*: like much else from Vatican II, it leaves us, in the words of the English poet Matthew Arnold (1822–88), "wandering between two worlds, one dead, / the other powerless to be born."[7] I go on to explain in the next section.

FROM ROME TO GENEVA TO OXFORD TO PARIS...

The moral theologians Michael Lawler and Todd Salzman recently published in the magazine *America* an article outlining what they term "the long-standing Catholic way to make a moral choice, namely, individual conscience," and delineating "two major approaches to conscience" since the Second Vatican Council.[8] On the one hand, they write, "conscience is ultimately about obedience to church teaching." To be clear, the position here is not that a Roman Catholic must abdicate his or her conscience; what is claimed, instead, is that the way to form it is "to conform

174

it to the teaching of the church," identified with the magisterium, the Vatican's teaching office.[9] The focus accordingly falls on what *Gaudium et Spes* calls "right conscience." A theologian whose sympathies do not lie with this view describes it as "magisterial positivism": being bound to do whatever the magisterium puts down is to be done.[10] On the other hand, Lawler and Salzman write, conscience "must be free and inviolable"; it "is not at the service of doctrine."[11] To be clear, the position here is not that a Roman Catholic may simply ignore the magisterium; what is claimed, instead, is that in conscience, the individual ultimately "is alone with God" (in the language of *Gaudium et Spes*) and must take sole responsibility for his or her own decision. A theologian whose sympathies do not lie with this view has remarked, "Firm, subjective conviction and the lack of scruples and doubts that follow from it do not justify man."[12]

As Lawler and Salzman also observe, different understandings or models of *church* coming out of the Council went on to underwrite different understandings of conscience: if in conscience a person is called to search for knowledge with the church, what is understood by *church* clearly makes a difference for the parameters of this search.[13] For example, when we say *church*, do we mean the pope, bishops, and other clergy, or do we mean the whole people of God, however they're to be determined? (Who's in, who's out?) I think it's crucial, however, to look beyond the church, in whatever sense, in order to understand our differences about conscience. For the reception of the teaching of *Gaudium et Spes* on conscience has taken place not only against the background of church documents and disputations, but against a centuries-long change in the understanding of conscience in Western culture, well beyond the bounds of Rome. Whereas conscience was conceived by the medieval Scholastics as part of a process by which we participate in God's providence, "directing all things toward their proper fulfillment in union with God,"[14] it came to be seen, in the aftermath of the Reformation, as a *faculty* providing authoritative, action-guiding moral knowledge, what one philosopher has termed "an agency within an agency," always on hand for our consultation, if only we would listen.[15] This change is apparent in the law, where the right of conscience has grown from a right "against government encroachment into a more generally applicable right to individual autonomy,"[16] most recently to refuse to provide such goods and services as cakes, flowers, and photography for gay weddings.[17]

Another moral theologian, Jennifer Herdt, has recently drawn attention to the role played by the great Reform theologian John Calvin (1509–64) in this changing conception of conscience. For Calvin, she writes, "It is by way of conscience that we become aware of the natural law written on our hearts. Conscience is a knowing-with God's knowledge of us; it is an immediate access to God's judgment."[18] Compare *Gaudium et Spes*:

> For man has in his heart a law written by God; to obey it is the very dignity of man; according to it he will be judged. Conscience is the most secret core and sanctuary of a man. There he is alone with God, Whose voice echoes in his depths. In a wonderful manner conscience reveals that law which is fulfilled by love of God and neighbor.

Certainly there are at least superficial similarities between Calvin and *Gaudium et Spes* (in particular, the third sentence of the quotation), but there are also quite significant differences between Calvin's conception of conscience and that of Aquinas, whose thinking so often figures in the background of contemporary Roman Catholic teaching, yet is still being retrieved from centuries of calcification.[19] What is novel about Calvin's conception of conscience is that, according to him, it offers quite specific moral knowledge. Calvin also holds, however, that this knowledge is often obscured by our depravity. Moreover, even if it were not disabled by self-deception and hardness of heart, conscience on Calvin's account would *not* enable us to be like gods, knowing good and evil of our own power. Instead, we may know how we are judged. So long as we do not hide ourselves from it, in conscience we may know ourselves as God knows us, which is to say we may experience God's infallible judgment of the morality of our actions. In Herdt's words, "Calvin's broader theological point is that fallen humanity has sufficient knowledge to justify being held responsible by God."[20] In brief, conscience functions "primarily as a theodicy,"[21] justifying the ways of God to men, as another great

Reformer, the English poet John Milton (1608–74), sought to do with his *Paradise Lost*.[22]

History then plays a trick. "This new understanding of conscience [as offering specific moral knowledge] was to take hold and outlive Calvin's understanding of the fall and what it has done to the natural gifts of intellect and will, giving rise in the seventeenth and eighteenth centuries to an understanding of conscience as a faculty which provides concrete, authoritative moral guidance to each individual."[23] In other words, married to the Enlightenment confidence in reason, conscience became a positive source of action-guiding moral knowledge, an "infallible voice within the breast,"[24] "the final safeguard of our moral nature"[25]—to repeat an earlier characterization of the so-called faculty view, an agency within an agency.

This conception of conscience is by no means unknown in Catholic circles. Instead, some of the great nineteenth-century historian and theologian John Henry Newman's oft-cited invocations of conscience fit squarely within this tradition.[26] Conscience, Newman writes, is

> that inward light, given...by God..., intended to set up within us a standard of right and of truth; to tell us our duty on every emergency, to instruct us in detail what sin is, to judge between all things which come before us, to discriminate the precious from the vile, to hinder us from being seduced by what is pleasant and agreeable, and to dissipate the sophisms of our reason.[27]

Newman lived, however, during darkening times. Against the confidence of the Enlightenment, he further holds that,

> even in countries called Christian, the natural inward light grows dim, because the Light, which lightens every one born into the world [that is, Christ], is removed out of sight. I say, it is a most miserable and frightful thought, that, in this country [namely, England], among this people which boasts that it is so Christian and so enlightened, the sun in the heavens is so eclipsed that the mirror of conscience can catch and reflect few

rays, and serves but poorly and scantily to preserve the foot from error. That inward light, given as it is by God, is powerless to illuminate the horizon, to mark out for us our direction, and to comfort us with the certainty that we are making for our Eternal Home.[28]

What is sorely needed, Newman claims, is right formation of conscience—a view that, echoing as it does in the present-day church, makes him a man of our time as well. For, he also writes, "Left to itself, though it tells truly at first, [conscience] soon becomes wavering, ambiguous, and false; it needs good teachers and good examples to keep it up to the mark and line of duty; and the misery is, that these external helps, teachers, and examples are in many instances wanting."[29]

What we need to appreciate is how far this view of conscience is from that of Aquinas. Aquinas followed already long-standing tradition in breaking what we call conscience into two. Like other medieval Scholastics, Aquinas distinguished what was called *synderesis*, understood as the natural habit by which we apprehend the first principles of practical reason,[30] from *conscientia*, understood as the act of applying our moral knowledge to a given case.[31] Otherwise put, *synderesis* is our innate disposition to grasp that good is to be pursued and evil avoided[32]—on pain of acting both irrationally (as we might accuse someone of doing who does not pursue what he takes to be good and does not avoid what he takes to be evil) and contrary to our nature as rational beings. *Synderesis* might then be likened to whatever we would want to call our innate disposition to language.[33] Strange though it sounds in English, a child develops the habit of understanding and speaking a language. Once this habit matures, a child can't but understand well-formed utterances in his or her language and comes to think and speak habitually in that language as well. On Aquinas's account, existing ethically—the quest for good over and against evil—likewise comes to be in time. The habit matures through example, teaching, practice, and reflection, to the point that we can't but apply our knowledge: as *Gaudium et Spes* puts it, we can't but know to "do this, shun that." Our moral knowledge comes to act, which is the experience named by *conscientia*.

There is, obviously, much to explain here—so much more to say about how being ethical belongs to being human, and about how the first principles of practical reason give rise to moral precepts or rules. For present purposes, the point to make is that there is a yawning gap between *synderesis* and *conscientia*. Take the principle that good is to be done and evil avoided. It's a start, but if that's all a child knew, how little would he or she know what to do in any given case! For what is good, and what evil? Again as a start, Aquinas also holds that the twofold command to love the Lord your God with all your being and to love your neighbor as yourself articulates self-evident principles of the natural law.[34] But these principles likewise need a lot of specification before they can be helpfully action guiding. In brief, for Aquinas, the interplay between *synderesis* and *conscientia* involves "active human judgment and a holistic reflection drawing on all possible sources of knowledge," human and divine.[35] Whereas for Calvin, "the accent falls on obedience to God's commands," for Aquinas, "the accent falls on rational creatures' participation, both by nature and in grace, in God's activity of directing all things to Godself."[36] For, in Aquinas's words, although "there is a certain necessity in the general principles, the more we descend to particulars, so much the more we encounter defect," which is to say occasions for disagreement and even irreducible diversity, where our freedom is put to the test.[37] Conscience also names how we come to terms with this freedom. In good conscience, we say, we cannot do this or that, or we can do no other, on pain of being unable to live with ourselves.[38]

BEYOND THE FACULTY VIEW

I hope it is clear by now in what sense the teaching on conscience in *Gaudium et Spes* may be described as wandering between two worlds. To put the point briefly, Aquinas is there in the document's teaching, but also Newman and maybe even Calvin: the teaching on conscience permits too many readings pulling in too many directions.

It's a further question which reading makes more sense. In this regard, there's much to recommend the Thomistic view of conscience over and against the faculty view—not merely because the Thomistic view might be considered traditionally Catholic whereas the faculty view is not so much, but because the faculty view has problems which the Thomistic view does not. The first problem is easy to see, but also relatively easy to dispatch. This is that what persons in good conscience can do, or in good conscience cannot do, varies profoundly, which we might think wouldn't be the case if conscience were a faculty providing authoritative knowledge. So Huck Finn, to cite a favorite example in the literature, suffered pangs of conscience when he was helping Jim escape from slavery.[39] Or think of how Catholics vary in conscience nowadays over the teaching of *Humanae Vitae*, or how soldiers may vary in conscience over going to war. The faculty view can counter this challenge, however, simply by acknowledging, with Newman and *Gaudium et Spes* alike, that conscience may grow sightless as a consequence either of want of "external helps" (Newman) or by reason of "habitual sin" (GS §16). Some will, some won't be persuaded by this solution.

A second problem for the faculty view is more difficult for it to dispatch. Consider how appeals to conscience function in today's "conscience wars" over cakes, flowers, photography, and the like. Once _____ (fill in the blank) is claimed to be against one's conscience, the argument is over before it even started. If conscience is thought to provide authoritative action-guiding knowledge, it serves not to open one to the demands of accountability to others, but to insulate one from the need to give an account of oneself.[40] The problem for the faculty view here is to "explain how conscience might profitably develop in response to experience and learning."[41] If conscience is supposed, as Newman claimed, "to tell us our duty on every emergency, to instruct us in detail what sin is, to judge between all things which come before us, to discriminate the precious from the vile," and so forth, what sense is there in telling someone that his or her conscience is malformed, for what reason is there for him or her to agree? On the faculty view, once conscience comes onto the scene, every exit would appear to be closed. By contrast, the Thomistic view of conscience has no trouble making sense of the development of conscience in response to experience and learning. If *conscientia* is our moral knowledge coming to act, then when our moral knowledge develops, so too will our conscience.

There is at least one respect, however, in which the Thomistic view does need development. Despite Aquinas's description of the experience of conscience as encompassing witnessing, inciting, binding, excusing, accusing, and tormenting,[42] inasmuch as conscience is understood as an act of our practical reason, it's liable to be understood merely as reflective thought. So one contemporary Thomistic philosopher advises, "Although conscience is sometimes portrayed as a feeling or instinct, [it] is better understood as an agent's best reasoned judgment of whether or not to perform an action."[43]

If the alternatives are feeling and instinct, no doubt conscience is better understood as "an agent's best reasoned judgment." But what it is to acquire a conscience is much more than to become skilled at practical reasoning; having a conscience means much more than acting conscientiously. Instead, experiences of conscience attest to what the French philosopher Paul Ricoeur (1913–2005) calls a "deeply hidden passivity" in our being, rooted in our embodiment.[44] As another philosopher has developed Ricoeur's thought here, "Conscience speaks to a series of experiences that we undergo or *suffer through*"; it is "the experience of being pulled into the world of norms, into the often hidden dialogue of reasons, the public space of other people."[45] In this regard, it makes sense to term conscience, as Ricoeur does, our experience of the voice of the Other, enjoining us to accountability, if not sometimes tormenting us as well.[46] Yes, in conscience, our moral knowledge comes to act; but the important point is that our moral knowledge is not just ours. In conscience, we experience, strangely, an otherness *in ourselves* that calls us to transcend ourselves. For "conscience voices how we ought to participate in the world of others."[47]

INTO THE BREACH: THE THEORY OF THE NEW NATURAL LAW

The question to consider now is what moral theory best accommodates the phenomena of conscience. In light of my claim that the Thomistic view of conscience has much to recommend it, it makes sense

181

to begin with Aquinas's natural law theory of morality. As I wrote in this book's introduction, according to the natural law tradition, to characterize it simply, through our natural reason, we can gain a basic understanding of the goods of human life and discern, through reflection upon experience and dialogue with others, precepts or rules corresponding to human needs and fulfillment.[48] Alas, we need at this point to make matters much more complex.

Readers might also recall from chapter 2 my introduction of the school of thought known as the new natural law, articulated and defended by the philosophers John Finnis, Germain Grisez, and Joseph Boyle. As I wrote, the name *the new natural law* indicates that its proponents aspire to renew the natural law tradition advanced by Aquinas, but there is some debate whether they have retrieved Aquinas's thinking or instead developed a new theory altogether. One way or the other, the new natural law is a powerful theory that has gained a strong following in Catholic philosophical circles. So it also makes sense to begin with it.

There are at least two ways to approach the new natural law. One is to situate it within the career of its principal founder, Germain Grisez. We would then connect the development of this theory with recent moral and ecclesiological controversies, like that over contraception, in which Grisez was involved;[49] and we would also connect it with controversies over the interpretation of Aquinas, to which he has made important contributions.[50] Another way to approach the theory is to situate it within what Elizabeth Anscombe called "modern moral philosophy."[51] This is my approach, and in taking it, I follow Finnis's lead in his excellent book *Fundamentals of Ethics*. The key figure in this account must be the Scottish Enlightenment philosopher David Hume (1711–76), since modern moral philosophy, as Anscombe uses the phrase, may be understood as an argument with Hume over the nature of practical reason: more precisely, whether reason can prescribe or proscribe actions as morally right or wrong.

Hume's answer to this question is well-known: no! "Reason alone," he claims in his great *Treatise of Human Nature*, "can never be a motive to any action of the will."[52] For, first, "abstract or demonstrative reasoning...never influences any of our actions" but in light of some "*design'd end or purpose*" that we bring to the reasoning to begin with.[53] By way of example, the result of a mathematical problem may move a person to action, but only because he or she already was moved by some end or purpose to solve the problem to begin with! Second, according to Hume, reasoning regarding the relations of objects—take cause-effect reasoning—is "nothing but the discovery of [these objects'] connexion" and so likewise cannot be invoked to explain why we cared to discover the connection in the first place.[54] It follows, on Hume's account, that morality is not based on reason. Here's why: (1) "common experience…informs us, that men are often govern'd by their duties, and are deter'd from some actions by the opinion of injustice, and impell'd to do others by that of obligation."[55] In other words, the rules of morality *do* move people to act, as we can see every day. (2) "Reason alone, as we have already prov'd, can never have any such influence" over the will.[56] So therefore (3) "the rules of morality…are not conclusions of our reason"—because the rules of morality move us to act, which Hume holds reason itself just can't do.[57] The upshot, to bring a long story to a quick close, is that "morality…is more properly felt than judg'd of."[58] The distinction between virtue and vice springs not from reason, but from "impression or sentiment."[59] Simply put, the virtuous is that which favorably impresses us as amiable and praiseworthy; the vicious is that which we feel to be odious and deserving of condemnation.

A further consequence, as Finnis has remarked, is that "'the foundation of ethics' (Hume's phrase) will be 'the particular fabric and constitution of the human species'" (again quoting Hume);[60] or, to put it less favorably, that ethics is reduced to an empirical inquiry into what "causes a pleasure or uneasiness of a particular kind."[61] Unfortunately for this strategy, as the Marquis de Sade (1740–1814) might be called on to witness, human beings exhibit great variability in this regard, and so it seems that turning to a "science of man" for the foundation of ethics will not do.[62] Against this background, it makes sense that many respectable philosophers turned instead to utilitarianism and its purportedly objective calculations of the greatest good for the greatest number.

The new natural law tells a rather different story, which we need to examine at greater length. In agreement with Hume, who after all must be engaged, Grisez, Finnis, and Boyle hold that "the moral *ought* cannot be derived from the *is* of theoretical truth," with the consequence that "the ultimate principles of morality cannot be theoretical truths" about human nature.[63] In other words, no *oughts* can be deduced from what's considered natural for human beings, or simply read off the alleged functions of our various body parts, as moralists about sex have sometimes proved wont to do. Instead, we learn what it is to be human by paying heed to what morality asks of us; the natural law illuminates our nature. What our authors disagree with is Hume's claim that "small attention" to this matter should "let us see, that the distinction of vice and virtue" is not "perceiv'd by reason" but founded in sentiment.[64] For they aim to pry practical reason from his grasp.

They begin by clarifying terms. "That for the sake of which one acts" they call one's *purpose* in acting.[65] "That about a purpose which makes one rationally interested in acting for it" is called a *good*.[66] To the question, "Why that purpose?" the answer is then, "Because of this good." Now comes a substantive claim: as "one does finish deliberating and begin acting," Grisez, Finnis, and Boyle write, "there cannot be a regress in the goods which are reasons for acting"; "[p]lainly..., there are reasons for acting which need no further reason."[67] These they term *basic goods*.[68]

The obvious question to ask at this point is this: How are the basic goods known? The answer that our authors give shows the influence of Anscombe. As she wrote in her book *Intention*,

> Can it be that there is something that modern moral philosophy has blankly misunderstood: namely what ancient and medieval philosophers meant by *practical knowledge*? Certainly in modern philosophy we have an incorrigibly contemplative conception of knowledge. Knowledge [according to this contemplative conception] must be something that is judged as such by being in accordance with the facts.[69]

For Grisez, Finnis, and Boyle, following Anscombe's lead, this "incorrigibly contemplative conception of knowledge" needs correcting, for it excludes *practical knowledge* properly speaking. Contra the contemplative conception of knowledge, the basic goods come to be known *in and through* action; they become apparent to us when we aim for some good, as Aristotle tells us that "every art and every inquiry, and likewise every action and choice," seem to do.[70] And they can be grasped only by reflection on practice, not by prior theoretical inquiry or contemplation. Otherwise put, what's known in practical knowledge isn't "out there" to be discovered by people with a lot of leisure for speculation. Instead, it can be known—it is revealed—when we act and reflect on why, ultimately, we do what we do.

In brief, the way that we can uncover the basic goods is by pursuing the question, "Why are you doing that?" or "What for?" to the end—to the point that it just does not make sense to keep asking.[71] Against Hume, it is claimed that what we discover is not some brute, blind desire that we just happen to have, but a *perception* of this or that basic good or form of human flourishing.[72] In other words, "persisting with such questions eventually uncovers a small number of basic purposes of diverse kinds" corresponding to "diverse basic goods" such as life itself, knowledge, aesthetic experience, friendship, and play.[73] These basic goods are the first principles of action. They are the first principles of action since "whenever one makes any choice, one's will, insofar as it is a rational appetite, must be specified by some intelligible good," and this specifying good, our authors claim, "either is or is reducible to the instantiation of one or more of the basic human goods."[74] Crucially, the basic goods "cannot be derived from any theoretical experience."[75] The way that they "function as principles of action is through being *known* as ultimate rational grounds…for proposing actions to be done."[76] To the question, "Why that purpose?" the *ultimate* answer is then, "Because of this or that *basic* good or set of basic goods." For example: because life is good! because knowledge is good! because aesthetic experience is good! because friendship is good! because play is good! and so on.

A natural question to ask at this point is the following: If all properly human actions—actions initiated by free choice guided by reason—are motivated by basic goods, what differentiates moral action from immoral action? To begin to answer, we need to consider what Grisez, Finnis, and Boyle call the "self-evident first principle, Good is to be done and pursued, [which] operates in all practical reasoning."[77] Practical reasoning that did not comply with this principle would be pointless: it would not be *practical* reasoning! This principle is then at work in all practical reasoning deserving of the name. What it does, they write, is to prohibit pointlessness by "requiring that every deliberate action be undertaken ultimately for the sake of some benefit—that is, something in which one is basically interested."[78] What it does not do, though, is to rule out morally bad actions, for "even [they] have their point."[79] Such actions comply, in other words, with the formal principle that good is to be done and pursued. After all, a person who commits a morally bad action does it for what he or she envisions as some good for him or herself. Where, then, lies the difference?

The rub, Grisez, Finnis, and Boyle claim, is that "morally wrong acts do not respond to this principle [of practical reasoning] as perfectly as morally good acts do."[80] For morally wrong acts are not as *reasonable* as morally good acts. This claim requires some explaining. According to our authors, "To be morally good is precisely to be completely reasonable."[81] That is, it is to be "alive" to all the basic reasons—all the basic goods— that there are for acting; to be fully committed to promoting and protecting the good in its diverse kinds. It follows that "*right reason* is nothing but *unfettered reason*."[82] By contrast, "Immoral choice fetters reason by adopting a proposal to act without adequate regard for some of the principles of practical reason [some of the basic goods], and so without a fully rational determination of action."[83]

This claim, too, needs explaining. Take Milton's Eve in his *Paradise Lost*. Eve was not wrong to consider knowledge a good, but it was wrong for her, fixed "wholly on her taste naught else" to regard, like her relationship with God.[84] Or consider the novelist Mary Shelley's Dr. Victor Frankenstein, who realizes too late, "'If the study to which you apply yourself has a tendency to weaken your affections [that is, to cut you off from the basic goods of human companionship in friendship or family], and to destroy your taste for those simple pleasures in which no alloy can possibly mix [say, the basic goods of play and aesthetic experience], then that study is certainly unlawful, that is to say, not befitting the human mind.'"[85] (Shelley lived 1797 to 1851.) Grisez, Finnis, and Boyle say more simply, "When an immoral choice is made, the principles of practical knowledge are embodied" imperfectly[86]—which Victor

Frankenstein, of course, came to know all too literally once his monster came to life! "Only morally right choices," our authors write, "respond fully to all of the principles of practical knowledge. Thus, only morally right choices respond perfectly to the first principle of practical reasoning."[87] To reiterate, they respond perfectly since they are alive to all the basic reasons—all the basic goods—that there are for acting.[88]

In sum, then, according to the new natural law, to act morally is to respond perfectly to the first principle of practical reasoning that good is to be done and pursued. According to this theory, virtues like justice, practical wisdom, courage, and temperance are "essential to *moral life*, because they are aspects of a person who is (more or less) wholly integrated with moral truth"—that is, aspects of a person who is in fact able to live in such a way as to respect all the basic goods.[89] But they are not themselves the starting points of morality: alleged virtues must be "evaluated by moral principles," and "only those character traits are true virtues which realize harmonies within the personality according to the demands of moral truth."[90] What's more, our authors claim that even "without having virtues at the outset, people can proceed soundly from practical principles [that is, the basic goods] to judgments about what they ought to do."[91] Without the virtues, one is admittedly liable to "shortcomings in judgments about what one is to do or ought to do" in concrete circumstances, but what Grisez, Finnis, and Boyle call the "core of the virtues" can be had even when one does not yet have the virtue of practical wisdom.[92] This so-called core is choice "in accord with soundly reasoned practical judgments": that is, choice that is fully respectful of the basic goods.[93]

Which brings us to this question: What to make of this theory?

AGAINST THE NEW NATURAL LAW

I want to preface my answer by noting points on which I agree with Grisez, Finnis, and Boyle. One is that *oughts* can't simply be deduced from what's considered natural for human beings, or read off the alleged functions of our body parts. Another is that the natural law is not to be discovered by looking outside ourselves toward, say, some ideal world that transcends our own. Instead, practical knowledge comes through reflection on action. As the moral theologian Jean Porter has nicely remarked in this regard, "Reason takes its starting points from inclinations which are not simply blind surges of desire, but intelligibly structured orientations toward goods connatural to the human creature."[94] That is, we can begin to discern how to live a good life by reflecting on the goods toward which we are naturally drawn, goods such as life, knowledge, and friendship, among others. A rather different philosopher put much the same point this way: "Ethical thought is the process of bringing objectivity to bear on the will," not the discovery of "a new aspect of the external world, called value," or the "bringing [of] our thoughts into accord with an external reality."[95] The upshot is that moral or evaluative truths do indeed exist, but the realism to which at least Thomistic natural law is committed might most accurately be called an *objectivism*: we discover real goods or values by thinking objectively (carefully, critically, in dialogue with others) about the goods toward which we're naturally drawn.

A basic disagreement I have with the new natural law, however, is with its claim that we inevitably discover *the basic goods*—"ultimate rational grounds (principles of practical reasoning)"—when we pursue the question, "What for?" to the end.[96] More precisely, what is implausible is the claim that there is a set of basic goods that, solely on the basis of practical reason, can be grasped with enough content and specificity to enable us to discriminate between right and wrong actions.

Porter also puts this criticism well and so can help to explain it. "It is one thing to say," she writes,

> that we are naturally oriented toward certain desiderata, and [that] this orientation provides a natural starting point for practical reflection and moral action. It is something else again to say that we have a rational grasp of certain basic goods, elemental enough to be regarded plausibly as self-evident to all and yet provided with enough content to [serve as] an immediate basis for practical reflection and moral action.[97]

Porter allows that "the claim that these goods are self-evidently manifest as such as soon as they are experienced is indeed plausible with respect

188

to some of these, such as life or knowledge," but notes, "even with respect to such goods…, Grisez and Finnis [and Boyle] find it necessary to qualify what these goods comprise in order to show how certain moral conclusions flow from them."[98] Her example is how the good of life "is expanded to include procreation, in order to justify the claim that the use of contraception involves 'acting against' the good of life."[99] What is difficult to see is how our practical knowledge that life is a basic good "can yield specific moral conclusions without the need of appealing to anything beyond the deliverances of practical reason."[100] For the deliverances of practical reason as described by Grisez, Finnis, and Boyle appear incapable of telling us just what the good of life comprises. Putting contraception aside—I return to it shortly—consider the question of whether suicide is wrong when it is done "to ensure the lives or the fundamental well-being of others," as when the British explorer Lawrence Oates (1880–1912), in an ill-fated expedition to the South Pole, deliberately wandered away from his fellow travelers lest they die caring for him.[101] Or, to consider other goods, just how to specify the key ingredients of, say, the good of family, and to determine what counts as an attack against this good? Must a family comprise "mothering and fathering"?[102] Would allowing gay couples to adopt children violate, or promote, the good of family life? And so on.

It is true that Grisez has applied his theory to derive answers to a host of sometimes idiosyncratic questions. Volume 3 of his work *The Way of the Lord Jesus*, titled *Difficult Moral Questions*, asks and answers two hundred such questions.[103] It is also true that proponents of the new natural law would reject Porter's criticism and thus mine. So I conclude my discussion here by presenting, in the Scholastic style that Grisez, Finnis, and Boyle occasionally deploy, an objection to this criticism (from the point of view of Grisez et al.) and a reply to this objection (from my own point of view).

Objection: You doubt that, in your words, there is a set of basic goods that, solely on the basis of practical reason, can be grasped with enough content and specificity to enable us to discriminate between right and wrong actions. To give your doubt the appearance of credibility, you cite the well-known moral theologian Jean Porter, who claims, "Even with respect to such goods [as life and knowledge], Grisez and Finnis [and Boyle] find it necessary to qualify what these goods comprise in order to show how certain moral conclusions flow from them." By way of example, she claims that the good of life "is expanded to include procreation, in order to justify the claim that the use of contraception involves 'acting against' the good of life." According to her, our practical knowledge that life is a basic good cannot yield this specific moral conclusion; in other words, she thinks that our specification of the good of life is at the very least not obvious. Based on her tone, we take it that she thinks, further, that it is unwarranted. And you apparently concur.

How wrong you are. Surely you cannot deny that "the contraceptive act seeks to impede *the beginning of the life of a possible person*";[104] otherwise, why do it? It follows that "contraception is a contralife act" that is in this regard "similar to deliberate homicide," as in fact was observed by "a canon…concerning contraception…included in the Church's universal law from the thirteenth century until 1917."[105] To make it perfectly clear for you: "Since contraception must be defined by its intention that a prospective new life not begin, every contraceptive act is necessarily contralife."[106] Like homicide, contraception "involve[s] a contralife will."[107] People who use contraception "look ahead and think about the baby whose life they might initiate"—and reject this baby, despite the fact, "which no one is likely to challenge," that "the coming to be of a new human person is a great human good."[108]

Reply: It is indeed undeniable that "the contraceptive act seeks to impede *the beginning of the life of a possible person*," as you say. But does it follow that contraception is then "contralife," or "involve[s] a contralife will"? In other words, is an act against the transmission of life an act against life itself? This is not at all self-evident. People who use contraception do not want to have *a* baby *now*, which is to say as a consequence of a particular act of sex; but it seems silly to say that they "look ahead and think about *the* baby whose life they might initiate [emphasis added]," and then reject *this* baby despite the goodness of "the coming to be of a new human person." People who did so look ahead and reject *the* baby might well be termed contralife, but who thinks about contraception in this way other than philosophers trying to press an implausible case against it?

You claim that people who use contraception "imagine that a new person will come to be if that is not prevented, they want *that* possible person not to be, and they effectively will that *he* or *she* not be [emphasis added]."[109] No: what they seek to prevent is that *a* baby should be conceived at this time. To say that they thereby exhibit a contralife will appears willful on your part—as if it is obvious and necessarily the case that they are opposed to procreating as a matter of principle, or would reject (that is, abort) *the* baby should *a* baby be conceived.[110] If a couple has decided not to have children, they *might* be termed contralife in some very extended and not at all charitable sense—no doubt no few would take great offense—but to say that by using contraception, they act against the basic good of human life appears even more extreme and peremptory. If a couple were to abort the baby should contraception fail, they would attack the good of life and so could be called contralife in a clear sense; but that the act of using contraception is in itself quite different in intent from homicide, thirteenth-century canons notwithstanding, is evident from the fact that many couples welcome the baby rather than abort it. Yes, these couples sought not to transmit life in having sex, but they did not thereby reject the good of life, or close themselves to procreation in principle.[111]

In sum, it is not at all self-evident that our practical knowledge that life is a basic good can yield the conclusion that contraception is an attack against life. The trouble is specifying the basic good. One of you once criticized Kant's moral theory on the ground that

> the notion of "respecting rational nature as an end in itself" is simply too vague to be decisively predicated…except perhaps in a few uncontroversial kinds of acts, like slavery and rape. Disagreements about what kinds of acts are properly described as acts of respecting rational nature or failing to respect it cannot…be settled except by compromise, intuition, or decision.[112]

But the new natural law is vulnerable to much the same criticism. For the new natural law, to repeat, the trouble is specifying the basic goods. Here "compromise, intuition, or decision" appears inescapable—and the temptation, some might say besetting sin, of new natural law theorists has been to *decide* that an action is an attack against a basic good and thus wrong without providing adequate argumentation in support.

BACK TO CONSCIENCE: THE VIRTUES REVISITED

There is at least this much to say in favor of the new natural law: it appears to fit well with the Thomistic view of conscience. Here's the story that could be told. Through *synderesis*, we apprehend the first principle of practical reason, "Good is to be done and pursued," which is then given direction by our natural inclinations toward various goods. Reflection on why, ultimately, we do what we do gives rise to moral knowledge, in particular to knowledge of the basic goods of human life, the so-called principles of action. *Conscientia* is this knowledge coming to act: it is the name we give the experience of knowing to "do this, shun that," which will be trustworthy to the extent that our penetration into the basic goods is profound and our reason is unfettered—that is, alive to all the basic goods there are.

But here is another way of putting my criticism of the new natural law: the role it envisions for conscience is unduly limited; the boundaries it would put around conscience are far too tightly drawn. Earlier in this chapter, I quoted Aquinas's remark that, although "there is a certain necessity in the general principles, the more we descend to particulars, so much the more we encounter defect," which is to say occasions for disagreement and even irreducible diversity, where our freedom is put to the test.[113] And I remarked that conscience also names how we come to terms with this freedom. By contrast, for the new natural lawyers, the moral knowledge we need is close at hand. "Defects" can be defeated. The way to form our conscience is simply to reflect on the meaning, so to speak, of our natural inclinations.

This book is nearing its conclusion, and it would be going well beyond its project to seek to present a thoroughgoing interpretation of Aquinas countering that of the new natural law.[114] Instead, what we need to do, in light of both the aims of this chapter and some of the arguments

I advanced in earlier chapters, is to consider the role of the virtues in Aquinas's theory of morality, which will bring us back to conscience again. As we have seen, examples of virtues are justice, practical wisdom, courage, and temperance: these are the so-called cardinal virtues, which are called that because they are thought to be "pivotal" for living an excellent human life. (The word *cardinal* is derived from the Latin *cardo*, "that on which a thing turns or depends.") Cardinal or not, what it means to call a character trait a virtue is precisely that it is needed for someone to flourish as a human being.[115] A human being who has, say, the virtue of temperance has a firm, stable disposition to *temper* his or her behavior: to bring it, we might say, to the proper pitch or measure, as when we speak of a tool that has been tempered, or of glass. Take the needs and desires of the human body, though we could also think about the emotions. A human being who has the virtue of temperance has a firm, stable disposition neither to overindulge in the needs and desires of the body, nor to starve him- or herself in this regard. To the contrary, the virtue enables him or her to act in a way that is rightly proportioned to the end of human well-being, or in a word, in a way that is *reasonable*.[116] Aquinas puts the point this way: "Virtues perfect us for following natural inclinations in an appropriate way."[117]

Recall that, according to the new natural law, the virtues have only a secondary role to play: they are those character traits that enable a person to live in a way that is fully respectful of the basic goods of human life—to follow the rules of morality. To stick with the same example, for the new lawyers, temperance is what we need to develop in order to be able to respect the basic good of human life in our sex lives, with all that means regarding the use of contraception. From this point of view, there is little sense in saying, as I did at the end of chapter 2, that the virtuous person *is* the rule. Instead, the virtuous person is simply he or she who has the strength—virtue shares a root with virility—to do as morality requires.

But note carefully what Aquinas says in full: "Virtues perfect us for following natural inclinations in an appropriate way." The statement, "Virtues perfect us for following natural inclinations" might be interpreted in line with the new natural law: on this interpretation, priority would go to the basic goods toward which we're pointed by our natural inclinations; the virtues simply enable us to toe the line. The qualification that "virtues perfect us for following natural inclinations *in an appropriate way*," however, suggests a subtle but quite significant difference between Aquinas and the new natural lawyers. In brief, for Aquinas, it is only *by virtue of the virtues*, so to speak, that we can know how to live out our natural inclinations appropriately, in a way that is befitting to us as the rational animals we are. In other words, the "meaning" or moral significance of our natural inclinations isn't given to us independently of the virtues. Contra the new natural law, it's not the case that, "without having virtues at the outset, people can proceed soundly from practical principles [that is, the basic goods] to judgments about what they ought to do."[118] Instead, we need the virtues—we need at least a vision of moral excellence—to know how to pursue and for that matter to construe the goods toward which our nature points us.[119]

Come at the point this way. Yes, as I quoted Jean Porter above, "reason takes its starting points from inclinations" orienting us "toward goods connatural to the human creature";[120] but what's important to see is that this is just a start. As Porter also writes, "The inclinations themselves are not moral norms."[121] Moral precepts or rules derive not directly from our natural inclinations, but from what we consider, on rational reflection, virtuous or excellent ways of pursuing the goods our nature opens and orients us to.[122] As one proponent of what has come to be called virtue ethics remarks, "Not only does each virtue generate a prescription—do what is honest, charitable, generous—but each vice a prohibition—do not do what is dishonest, charitable, mean."[123] Think here of someone who has moral wisdom to share when it comes to an unwanted pregnancy, or to a pregnancy in which the child has been found to have Downs or Turner's syndrome, or to a pregnancy that threatens the mother's life, subjects of chapters 1 and 2. If we want to know how to act rightly in these circumstances, we want to know what this person thinks we should do: how this morally excellent person (compassionate yet exacting, caring yet truth telling, humble yet steadfast—and so on) would direct us to act in order to protect, promote, and pursue the goods of life and family in the concrete case in question.

Natural questions to ask here include the following: How do we know a person has moral wisdom? Otherwise put, how can we know that our account of the virtues, or our vision of moral excellence, is correct—for example, to think again of chapter 1, that vision to which being pro-life belongs and which it helps support? If, as Aquinas claims, the "virtues perfect us for following natural inclinations in an appropriate way," what's the criterion for appropriateness (or reasonableness), and how can we know that we know it? These are questions that proponents of virtue ethics have long recognized: "But how do we know...*which* character traits are the virtues?"[124] "Can we hope to achieve a justified conviction that certain views about which character traits are the virtues (and which not) are objectively correct?"[125] Kant can serve as an example of a skeptic about the project of virtue ethics as it's developed today. Like the new natural lawyers, he believed that we need to work out the rules of morality independently of our account of the virtues in order to be able to judge which character trait is a virtue and which is not. And so, he notoriously wrote, "Even the Holy One of the Gospel [that is, Jesus] must first be compared with our ideal of moral perfection before we can recognize Him as such."[126] In other words, even Jesus—the Way, the Truth, and the Life, according to the Gospel of John (14:6)—must prove his virtue before the bar of the moral law.

I think a natural law framework can help us answer these questions and concerns. A first point to make, as Jeff McMahan observed with tongue partly in cheek, is that "we have been impressed for so long by the claims of cultural anthropologists, postmodern relativists, undergraduates, and others about the diversity of moral opinion that we have tended to overlook how much agreement there really is."[127] All cultures show care for physical life and well-being, value marriage and family in some form or other, make provisions for education of some kind or other, and recognize that human beings have not only bodily needs but spiritual yearnings.[128] And this is no surprise, for our common human experiences of need and deprivation, and of fulfillment and flourishing, put us onto common goods.[129] For sure, our common human nature *underdetermines* what is the good life for a human being. "Ethical evaluation," a virtue ethicist has remarked, "cannot be a branch of biology or ethology because neither we, nor our concepts of 'a good human being' and 'living well as a human being,' are completely constrained by nature."[130] But human nature nonetheless sets the parameters for meaningful moral inquiry. For example, whatever else we are, we are *dependent* rational animals.[131] We come into the world profoundly needy and very often leave it that way as well. Any account of the virtues that did not recognize this fact about us would be deficient. More precisely and to the point, any account of the virtues that did not include such virtues as self-giving love, patience, forbearance, forgiveness, and a host of others—the virtues that enable the development of dependent rational animals like us into more or less independent agents for a while—would need to be accounted either inadequate, if it just needed filling out, or delusional, if those virtues were rejected altogether.

A way to rephrase this last point is that our account of the virtues must pass muster with human nature. That said, it also bears repeating that human nature underdetermines what is the good life for a human being. To paraphrase Aquinas, although we can agree on the basics, which are all clear enough, the more we descend to particulars, the more we can expect disagreement and diversity. No appeal to what's allegedly natural can carry the day. Porter has put the upshot exactly: "Any attempt to specify the general precepts of the natural law, will remain indeterminate and incomplete, apart from the traditions and practices of some specific community."[132] In other words, different communities will propose different answers to just what is the way, the truth, and the life, so to speak. They will point to different exemplars, draw from different traditions, and be informed by different practices, say with respect to marriage and the family. Sometimes, accordingly, we can have great trouble understanding one another across cultural traditions.[133] But the roots of morality in our common human nature also hold us together and allow us both to understand and to challenge one another's views and ways—so long, anyway, as the temptation to violence to see that our views and ways rule unchallenged does not cut the conversation short.

At the end of the analysis, natural law on this understanding is a framework for a theory of the virtues. Within this framework, the importance of conscience can hardly be overstated. Here's the story, which is familiar at first but soon takes a new turn. Through *synderesis*, we apprehend the first principle of practical reason, "Good is to be done and pursued," which is then given direction by our natural inclinations toward various goods. So far, so good—been there, done that. These goods are interpreted for us, however, by the traditions in which we come of age. By *tradition*, I have in mind again, as I did in this book's introduction, what Alasdair MacIntyre calls a living tradition: "an historically extended, socially embodied argument, and an argument precisely in part about the goods which constitute that tradition."[134] The important point for present purposes is that our moral knowledge, or at least what we claim to know about how to live an excellent human life, comes to us not merely through reflection on the "meaning" of our natural inclinations, but through participation in the life of a tradition: in its arguments about virtues, vices, controversies, concepts, authority, and institutions—arguments that this book has sought to make alive for readers. For Christian Catholics, Jesus Christ shows us the way, the truth, and the life: how to have life most fully. But though Jesus is our exemplar, and we believe he is present to us through the Spirit and enlivens us in the Eucharist, just how to live faithful to his example is by no means always clear. Just remember, as noted in chapter 4, both that Jesus radically rejected violence and that just war theory was developed by self-professed followers of him![135] And remember, too, the crookedness of the human heart, mysteriously vulnerable to evil (compare Gen 4:7), which to overcome, Christians believe we need divine grace. Our freedom is often put to the test. What's more, sometimes our moral knowledge comes to act—the experience of *conscientia*—but leads us to see precisely that we *don't know* just what to do in this or that particular case. Think here of the cases of conscience discussed in chapter 2, or again of the narrator in Tim O'Brien's *The Things They Carried*, cited in chapter 4, struggling with whether "to fight a war I hated." In these cases, in the words of *Gaudium et Spes*, we are apt to find ourselves "alone with God." What we must hope is that our traditions have the resources to enable us to make an answer for ourselves.

197

ACCOUNTABILITY, FINALLY

Though it is true that each virtue generates a prescription—do what is honest, charitable, generous!—and each vice a prohibition—don't do what is dishonest, uncharitable, mean!—there is an important difference between these so-called v-rules, on the one hand, and moral obligations, on the other, which one must satisfy or observe on pain of being culpable and incurring guilt and blame.[136] This point can be appreciated by considering the distinction drawn by the formidable British philosopher Thomas Hobbes (1588–1679) between counsel and command. "Now COUNSELL," Hobbes writes, "is a *precept* in which the reason of my obeying it, is taken from *the thing it self* which is advised; but COMMAND is a *precept* in which the cause of my obedience depends on the *will of the Commander.*"[137] Let's say that, not knowing what to do in a given case—whether involving pregnancy (chapters 1 and 2), war (chapter 4), or for that matter diet (chapter 5)—you know enough to seek out someone who has moral wisdom to share. This morally excellent person advises you what would be best to do in the case in question. Would you be culpable and incur guilt and blame if you didn't do it? Perhaps you would, but if so it wouldn't be simply because you didn't follow the advice or counsel given to you. The morally excellent person who counseled you made a claim on your beliefs. *This*, he or she told you, is what there's reason to do.[138] But the counsel itself didn't generate an obligation to do it. Command is different in this regard so long as the commander has the rightful authority to exact your obedience. Likewise, whether it is *obligatory*, or in Kant's language *categorically imperative*, to do this or that is different from whether it is *well-advised* to do so in order to live an excellent human life.

Pursuing this point to its end would draw us deep into the difference between virtue ethics and, to use Elizabeth Anscombe's phrase again, modern moral philosophy. On Anscombe's account, the concept of obligation, as well as what she calls "the emphatic, 'moral,' *ought*," is foreign to the virtue ethics of an ancient Greek philosopher like Aristotle, whose thought contemporary virtue ethics seeks to retrieve and who stands in the background of Aquinas's thinking. What separates us from Aristotle,

Anscombe claims, is Christianity, "with its *law* conception of ethics" derived from the Jewish Torah (aka the five books of Moses).[139] "In consequence of the dominance of Christianity for many centuries, the concepts of being bound, permitted, or excused became deeply embedded in our language and thought."[140] Now this picture holds us captive, as Anscombe's teacher Ludwig Wittgenstein might have put it,[141] despite the fact that many people nowadays "reject the notion of a divine lawgiver" and so the corresponding conception of ethics.[142]

Anscombe's historical answer to the question of how we came into the "the emphatic, 'moral,' *ought*" no doubt has a lot going for it. Our conception of ethics or morality—I use these terms interchangeably—does indeed reflect "the dominance of Christianity for many centuries." Despite the impression one could take away from much Catholic moral philosophy, including this book to this point, natural law theory didn't come to an end with Aquinas. Instead, it developed after him in a new direction, which we can see with the Spanish Jesuit Francisco Suárez (1548–1617), a leading figure of the Salamanca School and the so-called Second Scholasticism of the sixteenth and seventeenth centuries. As the contemporary American philosopher Stephen Darwall has remarked, "Suárez was in many ways a classical (Thomist) natural lawyer, but he thought that Aquinas's view left out an essential element: morality's distinctive power to bind or obligate those subject to it."[143] Suárez also thought that morality's power to obligate could be accounted for only by seeing moral precepts "as commands that are addressed to us by a superior authority, that is, by God."[144] In a word, Suárez was a *voluntarist* about morality: its precepts obligate us because we are accountable to God who by rights commands us—recall Hobbes's distinction between command and counsel—to obey. God's *will* does the work Suárez found missing in Aquinas's natural law.

Anscombe also holds that, without belief in God as lawgiver, the law conception of ethics loses its root and must in time wither away.[145] This thesis of hers, however, is not as convincing as her history. To begin with, I noted some while ago in this chapter, just before we turned to consider theories of the natural law, that there is at least one respect in which the Thomistic view of conscience needs development: inasmuch as conscience

199

is understood as an act of our practical reason, as Aquinas describes it, it's liable to be understood merely as reflective thought. But, as I also noted then, what it is to acquire a conscience is much more than to become skilled at practical reasoning; having a conscience means much more than acting conscientiously. Instead, conscience names, as Paul Ricoeur suggests, our experience of the voice of the Other, enjoining us to accountability. The voice of conscience, otherwise put, speaks the language of the emphatic, moral, *ought*. Admittedly, it could be that this conception of conscience—or this experience that we name by it—likewise reflects "the dominance of Christianity for many centuries," which is to say likewise originated with a divine law conception of ethics. But the history of conscience reaches further back than the history of Christianity, and the early invocations of the idea in the classical Greek playwrights, while presupposing knowledge of wrong, do not presuppose either natural or divine law.[146]

In any event, I don't think conscience must change its language—must cease speaking in terms of the emphatic, moral, *ought*—without belief in God as lawgiver. Instead, it's more than imaginable that the experience of accountability could give rise to the search for a higher power. After all, yet another way to describe the experience of conscience is to say that, in it, we experience ourselves as beings with obligations, not as absolutes, which is to say not as gods.[147] To whom are we obligated and for what? Who is this Other whom, in conscience, I experience as at once distinct from me *and* more inner to me than I am to myself? These questions are summons to a quest of self-discovery that points beyond the self. One theologian suggests, accordingly, that experiences of conscience may be described as "*implicitly* or *virtually* religious experience," even if a person does not yet know or believe in God as such.[148]

God, however, is not the only candidate to whom we might have moral obligations. In fact, the idea of voluntarists like Suárez that we are accountable to God arguably put pressure on the early modern natural law conception of *morality as accountability to God* and thereby gave rise in the eighteenth and nineteenth centuries to another conception of morality, namely, *morality as equal accountability* to one another as free and rational beings.[149] This conception of morality was developed most prominently by Kant, who claimed, as we saw in chapter 6, that a human being is never to be used merely as a means, but must always be respected as an end in view of the dignity that each and every one of us has. Morality on this conception is about what *you and I* can rightfully demand of one another, which we can seek to determine by considering what demands any one of us could reasonably make of anyone else from a standpoint everyone could share—the Golden Rule as a philosopher would formulate it. Morality is not about, or anyway not just about, what would be best as determined from an impersonal, third-person point of view. Instead it is about what we owe to each other: what you can rightfully demand of me and I of you, relating to one another second-personally as free and rational beings.[150]

How morality as accountability to God might have given rise to morality as equal accountability is easy to grasp once we think some about what is presupposed in holding someone accountable. Take the story in Genesis 2 and 3 of God holding Adam and Eve accountable for eating from the tree of knowledge of good and evil, however we are to interpret this wonderful tale, which is splendidly represented by the artwork on this book's cover. Imagine, however, that some other animal in the garden, say a very hungry rabbit, had eaten from this same tree before Adam and Eve got to it. Other than being quite athletic, this rabbit, I am supposing, is like all other rabbits we know today. Would it have made sense for God to hold this rabbit to account? Could God justifiably have demanded of this rabbit, before it ate from the tree, that it heed the command not to do so, on pain of being culpable and incurring guilt and blame? This is nonsense. "Being thus accountable is only possible for free rational agents who are able to hold themselves responsible."[151] Rabbits can't.

We human beings, however, can hold ourselves responsible; accountability is thus possible for us, as the story of Adam and Eve illustrates. But this is not just some value-free fact about us. That we are accountable bespeaks our freedom and our rationality: we have some measure of mastery over ourselves and our actions, which inasmuch as they are properly human do not simply proceed from whatever allegedly comes naturally to us, but correspond to reasons. It's clear from the story in Genesis, as well as any newspaper, that our freedom and rationality can be used for ill. But they also introduce to the world a new good, that of moral worth. The human being whose will is committed to observing his or her moral duty has a goodness in him- or herself, even apart from whether he or she is in fact able to carry through.[152] That we can hold ourselves accountable to do what we ought redounds to our own credit; it is an earnest of our own value. It's no logical leap to conclude from here that human beings ought to respect one another. For a being that can hold itself accountable to do as it ought itself has moral worth. It has, in a word, dignity. In terms drawn from Genesis 1, we can see in one another, in this regard, a glimmer of the image of God whose likeness it is claimed we bear (1:27).

To my mind, the upshot is that Catholic moral philosophy can forsake neither the virtue ethics of the ancients, nor the moral philosophy of the moderns. Instead, as in chapter 6, Aquinas and Kant, and so Aristotle and the Torah, must meet. This is this chapter's, and this book's, last lesson of conscience. As harmonizing these traditions of moral thought presents no little challenge,[153] this book then closes, appropriately for an introduction, with the acknowledgement that it is, after all, only a beginning.

QUESTIONS FOR FURTHER REFLECTION/PAPER QUESTIONS

(1) It's claimed toward the end of this chapter that, while our common human nature *underdetermines* what is the good life for a human being, human nature nonetheless sets the parameters for meaningful moral inquiry. It's then claimed further that, because of the fact that we are *dependent* rational animals, any account of the virtues that didn't include such virtues as self-giving love, patience, forbearance, and forgiveness—the virtues that enable the development of dependent rational animals—would need to be accounted either inadequate or delusional. But isn't this move made too fast? For, though virtues like these might be necessary, need they be common to all persons? Historically,

the virtues have been *gendered*: some have been coded feminine, others masculine. So why couldn't the masculine virtues be spiritedness, aggression, fierceness, self-affirmation, pride, self-reverence, and so forth—all likewise expression of natural tendencies?[154] What, by contrast, recommends the Hebrew-Christian, egalitarian vision of the good life, secularized in our modern liberal democracies? How to answer the (Nietzchean) charge that such a vision of the good life is *slavish*—and that what the noble among us need to do is to free themselves from its strictures? In a series of letters between two fictional characters, develop this charge (ideally after reading Nietzsche's 1887 *On the Genealogy of Morality*), rebut it, reply in turn, and so on until the letter writers come to some resolution.

(2) This chapter's criticism of the so-called new natural law concludes with a Scholastic-style exchange consisting of one objection and one reply. What's missing is the response setting forth the position that, in the end, the Scholastic master thinks ought to be affirmed. Be that Scholastic master; write the response. Otherwise put, finish the dialogue, giving of course reasons for how you come down.

(3) It's been argued here that the Thomistic view of conscience has more to recommend it than the faculty view does, in part because the faculty view faces problems the Thomistic view is able to avoid. But does *morality as accountability*, whether to God or to one another as free and equal rational beings, push toward the faculty view of conscience—and away from the Thomistic view? In other words, is there a reason why the Thomistic view gave way to the faculty view in the early modern period, just when thinkers like Suárez were emphasizing morality's power to bind or obligate those subject to it? Can the Thomistic view of conscience be developed to capture the experience of accountability, or is what's needed an altogether different view, perhaps more like the faculty view after all?

(4) A basic claim of natural law theorists, "new" or not, is that our natural inclinations open us to goods that really are

good—to evaluative truths, such as that life is good or pain is bad, the truth of which *does not depend* on the attitudes or dispositions we just happen to have, but which we recognize on reflection as objectively the case. Arguably, however, such a value realism, as it might be called, is vulnerable to the charge that it reflects or is dependent on a discredited worldview according to which "there is inherent in each natural kind of thing an appropriate way for things of that kind to behave": in other words, values in place for it to recognize.[155] Has not Darwin's theory of evolution made this view untenable? Must we not then, if we're honest, admit that value realism has become untenable? Must we not abandon the claim that we apprehend objective goods and values? Must we not acknowledge, instead, that the goods we value are valuable precisely because they are valuable to us, not because they are valuable independently of the attitudes and dispositions evolution has just happened to give us?

What should we make of this charge? To understand and evaluate it, do some reading going beyond this introductory book.[156] Then seek to make a contribution of your own to the philosophical literature.

NOTES

INTRODUCTION

1. Going forward, I refer for the sake of simplicity to *Catholic* moral philosophy, though it's worth remembering that besides Roman Catholics, there are Armenian, Coptic, and Greek Byzantine Catholics, among others in union with Rome.

2. See my paper "The Idea of a Catholic College: Charism, Curricula, and Community," *Journal of Catholic Higher Education* 34, no. 1 (2015): 1–9.

3. See Melanie M. Morey and John J. Piderit, *Catholic Higher Education: A Culture in Crisis* (Oxford: Oxford University Press, 2006), chap. 9, "Cultural Collapse and Religious Congregations of Women," 245–73; and Christian Smith, Kyle Longest, Jonathan Hill, and Kari Christoffersen, *Young Catholic America: Emerging Adults in, out of, and Gone from the Church* (Oxford: Oxford University Press, 2014), 59, observing that, in recent decades, "the Catholic Church has struggled more than Protestants to pull emerging adults back into patterns of regular church attendance in adulthood." The Pew Research Center's 2015 report "America's Changing Religious Landscape" further supports this observation. This report is available online through the Center's Web site (http://www.pewforum.org/2015/05/12/americas-changing-religious-landscape/).

4. My father was granted a dispensation to marry; my mother had not taken final vows.

5. David Cloutier, "Introduction: The Trajectories of Catholic Sexual Ethics," in *Leaving and Coming Home: New Wineskins for Catholic Sexual Ethics*, ed. David Cloutier (Eugene, OR: Wipf and Stock, 2010), 1–26, at 10.

6. Alasdair MacIntyre, *After Virtue*, 2nd ed. (Notre Dame, IN: University of Notre Dame Press, 1984), 222.

7. Ibid. Cf. John Henry Newman, *An Essay on the Development of Christian Doctrine* (London: Longmans, Green, 1909), chap. 1, sec. 1, §7, http://www.newmanreader.org/works/development/: "Here below to live is to change, and to be perfect is to have changed often."

8. See for discussion Mary Ellen Konieczny, *The Spirit's Tether: Family, Work, and Religion among American Catholics* (Oxford: Oxford University Press, 2013), 236–37, 246.

9. Georg Simmel, *On Individuality and Social Forms*, ed. Donald N. Levine (Chicago: The University of Chicago Press, 1971), chap. 6, "Conflict," trans. Kurt H. Wolff, 70–95, at 92.

10. I follow here Konieczny, *The Spirit's Tether*, 3.

11. See Massimo Faggioli, *Vatican II: The Battle for Meaning* (New York: Paulist Press, 2012), 133.

12. See Pope Francis, "A Big Heart Open to God," interview by Antonio Spadaro, SJ, trans. Massimo Faggioli et al., *America*, September 30, 2013, 15–38, at 30, and Francis's 2013 apostolic exhortation *Evangelii Gaudium* (*The Joy of the Gospel*), §84, citing Pope John XXIII's 1962 "Address on the Occasion of the Solemn Opening of the Most Holy Council." Every papal and conciliar document cited in this book is available in English on the Vatican's Web site (vatican.va) with the sole exception of John XXIII's opening address, which is available online in Italian, Latin, Portuguese, and Spanish, but not in English.

13. Pope Francis, *Evangelii Gaudium*, §§222, 223.

14. Ibid., §223. See also §§49, 95; cf. "A Big Heart Open to God," 30.

15. Pope Francis, "A Big Heart Open to God," 26.

16. Ibid.

17. Pope Francis, *Evangelii Gaudium*, §39.

18. Pope Francis, "A Big Heart Open to God," 26; cf. *Evangelii Gaudium*, §39.

19. The *Didache* is easily found online. See, for discussion, John T. Noonan Jr., "An Almost Absolute Value in History," in *The Morality of Abortion: Legal and Historical Perspectives*, ed. John T. Noonan Jr. (Cambridge, MA: Harvard University Press, 1970), 1–59, at 9–10.

20. Pope Francis, *Evangelii Gaudium*, §214.

21. See Thomas Merton and Czesław Miłosz, *Striving towards Being: The Letters of Thomas Merton and Czesław Miłosz*, ed. Robert Faggen (New York: Farrar, Straus and Giroux, 1996), letter from Miłosz to Merton, November 28, 1960, p. 66. In his work *Pensées*, Pascal famously addresses a nameless interlocutor who stands, wavering, at the threshold of Christian faith. See *Pensées*, ed. Léon Brunschvicg (Paris: Garnier-Flammarion, 1976), no. 233, pp. 114–16.

22. See, in this regard, Michael J. Buckley, *At the Origins of Modern Atheism* (New Haven: Yale University Press, 1987) and *Denying and Disclosing God: The Ambiguous Progress of Modern Atheism* (New Haven: Yale University Press, 2004).

23. John Paul II, *Fides et Ratio*, §76.

24. See, for example, Friedrich Nietzsche, *On the Genealogy of Morality*, trans. Maudemarie Clark and Alan J. Swensen (Indianapolis: Hackett, 1998), pt. 1, §§6–8, pp. 14–18.

25. I draw some of this language from Primo Levi, *The Drowned and the Saved*, trans. Raymond Rosenthal (New York: Vintage, 1989), 43.

26. I draw here from Jeff McMahan, *Killing in War* (Oxford: Oxford University Press, 2009), 199.

27. Tertullian, "Athens and Jerusalem," in *The Sheed & Ward Anthology of Catholic Philosophy*, ed. James C. Swindal and Harry J. Gensler (Lanham, MD: Rowman & Littlefield, 2005), 61–62, at 62.

28. See John W. O'Malley, *Four Cultures of the West* (Cambridge, MA: Harvard University Press, 2004), 38–42.

29. A fascinating way to appreciate this difference is to compare and contrast the flood story in the ancient epic *Gilgamesh,* as rendered by the poet David Ferry (New York: Farrar, Straus and Giroux, 1993) with the flood story in Genesis as rendered by Robert Alter in *The Five Books of Moses* (New York: W. W. Norton, 2004).

30. God's answer to Moses when he asked for God's name was " *'Ehyeh-'Asher-'Ehyeh*, I-Will-Be-Who-I-Will-Be," sometimes also translated as "I-Am-That-I-Am," or "I-Am-He-Who-Endures," but sometimes also understood as rejecting the question, as if implying that Moses could never understand (Exod 3:14). See Alter's commentary in *The Five Books of Moses*, 321n14. Consider also Cardinal Walter Kasper's reflections in "Merciful God, Merciful Church," interview by Matthew Boudway and Grant Gallicho, *Commonweal*, June 13, 2014, 14–19, at 14: "The doctrine on God was arrived at by ontological understanding—God is

absolute being and so on—which is not wrong. But the biblical under-standing is much deeper and more personal. God's relation to Moses in the Burning Bush is not 'I am,' but 'I am *with* you. I am *for* you. I am going with you.'"

31. See Rémi Brague, *On the God of the Christians (and on One or Two Others)*, trans. Paul Seaton (South Bend, IN: St. Augustine's Press, 2013), 21–22.

32. Ibid., 21.

33. Cf. Jacques Maritain, *An Essay on Christian Philosophy*, trans. Edward H. Flannery (New York: Philosophical Library, 1955), 15.

34. Eva Brann, "A Call to Thought," *The St. John's Review* 45 (1999): 108–18, at 116. This paper is a reflection on John Paul II's *Fides et Ratio*.

35. See, for example, Richard Sorabji, *Animal Minds and Human Morals: The Origins of the Western Debate* (Ithaca, NY: Cornell University Press, 1993), 12, on Aristotle's denial of reason to animals. As Sorabji later comments, given that "it is hard to deny that the chimpanzee who put two sticks together to extend his reach for a banana was exercising reason in *some* sense," the question for the argumentative Greeks was just what sense to give this term in order for reason to belong exclusively to human beings, if in fact it does (78).

36. Pope Benedict XVI, *Spe Salvi*, §6.

37. Étienne Gilson, *The Spirit of Medaeval Philosophy*, trans. A. H. C. Downes (New York: Charles Scribner's Sons, 1940), 22. See also 23: for Paul, "as far as concerns the interests of salvation, faith really and totally absolves us from all need of philosophy."

38. See again Pope Benedict XVI, *Spe Salvi*, §6.

39. See Michael J. Himes, "'Finding God in All Things': A Sacramental Worldview and Its Effects," in *As Leaven in the World: Catholic Perspectives on Faith, Vocation, and the Intellectual Life*, ed. Thomas M. Landy (Franklin, WI: Sheed & Ward, 2001), 91–103, at 101.

40. See Pope Leo XIII, *Aeterni Patris*, §§7 and 18.

41. See Jean Porter, *Natural and Divine Law: Reclaiming the Tradition for Christian Ethics* (Grand Rapids: Eerdmans, 1999), 41–44, and O'Malley, *Four Cultures of the West*, 87–103.

42. See Brian J. Shanley, "Perspectives in Catholic Philosophy I," in *Teaching the Tradition: Catholic Themes in Academic Disciplines*, ed. John

J. Piderit and Melanie Morey (Oxford: Oxford University Press, 2012), 65–83, at 67, 75.

43. Pope John Paul II, *Fides et Ratio*, §77.

44. See, for example, Herbert Feigl, "Logical Empiricism," in *Readings in Philosophical Analysis*, ed. Herbert Feigl and Wilfrid Sellars (New York: Appleton-Century-Crofts, 1949), 3–26, at 3.

45. Pope John Paul II, *Fides et Ratio*, §77.

46. Martin Heidegger, *Phänomenologie und Theologie* (Frankfurt am Main: Vittorio Klostermann, 1970), 27, 30. Heidegger's italics.

47. Pope John Paul II, *Fides et Ratio*, §77.

48. See, for example, Hans Jonas, "Heidegger and Theology," in *The Phenomenon of Life: Toward a Philosophical Biology* (Evanston, IL: Northwestern University Press, 2001), 235–61; and Jean-Luc Marion, *Dieu sans l'être* (Paris: Presses universitaires de France, 1991), 39–80.

49. Clement of Alexandria, "Philosophy and Christianity," in *The Sheed & Ward Anthology of Catholic Philosophy*, 58–60, at 59.

50. Newman, *The Idea of a University* (London: Longmans, Green, 1907), discourse 8, §3, http://www.newmanreader.org/works/idea/. The phrase "the evil of sensuality" appears in discourse 8, §2. Compare, more recently, Daniel O. Dahlstrom, "Philosophy as an Opening for Faith," *Journal of Catholic Higher Education* 34, no. 1 (2015): 27–41.

51. See Augustine, *Confessions*, bk. 3, chap. 4.

52. Robert Sokolowski, *The God of Faith and Reason: Foundations of Christian Theology* (Washington, DC: The Catholic University of America Press, 1995), 43.

53. See further David B. Burrell, "Perspectives in Catholic Philosophy II," in *Teaching the Tradition*, 85–106, at 96; and Alasdair MacIntyre, *God, Philosophy, Universities: A Selective History of the Catholic Philosophical Tradition* (Lanham, MD: Rowman & Littlefield, 2009), 53.

54. Sokolowski, *The God of Faith and Reason*, 70. See 1 John 4:8. Marion's *Dieu sans l'Être* represents a further exploration of this line of thought.

55. Pascal, *Pensées*, no. 277, p. 127.

56. I take this wonderful characterization of the philosopher from Rémi Brague, *Europe, la Voie Romaine* (Paris: Gallimard, 1992), 9–10: "Étant philosophe de métier, j'appartiens à cette race de gens un peu obtus 'à qui il faut vraiment tout expliquer,' même les choses les plus

claires—l'Être, le Bien, la Cité, l'Homme, et quelques autres prétendues evidences."

57. Gilson, *The Spirit of Mediæval Philosophy*, 37 (his italics).

58. Jean-Luc Marion, "'Christian Philosophy': Hermeneutic or Heuristic?" in *The Question of Christian Philosophy Today*, ed. Francis J. Ambrosio (New York: Fordham University Press, 1999), 247–64, at 255.

59. Ibid.

60. See, for a fine discussion, John C. Cavadini, "Why Study God? The Role of Theology at a Catholic University," *Commonweal*, October 11, 2013, 12–18.

61. I have cobbled together this characterization of natural law from Lisa Sowle Cahill, *Sex, Gender, and Christian Ethics* (Cambridge: Cambridge University Press, 1996), 2–3.

62. Porter, *Natural and Divine Law*, 305.

63. See, in addition to Pope Leo XIII's *Aeterni Patris*, Pope Pius XII's 1950 encyclical *Humani Generis* (*Of the Human Race*), §29, which praises "that sound philosophy which has long been, as it were, a patrimony handed down by earlier Christian ages."

64. For example, in §4 of his 1968 encyclical *Humanae Vitae* (*Of Human Life*) concerning contraception, Pope Paul VI even declared, "No member of the faithful could possibly deny that the Church is competent in her magisterium to interpret the natural moral law. It is in fact indisputable, as Our predecessors have many times declared, that Jesus Christ, when He communicated His divine power to Peter and the other Apostles and sent them to teach all nations His commandments, constituted them as the authentic guardians and interpreters of the whole moral law, not only, that is, of the law of the Gospel but also of the natural law." The pope cites here Matthew 28:18–19. See further John Mahoney, *The Making of Moral Theology: A Study of the Roman Catholic Tradition* (Oxford: Oxford University Press, 1987), 173–74, 222, and 278. Mahoney contrasts "the Matthean theology of authoritative moral teaching" with the Johannine theology of the Spirit as inner teacher.

65. Porter, *Natural and Divine Law*, 282.

66. Ibid., 177.

67. Ibid., 284–87. Cf. John Webster, "God and Conscience," in *The Doctrine of God and Theological Ethics*, ed. Alan J. Torrance and Michael Banner (New York: T & T Clark, 2006), 147–65, at 158, citing John Calvin and Karl Barth "against the fantasy of being our own judges,

finding a source of moral truth in ourselves independent of any reference to the presence and action of God."

68. See, for starters, the entry "The Moral Autonomy School and the Faith Ethics School," in *Handbook of Roman Catholic Moral Terms*, by James T. Bretzke (Washington, DC: Georgetown University Press, 2013), 152; and *A Morally Complex World* (Collegeville, MN: Liturgical Press, 2004), 44–47, 86–93. It is interesting to note that theologians as otherwise different as Joseph Ratzinger (later Pope Benedict XVI) and Charles Curran agree as to the inadequacy of our natural knowledge of the moral law. Curran, for example, has criticized *Humane Vitae* for presuming to interpret the natural law without reference to Scriptures, despite the fact that "sin affects reason itself and the very nature on which natural law theory is based." See his "Natural Law and Contemporary Moral Theory," in *Contraception: Authority and Dissent*, ed. Charles Curran (New York: Herder and Herder, 1969), 151–75, at 156.

69. See, for an insightful discussion, O'Malley, *Four Cultures of the West*, 208–18.

70. See, for a fascinating discussion (and examples), the poet Christian Wiman, "Being Prepared for Joy," interview by Anthony Domestico, *Commonweal*, May 2, 2014, 11–16, at 15–16.

71. John Paul II, *Fides et Ratio*, §49.

72. Ibid., §§57 and 78. For discussion of "the Thomism of the encyclical," see Cyrille Michon, "Faith and Reason: Aquinas's Two Strategies," in *Faith and Reason: The Notre Dame Symposium 1999*, ed. Timothy L. Smith (South Bend, IN: St. Augustine's Press, 2001), 283–300, at 291–96.

73. Pope John Paul II, *Fides et Ratio*, §73.

74. *Lumen Gentium* (1964), §25.

75. See Bretzke, *Handbook of Roman Catholic Moral Terms*, 163–64.

76. See Germain Grisez, *Christian Moral Principles*, vol. 1 of *The Way of the Lord Jesus*, chap. 36, http://www.twotlj.org/G-1-V-1.html. Cf. Joseph Ratzinger, *On Conscience: Two Essays* (Philadelphia/San Francisco: National Catholic Bioethics Center/Ignatius Press, 2007), 63.

77. The *locus classicus* is John Henry Newman's 1875 "Letter Addressed to the Duke of Norfolk," in *Certain Difficulties Felt by Anglicans in Catholic Teaching* (London: Longmans, Green, 1900), vol. 2, §5, http://newmanreader.org/works/anglicans/volume2/gladstone/index .html. Compare, more recently, Josef Fuchs, *Christian Morality: The Word*

Becomes Flesh, trans. Brian McNeil (Washington, DC: Georgetown University Press, 1987), 138; and *Moral Demands and Personal Obligations*, trans. Brian McNeil (Washington, DC: Georgetown University Press, 1993), 165.

78. Ladislas Orsy, "Magisterium: Assent and Dissent," *Theological Studies* 48 (1987): 473–97, at 490.

79. Ibid.

80. Pope John Paul II, *Fides et Ratio*, §73. Avery Dulles has noted John Paul's subtle but it seems significant differences from Vatican I. John Paul, Dulles writes, "softens [Vatican I's] dualism of faith and reason" and "shows a marked preference for circular images." See Dulles's "Faith and Reason: From Vatican I to John Paul II," in *The Two Wings of Catholic Thought: Essays on Fides et Ratio*, ed. David Ruel Foster and Joseph W. Koterski (Washington, DC: Catholic University of America Press, 2003), 193–208, at 201. Cf. *Fides et Ratio*, §73.

81. See John T. Noonan Jr., "Development in Moral Doctrine," *Theological Studies* 54 (1993): 662–77; and at greater length *A Church That Can and Cannot Change* (Notre Dame, IN: University of Notre Dame Press, 2005).

82. Noonan, "Transparency in Theology," in *The Foundation of Freedom*, ed. William Hund and Margaret Monahan Hogan (Portland: The University of Portland Press, 2006), 23–28, at 24.

CHAPTER 1

1. Pope Francis, "A Big Heart Open to God," interview by Antonio Spadaro, SJ, trans. Massimo Faggioli et al., *America*, September 30, 2013, 15–38, at 26.

2. It should be acknowledged that, well into the nineteenth century, most Catholic authorities believed that *hominization*—that strange and remarkable event when a human being comes into existence—occurred not immediately with conception, but some time into a woman's pregnancy, typically put at forty days; see John T. Noonan Jr., "An Almost Absolute Value in History," in *The Morality of Abortion: Legal and Historical Perspectives*, ed. John T. Noonan Jr. (Cambridge, MA: Harvard University Press, 1970), 1–59, at 38. Disagreement about the timing of hominization did not lead, however, to approval of even very early abortion,

though it was generally legally ignored; see Kristin Luker, *Abortion and the Politics of Motherhood* (Berkeley: University of California Press, 1984), 13–14. What's more, opposition to abortion once the fetus is considered "formed" has been nearly absolute in the tradition, qualified only by long-standing, nuanced arguments over abortion when the life of the mother is at risk.

3. 410 U.S. 113, 152, 153 (1973).

4. Luker, *Abortion and the Politics of Motherhood*, 126–57.

5. Christopher Kaczor, *The Ethics of Abortion: Women's Rights, Human Life, and the Question of Justice* (New York: Routledge 2011), 179.

6. Patrick Lee, *Abortion and Unborn Human Life*, 2nd ed. (Washington, DC: The Catholic University of America Press, 2010), 55.

7. Robert P. George and Christopher Tollefsen, *Embryo: A Defense of Human Life* (New York: Doubleday, 2008), 134.

8. Ibid.

9. What's more, contemporary science indicates that there is no "moment" of conception, but that it is instead a process taking place over two to four days. See Scott F. Gilbert, "When 'Personhood' Begins in the Embryo: Avoiding a Syllabus of Errors," *Birth Defects Research* Part C 84 (2008): 164–73, at 168.

10. See, principally, Judith Jarvis Thomson, "A Defense of Abortion," *Philosophy and Public Affairs* 1 (1971): 47–66.

11. See Gilbert, "When 'Personhood' Begins in the Embryo," 169.

12. Luker, *Abortion and the Politics of Motherhood*, 180.

13. Andrew Peach, "Late- vs. Early-Term Abortion: A Thomistic Analysis," *The Thomist* 71 (2007): 113–41, at 119.

14. Ibid.

15. Warren Quinn, "Abortion: Identity and Loss," *Philosophy and Public Affairs* 13 (1984): 24–54, at 25.

16. Ibid.

17. Ibid., 33.

18. Ibid., 37.

19. Quinn introduces further distinctions that, while not necessary for purposes of this chapter, may be worthwhile to think through. Briefly, *generic* sortals "preserve the distinction between partial and full reality found within the [complex] substance sortal": that is, they are kinds of things that a complex substance sortal may be classified as that are themselves complex and so themselves admit of two classes of things,

fully realized and partly realized (ibid., 37). For example: houses may be classified as buildings; buildings, like houses, can be fully or partly realized. By contrast, *mock-generic* sortals are simple sortals that "apply to all the individuals, whether fully or partly real, falling under the [complex] substance sortal": that is, they are kinds of things that a complex sortal may be classified as that do *not* admit of or break down into two classes of things (37). For example: all houses may be classified as construction, but there aren't two classes of construction, fully realized and partly realized; instead, something is an instance of construction or it isn't. Another example: all human beings—supposing that the concept human being is a complex substance sortal—may be classified as biological organisms, but there aren't two classes of biological organisms, as instead something simply is or it isn't. Finally, *proto-stage* sortals "apply exclusively to partly real individuals of a given kind": these are again simple sortals, naming an early or "proto" stage of a thing that has not yet been fully realized (38). For example: house-under-construction refers to an early stage of a house; fetus refers to an early stage of a human being.

Mock-generic sortals are potentially misleading. When we classify a complex substance sortal as a mock-generic sortal (house as construction, human being as biological organism), because the mock-generic sortal doesn't break down into two classes, we are liable to lose sight of the fact that the complex substance sortal does. Consider this claim: "Medical science has confirmed that an embryo is human life." The concept *human life*, however, appears to be a mock-generic sortal. It does not admit of the distinction made by the process theory between fully realized and partly realized human beings. This distinction is lost when the debate is cast in terms of whether or not a zygote or an embryo or a fetus is human life. For of course it is. An advocate of the process theory would claim that whether the human life in question is a fully realized human being is a different matter that must not be obscured.

Proto-stage sortals are likewise potentially misleading. In Quinn's words, "Partly real individuals can fully and unambiguously satisfy the criteria associated with such sortals....We must be on guard not to infer from the fact that we have found a full-fledged S that we have found a fully-real individual" (38). Here is the same example: "Medical science has confirmed that an embryo is human life." *Embryo* is a proto-stage sortal. Something is an embryo or it isn't. An advocate of the process theory would claim that whether an embryo is a fully realized human being is a different matter that must not be obscured.

20. Peach, "Late- vs. Early-Term Abortion," 140.

21. See, for example, Michael J. Sandel, *The Case against Perfection* (Cambridge, MA: Harvard University Press, 2007), 102–3, commenting on the muddle a spokesperson for President George W. Bush made for himself in trying to clarify the administration's opposition to the destruction of human embryos for research: at first, the spokesperson termed this destruction murder, then retracted this designation without proffering another.

22. Peter Steinfels, "Beyond the Stalemate: Fifty Years after 'Roe,'" *Commonweal*, June 14, 2013, 12–18, at 15. Steinfels's fine article is worth reading in full.

23. See Michael S. Gazzaniga, "Human Being Redux," *Science* 304 (2004): 388–89, at 389.

24. Rosalind Hursthouse, "Virtue Theory and Abortion," *Philosophy and Public Affairs* 20 (1991): 223–46, at 237.

25. Ibid.

26. Ibid., 236.

27. Peach, "Late- vs. Early-Term Abortion," 119.

28. Ibid., 119, 139.

29. Ibid., 126.

30. Ibid., 126–27.

31. Ibid., 132.

32. Ibid., 134.

33. Ibid., 135–36.

34. Ibid., 136.

35. Ibid., 139.

36. Lee, *Abortion and Unborn Human Life*, 54.

37. Quinn, "Abortion," 40.

38. Ibid., 54.

39. Ibid.

40. Gilbert, "When 'Personhood' Begins in the Embryo," 165.

41. Hursthouse, "Virtue Theory and Abortion," 236. Cf. Beverly Wildung Harrison and Shirley Cloyes, "Theology and Morality of Procreative Choice," in Beverly Wildung Harrison, *Making the Connections: Essays in Feminist Social Ethics*, ed. Carol S. Robb (Boston: Beacon Press, 1985), 115–34, at 123, who claim, provocatively, that the

fact that "the abortion decision is never [*sic*] treated in the way it arises as part of the female agent's life process" stands as evidence of our culture's fundamental misogyny.

42. Ruth Padawer, "The Two-Minus-One Pregnancy," *New York Times Magazine*, August 10, 2011, 22ff., at 24.

43. Ibid.

44. Ibid., 25.

45. Shelley Burtt, "Which Babies? Dilemmas of Genetic Testing," *Tikkun* 16, no. 1 (January/February 2001): 45–47, at 47.

46. See Hursthouse, "Virtue Theory and Abortion," 235. Cf. Harrison and Cloyes, "Theology and Morality of Procreative Choice," 130: "Even so, we must be careful, when we make the case for our right to bodily integrity, not to confuse moral rights with mere liberties. To claim that we have a moral right to procreative choice does not mean we believe that women can exercise this right free from all moral claims of the community."

47. See, for example, Lee, *Abortion and Unborn Human Life*, xi, and Joseph Bernardin, "The Consistent Ethics of Life after *Webster*," in *The Seamless Garment: Writings on the Consistent Ethic of Life*, ed. Thomas A. Nairn (Maryknoll, NY: Orbis, 2008), 188–99, at 191.

48. Bernardin, "Linkage and the Logic of the Abortion Debate," in *The Seamless Garment*, 21–32, at 22.

49. Kaczor, *The Ethics of Abortion*, 178.

50. As the Catholic theologian and legal scholar Cathleen Kaveny has remarked, "Any acknowledgement of the objective wrongness of abortion must have as its counterpoint utmost sensitivity to the difficulties facing women who confront unplanned pregnancies in this society. These difficulties seem insuperable because our society does not treat with gentleness the weak or vulnerable at any stage in life." See M. Cathleen Kaveny, "Toward a Thomistic Perspective on Abortion and the Law in Contemporary America," *The Thomist* 55 (1991): 343–96, at 362. See also her contribution to an exchange with Dennis O'Brien and Peter Steinfels, "Can We Talk about Abortion?" in *Commonweal*, September 23, 2011, 12–19, at 19: "Abortion is a heart-wrenching and difficult problem because the most vulnerable class of human beings—the unborn—are totally dependent on human beings who are themselves very vulnerable—women facing crisis pregnancies."

51. See Hursthouse, "Virue Theory and Abortion," 240.

52. Luker, *Abortion and the Politics of Motherhood*, 242.

53. See the Pew Research Center's 2013 report "Roe at 40: Most Oppose Overturning Abortion Decision," available online through the Center's Web site (http://www.pewforum.org/2013/01/16/roe-v-wade-at-40/).

54. Luker, *Abortion and the Politics of Motherhood*, 243.

55. See for this data Charles Camosy, *Beyond the Abortion Wars: A Way Forward for a New Generation* (Grand Rapids: Eerdmans, 2015), 17.

56. John Boswell, *The Kindness of Strangers: The Abandonment of Children in Western Europe from Late Antiquity through the Renaissance* (New York: Pantheon, 1988), 13–14.

57. Bernardin, "The Consistent Ethics of Life after *Webster*," 191.

58. Lori Freedman and Tracy A. Weitz, "The Politics of Motherhood Meets the Politics of Poverty," *Contemporary Sociology* 41 (2012): 36–42, at 40. See also Caveny, "Toward a Thomistic Perspective on Abortion and the Law in Contemporary America," 377, from whom I have adapted the phrase "a legal policy which is truly pro-life (and not simply anti-abortion)."

59. Freedman and Weitz, "The Politics of Motherhood Meets the Politics of Poverty," 377.

60. See, in this regard, Lisa Selin Davis, "I Couldn't Turn My Abortion into Art," *New York Times*, July 2, 2014, available online through the *New York Times* Web site (http://opinionator.blogs.nytimes.com/2014/07/02/i-couldnt-turn-my-abortion-into-art/?_r=0).

61. Caveny, "Toward a Thomistic Perspective on Abortion and the Law in Contemporary America," 393.

62. Freedman and Weitz, "The Politics of Motherhood Meets the Politics of Poverty," 37.

63. Luker, *Abortion and the Politics of Motherhood*, 7.

64. Ibid., 244: "How people think about abortion is intimately tied to their thoughts about women, children, and the family; and their feelings on these topics will undoubtedly be affected by large-scale social and economic changes now in progress."

65. Ibid., 194.

66. Jon A. Shields, "The Politics of Motherhood Revisited," *Contemporary Sociology* 41 (2012): 43–48, at 43.

67. Ibid., 44–45.

68. See Mary Ellen Konieczny, *The Spirit's Tether: Family, Work, and Religion among American Catholics* (Oxford: Oxford University Press, 2013), 120. Cf. Luker, *Abortion and the Politics of Motherhood*, 8: "If the status of the embryo has always been ambiguous…, then to attribute personhood to the embryo is to make the social statement that pregnancy is valuable and that women should subordinate other parts of their lives."

69. Caveny, "Toward a Thomistic Perspective on Abortion and the Law in Contemporary America," 377.

70. Ibid., 395.

71. Edward Vacek, SJ, "Conditions May Apply: Relativity without Relativism," *Commonweal*, March 11, 2011, 14–17, at 15. The sentence in full reads, "Fortunately, the abortion debate has more and more turned toward the question of whether the fetus possesses the properties that constitute personhood, a question whose answer does not depend on the attitude of its mother."

72. Search online or see chapters 4 and 6 of Camosy's book *Beyond the Abortion Wars*.

73. See Kaveny, "Toward a Thomistic Perspective on Abortion and the Law in Contemporary America," *The Thomist* 55 (1991): 343–96.

74. George McKenna, "On Abortion: A Lincolnian Position," *The Atlantic Monthly*, September 1995, 51–68.

75. Peter Steinfels's "Beyond the Stalemate: Fifty Years after 'Roe'" is especially valuable.

CHAPTER 2

1. Search *casuistry* at oed.com.

2. Ibid.

3. Alexander Pope, "The Rape of the Locke," in *The Rape of the Locke and Other Poems*, ed. Geoffrey Tillotson, vol. 2 of *The Poems of Alexander Pope* (London: Methuen, 1940), canto 5, lines 109–10 and 113–14, p. 208.

4. Ibid., lines 119–22, p. 209.

5. Ralph Waldo Emerson, "The Times," in *The Complete Writings of Ralph Waldo Emerson*, vol. 1 (New York: W. H. Wise, 1929), 83.

6. According to media reports, the doctors estimated the likelihood of death at "close to 100 percent." See Barbara Bradley Hagerty,

"Nun Excommunicated for Allowing Abortion," National Public Radio, May 19, 2010, available online through NPR's Web site (http://www.npr.org/templates/story/story.php?storyId=126985072). The fullest account of the facts we have is M. Therese Lysaught's "Moral Analysis of Procedure at Phoenix Hospital," *Origins* 40 (2011): 537–49, at 537–39, which Lysaught wrote, in the aftermath of the case, at the behest of St. Joseph's Hospital and Catholic Healthcare West.

7. See Denise Grady, "The Mysterious Tree of a Newborn's Life," *New York Times*, July 14, 2014, D1, available online through the *New York Times* Web site (http://www.nytimes.com/2014/07/15/health/the-push-to-understand-the-placenta.html).

8. Lysaught, "Moral Analysis of Procedure at Phoenix Hospital," 539.

9. See "Statements from the Diocese of Phoenix and St. Joseph's," *The Arizona Republic*, May 15, 2010, available through *The Arizona Republic*'s Web site (http://archive.azcentral.com/community/phoenix/articles/2010/05/14/20100514stjoseph0515bishop.html).

10. Ibid.

11. Pope John Paul II, *Evangelium Vitae* (1995), §62, available through the Vatican's Web site (http://w2.vatican.va/content/john-paul-ii/en/encyclicals/documents/hf_jp-ii_enc_25031995_evangelium-vitae.html).

12. United States Conference of Catholic Bishops, *Ethical and Religious Directives for Catholic Healthcare Services*, 5th ed., §45, available online through the USCCB Web site (http://www.usccb.org/issues-and-action/human-life-and-dignity/health-care/upload/Ethical-Religious-Directives-Catholic-Health-Care-Services-fifth-edition-2009.pdf).

13. *Catechism of the Roman Catholic Church*, pt. 3, sec. 2, art. 5, §2271, available online through the Vatican's Web site (http://www.vatican.va/archive/ENG0015/_INDEX.HTM).

14. Search online for Father John Ehrlich's May 17, 2010 statement, "Catholic Morality and Mothers Who Are at Risk," though unfortunately it is no longer available through the Phoenix diocese's Web site. See also his comment to Hagerty in "Nun Excommunicated for Allowing Abortion": Sister McBride "consented in the murder of an unborn child....But—and this is the Catholic perspective—you can't do evil to bring about good. The end does not justify the means."

15. See Hagerty, "Nun Excommunicated for Allowing Abortion."

16. See Christopher Kaczor, "Double-Effect Reasoning from Jean Pierre Gury to Peter Knauer," *Theological Studies* 59 (1998): 297–316, at 297.

17. Joseph M. Boyle Jr., "Toward Understanding the Principle of Double Effect," *Ethics* 90 (1980): 527–38, at 530. See further for this history Joseph T. Mangan, "An Historical Analysis of the Principle of Double Effect," *Theological Studies* 10 (1949): 41–61; Josef Ghoos, "L'acte à double effet. Étude de théologie positive," *Ephemerides Theologicae Lovanienses* 27 (1951): 30–52; James F. Keenan, "The Function of the Double Effect Principle," *Theological Studies* 54 (1993): 294–315; and Thomas A. Cavanaugh, *Double-Effect Reasoning: Doing Good and Avoiding Evil* (Oxford: Oxford University Press, 2006), 1–26. As Cavanaugh nicely remarks, whoever it was who should be counted as the originator of the PDE, "the Thomistic tradition…serves as the matrix of double-effect reasoning" (15).

18. Mangan, "An Historical Analysis of the Principle of Double Effect," 43. See also, more recently, Alfonso Gómez-Lobo, *Morality and the Human Goods: An Introduction to Natural Law Ethics* (Washington, DC: Georgetown University Press, 2002), 80; and the National Catholic Bioethics Center's "Commentary on the Phoenix Situation," *Origins* 40 (2011): 549–51, at 550.

19. United States Conference of Catholic Bishops, *Ethical and Religious Directives for Catholic Healthcare Services*, §47. Cf. §61, on the alleviation and suppression of pain.

20. United States Conference of Catholic Bishops Committee on Doctrine, "The Distinction between Direct Abortion and Legitimate Medical Procedures," June 23, 2010, 1–4, at 2, available online through the USCCB's Web site (http://www.usccb.org/about/doctrine/publica tions/upload/direct-abortion-statement2010-06-23.pdf).

21. See, for example, Germain G. Grisez, "Toward a Consistent Natural-Law Ethics of Killing," *The American Journal of Jurisprudence* 15 (1970): 64–96, at 94; and Cavanaugh, *Double-Effect Reasoning*, 113–14.

22. Matthew B. O'Brien and Robert C. Koons, "Objects of Intention: A Hylomorphic Critique of the New Natural Law Theory," *American Catholic Philosophical Quarterly* 86 (2012): 655–703, at 669.

23. Alan Donagan, *The Theory of Morality* (Chicago: The University of Chicago Press, 1977), 149.

24. Aristotle, *Nicomachean Ethics*, trans. Joe Sachs (Newburyport, MA: Focus Publishing, 2002), bk. 2, chap. 6, p. 30, 1107a.

25. Rosalind Hursthouse, *On Virtue Ethics* (Oxford: Oxford University Press, 1999), 46–47. See also her paper "Discussing Dilemmas," *Christian Bioethics* 14 (2008): 141–50, at 146–48.

26. John Zeis, "Killing Innocents and the Doctrine of Double Effect," *Proceedings of the American Catholic Philosophical Association* 78 (2005): 133–44, at 138–39.

27. Ibid., 134.

28. See John R. Connery, *Abortion: The Development of the Roman Catholic Perspective* (Chicago: Loyola University Press, 1977), 240. Cf. 162.

29. See the Associated Press story by Amanda Lee Myers, "Ariz. Hospital Loses Catholic Status over Surgery," disseminated December 21, 2010, and available online through various Web sites.

30. See, for citations, Keenan, "The Function of the Principle of Double Effect," 301. Perhaps the most important development of this interpretation in the twentieth century was that of Peter Knauer, "La détermination du bien et du mal moral par le principe du double effet," *Nouvelle Revue Théologique* 87 (1965): 356–76. See, for example, 371 on his understanding of proportionate reason: "On doit admettre un mal si c'est la seule manière de ne pas contredire exactement le maximum du valeur qui s'y oppose."

31. Alison McIntyre, "Doing Away with Double Effect," *Ethics* 111 (2001): 219–55, at 222. Cf. Elizabeth Anscombe, "Action, Intention and 'Double Effect,'" *Proceedings of the American Catholic Philosophical Association* 56 (1982): 12–25, at 21; and Grisez, "Toward a Consistent Natural-Law Ethics of Killing," 78–79.

32. Joseph M. Boyle Jr., "Who Is Entitled to Double Effect?" *Journal of Medicine and Philosophy* 16 (1991): 475–94, at 476.

33. Cf. McIntyre, "Doing Away with Double Effect," 223.

34. Whether it was a mistake to apply the PDE to this case is a disputed point in the literature, but as I have also noted the USCCB's Committee on Doctrine cites just this example in its defense of Bishop Olmsted, and in fact it's nearly always cited in discussions of the PDE. See Daniel P. Sulmasy, "'Reinventing' the Rule of Double Effect," in *The Oxford Handbook of Bioethics*, ed. Bonnie Steinbock (Oxford: Oxford University Press, 2007), 114–49, at 117–18. Sulmasy claims that it was a

mistake, originating in the early twentieth century, to apply the principle (which he prefers to call a rule) to the cases of the cancerous gravid uterus and tubal ectopic pregnancy. Yet he acknowledges that "the traditional view" is that "these are typical applications of the RDE (even paradigmatic instances of its use)."

35. See, for this language, the *Catechism of the Catholic Church*, pt. 3, sec. 1, chap. 1, §1751.

36. Thomas Aquinas, *Summa Theologiae*, ed. Thomas Gilby, bilingual ed. (New York: McGraw Hill/Blackfriars, 1975), vol. 38, II-II, q. 64, a. 7, p. 42: "Actus ergo hujusmodi, ex hoc quod intenditur conservatio propriæ vitæ, non habet rationem illiciti, cum hoc sit cuilibet naturale quod se conservet in esse quantum potest."

37. See, on this point, Kaczor, "Double-Effect Reasoning from Jean Pierre Gury to Peter Knauer," 310–11, from whom I also take the phrase "the prerogative of self-defense arising from the natural inclination to self-preservation" (311).

38. Aquinas, *Summa Theologiae* II-II, q. 64, a. 7, p. 42: "Potest tamen aliquis actus ex bona intentione, proveniens, illicitus reddi, si non sit proportionatus fini. Et ideo si aliquis ad defendendum propriam vitam utatur maiori violentia quam oporteat, erit illicitum."

39. Ibid.: "Nec est necessarium ad salutem ut homo actum moderatæ tutelæ prætermittat ad evitandum occisionem alterius; quia plus tenetur homo vitæ suæ providere quam vitæ alienæ."

40. See, for an instructive though doleful discussion of fetal craniotomy, from a medical perspective, Mahendra N. Parikh, "Destructive Operations in Obstetrics," *Journal of Obstetrics and Gynecology of India* 56, no. 2 (March–April 2006): 113–14.

41. Warren Quinn, "Actions, Intentions, and Consequences: The Doctrine of Double Effect," *Philosophy and Public Affairs* 18 (1989): 334–51, at 335n4.

42. Kevin O'Rourke, "Complications," *America*, August 2–9, 2010, 15–16, at 16.

43. See J. H. Keffer, "The Placenta Is Key," *America*, August 16–23, 2010, 28–29.

44. Lysaught, "Moral Analysis of Procedure at Phoenix Hospital," 546–47. Cf. Gerard Magill, "Threat of Imminent Death in Pregnancy: A Role for Double-Effect Reasoning," *Theological Studies* 72 (2011): 848–76, at 854–55 and 868.

45. Lysaught, "Moral Analysis of Procedure at Phoenix Hospital," 539.

46. Nicanor Pier Giorgio Austriaco, "Abortion in a Case of Pulmonary Arterial Hypertension: A Test Case for Two Rival Theories of Human Action," *National Catholic Bioethics Quarterly* 11 (2011): 503–18, at 516–17.

47. Gerald D. Coleman, "Direct and Indirect Abortion in the Roman Catholic Tradition: A Review of the Phoenix Case," *HEC Forum* 25 (2013): 127–43, at 141–42.

48. Kevin L. Flannery, "Vital Conflicts and the Catholic Magisterial Tradition," *National Catholic Bioethics Quarterly* 11 (2011): 691–704, at 702; cf. Magill, "Threat of Imminent Death in Pregnancy," 854.

49. Flannery, "Vital Conflicts and the Catholic Magisterial Tradition," 702.

50. See Keenan, "The Function of the Principle of Double Effect," 295 (on the geometric method) and 311 (on turning to the geometric method to justify a controversial action). Keenan takes this terminology from Albert R. Jonsen and Stephen Toulmin, *The Abuse of Casuistry: A History of Moral Reasoning* (Berkeley: University of California Press, 1988).

51. See Donald B. Marquis, "Four Versions of Double Effect," *Journal of Medicine and Philosophy* 16 (1991): 515–44, at 524–25.

52. See Donagan, *The Theory of Morality*, 160. Cf. Grisez, "Toward a Consistent Natural-Law Ethics of Killing," 88: "A performance considered as a process of causation in the order of nature includes not only the bodily movements of the agent but also the inevitable physical effects which naturally follow from those movements. For example, the performance of lighting a match includes the match igniting; the performance of eating includes eliminating hunger." The claim that one's agency is identical "with the causing of each and every consequence to which the doer's agency in doing it extends" requires, however, two qualifications. First, one's agency is cut short, so to speak, by the intervention of a new agent. Second, one's agency does not extend to abnormal events, which is to say to events not reasonably expected to follow. See, for discussion of these qualifications, Donagan, *The Theory of Morality*, 43–47.

53. Austriaco, "Abortion in a Case of Pulmonary Arterial Hypertension," 510.

54. Cf. Lysaught, "Moral Analysis of Procedure at Phoenix Hospital," 546.

55. John Finnis, Germain Grisez, and Joseph Boyle, "'Direct' and 'Indirect': A Reply to Critics of Our Action Theory," *The Thomist* 65 (2001): 1–44, at 19.

56. Ibid., 20.

57. Finnis, "Object and Intention in Moral Judgments according to Aquinas," *The Thomist* 55 (1991): 1–27, at 25. See also 26: "Intention cannot be explained, and intentions cannot be identified, by reference to what one 'knowingly gives rise to' or 'deliberately causes' or 'immediately and necessarily causes' but only by attending to the course of practical reasoning in the deliberation which ends in choice."

58. Finnis, Grisez, and Boyle, "'Direct' and 'Indirect,'" 5.

59. Finnis, "Reflections and Responses," in *Reason, Morality, and Law: The Philosophy of John Finnis*, ed. John Keown and Robert P. George (Oxford: Oxford University Press, 2013), 459–584, at 481. I have changed the order of presentation of the examples: Finnis gives the third example first.

60. Finnis, Grisez, and Boyle, "'Direct' and 'Indirect,'" 25.

61. Ibid., 24.

62. *Catechism of the Catholic Church*, pt. 3, sec. 1, chap. 1, §1751.

63. Pope John Paul II, *Veritatis Splendor* (1991), §78. Italics in the original.

64. Finnis, "Object and Intention in Moral Judgments according to Aquinas," 18.

65. Finnis, Grisez, and Boyle, "'Direct' and 'Indirect,'" 29.

66. H. L. A. Hart, "Intention and Punishment," in *Punishment and Responsibility: Essays in the Philosophy of Law* (Oxford: Oxford University Press, 1968), 113–35, at 123.

67. Philippa Foot, "The Problem of Abortion and the Doctrine of Double Effect," in *Virtues and Vices and Other Essays in Moral Philosophy* (Berkeley: University of California Press, 1978), 19–32, at 21–22.

68. Cf. Peter A. Clark, "Methotrexate and Tubal Pregnancies: Direct or Indirect Abortion?" *Linacre Quarterly* 16 (2000): 7–24, at 16, on the use of MTX for tubal pregnancies: "A foreseen consequence of this action is the death of the embryo but this is not intended as a means or an end. What is directly intended is to stop the DNA synthesis so that the life-threatening condition to the mother is avoided." But can one aim at stopping DNA synthesis without aiming at the death of the fetus whose DNA is being targeted?

69. Cf. Cavanaugh, *Double-Effect Reasoning*, 107–14.

70. Alan Donagan, "Moral Absolutism and the Double-Effect Exception: Reflections on Joseph Boyle's 'Who Is Entitled to Double Effect?'" *Journal of Medicine and Philosophy* 16 (1991): 495–509, at 496.

71. Cf. Aquinas, *Summa Theologiae* I-II, q. 12, a. 4, ad 3. See also J. L. Austin, "Three Ways of Spilling Ink," in *Philosophical Papers*, ed. J. O. Urmson and G. J. Warnock, 3rd ed. (Oxford: Oxford University Press, 1979), 273–87, at 279: "'I intend to X' is, as it were, a sort of 'future tense' of the verb 'to X.' It has a vector, committal effect."

72. Austin, "Three Ways of Spilling Ink," 283.

73. See, for a nice discussion, Donagan, *The Theory of Morality*, 125. To explain a bit, propositions can be what is called (1) extensional and what is called (2) intensional. A proposition is *extensional* if it will yield propositions of the same truth value when the individuals or objects designated in the proposition are described by different designations. For example, it is true that "___My copy of *The Theory of Morality*___is missing its cover." It is also true that "___My copy of Alan Donagan's book on moral philosophy___is missing its cover." Both these designations describe the same object. By contrast, a proposition is *intensional* if it will yield propositions of the same truth value only when the individuals or objects designated in the proposition are described in a certain way or with certain properties. Here the relation of the mind to its object is crucial. For example, it is true that "Oedipus chose to kill___the haughty stranger who ordered him to give way___," but it is not true that "Oedipus chose to kill___his father___," even though *his father* designates the same individual as *the haughty stranger*. Like propositions: "_____ is voluntary," propositions: "_____ is intentional" are *intensional*. That is, to quote Donagan, "They are true of a given action only under certain descriptions" (125).

74. Anscombe, "Action, Intention and 'Double Effect,'" 23.

75. Anscombe, *Intention*, 2nd ed. (Cambridge, MA: Harvard University Press, 1963), 36.

76. Blaise Pascal, *Les Provinciales*, in *Oeuvres Complètes*, ed. Michel Le Guern (Paris: Gallimard, 1998), vol. 1, 648–49. Cf. Anthony Kenny, "Intention and Side Effects: The Mens Rea for Murder," in Keown and George, *Reason, Morality, and Law*, 109–17, at 114: "Surely focusing on the description [of an action] that promises to yield [a] benefit—rather than

the other descriptions indicating the impermissibility of the means—is precisely what constitutes 'direction of intention.'"

77. See, on Aquinas, Flannery, "Vital Conflicts and the Catholic Magisterial Tradition," 693–94 and 696–97, and "John Finnis on Thomas Aquinas on Human Action," in Keown and George, *Reason, Morality, and Law*, 118–32, to which Finnis replies in "Reflections and Responses," 489–98.

78. Finnis, "Object and Intention in Moral Judgments according to Aquinas," 18.

79. Finnis, Grisez, and Boyle, "'Direct' and 'Indirect,'" 29.

80. Austriaco, "Abortion in a Case of Pulmonary Arterial Hypertension," 514.

81. Koons and O'Brien, "Objects of Intention," 668.

82. Anscombe, "Action, Intention and 'Double Effect,'" 23.

83. Anscombe, *Intention*, 34.

84. I take this example from McIntyre, "Doing Away with Double Effect," 241.

85. Ibid., 250. McIntyre took this example in turn from *The New Catholic Encyclopedia*.

86. Aquinas, *Summa Theologiae* II-II, q. 64, a. 7.

87. See, for much more on this qualification, Jeff McMahan, *Killing in War* (Oxford: Oxford University Press, 2009), to begin with 15–37.

88. An interesting question is whether soldiers with a just cause may rightly kill the enemy if they *are* motivated by malice. I am inclined to say that killing the enemy in this case is morally permissible, but that the soldiers would be morally blameworthy because of the reasons they saw as decisive. Cf. Judith Jarvis Thomson, "Self-Defense," *Philosophy and Public Affairs* 20 (1991): 283–310, at 292–96; T. M. Scanlon, *Moral Dimensions: Permissibility, Meaning, Blame* (Cambridge, MA: Harvard University Press, 2008), 19–36; and Niko Kolodny, "Scanlon's Investigation: The Relevance of Intent to Permissibility," *Analytic Philosophy* 52 (2011): 100–23, especially 122. At the same time, as Cathleen Kaveny has remarked, according to the Catholic moral tradition, "the most significant aspect of a human action is the way in which it shapes the character of the person who performs it," such that "individuals who engage in deliberate evildoing harm themselves far more than they [harm] those who suffer injustice at their hands." What's tricky about the case of wrongly motivated soldiers with a just cause is that they do evil

to themselves in doing precisely what, from another angle, they should be doing. See Kaveny, "Appropriation of Evil: Cooperation's Mirror Image," *Theological Studies* 61 (2000): 280–313, at 303. Cf. Plato's *Gorgias*, 470e–479e, and *Republic*, bk. 2.

89. Thomas Nagel, *The View from Nowhere* (Oxford: Oxford University Press, 1986), 181–82.

90. See McIntyre, "Doing Away with Double Effect," 227.

91. By the way, a dentist who inflicted pain in all instances both as a rightly proportioned means *and* as an end likely would not be as dangerous as a dentist who inflicted pain as an end all on its own, but still there would be reason to criticize both dentists morally. Moral evaluation concerns, after all, not only what is done, but the reasons for actions.

92. Cf. Knauer, "La détermination du bien et du mal par le principe du double effet," 360–1, who is especially clear on the mistake of "le morcelage des actes selon leur structure physique extérieure, alors qu'il faudrait les considérer dans l'unité de l'objet moral" (360).

93. It is worth recalling the context of Romans 3:8: Paul is not systematically developing a moral theology or philosophy, but countering the slander, perhaps directed against him in particular, that Christians believe it permissible to do evil so that God might counter by bringing forth good things in abundance (cf. 6:1).

94. See the title of McIntyre's paper: "Doing Away with Double Effect."

95. John T. Noonan Jr., "An Almost Absolute Value in History," in *The Morality of Abortion: Legal and Historical Perspectives*, ed. John T. Noonan Jr. (Cambridge, MA: Harvard University Press, 1970), 1–59, at 50.

96. Ibid.

97. Quinn, "Actions, Intentions, and Consequences," 335n4.

98. See Keenan, "The Function of the Principle of Double Effect," 296, again drawing from Jonsen and Toulmin's *The Abuse of Casuistry*. The claim that casuistry proceeds not "geometrically" but "taxonomically" needs, however, to be qualified: sixteenth-century "high casuistry" proceeded taxonomically; what Keenan calls the seventeenth-century "casuistry of accommodation" became deductive in its method. See, on this change, Keenan's "The Return of Casuistry," *Theological Studies* 57 (1996): 123–38, at 129–30; and "Applying the Seventeenth-Century Casuistry of Accommodation to HIV Prevention," *Theological Studies* 60 (1999): 492–512, at 497–98.

99. Keenan, "The Function of the Principle of Double Effect," 295; see also 298 and 300.

100. John C. Ford, "The Morality of Obliteration Bombing," *Theological Studies* 5 (1944): 261–309, at 289, 290.

101. Cf., for example, R. M. Hare, "Is Medical Ethics Lost?" *Journal of Medical Ethics* 19 (1993): 69–70, who speaks witheringly of "some ecclesiastics and lawyers, who simply make the old casuistical moves without any attempt to justify them" (70).

102. Keenan, "The Function of the Principle of Double Effect," 313.

103. See M. V. Dougherty, *Moral Dilemmas in Medieval Thought: From Gratian to Aquinas* (Cambridge: Cambridge University Press, 2011), 21–22.

104. See for discussion James T. Bretzke, "The Lesser Evil," *America*, March 26, 2007, 16–18.

105. See David Gibson, "The Catholic Church, Condoms, and 'Lesser Evils,'" *New York Times*, November 28, 2010, Week-in-Review, 4 (also available online through the *New York Times* Web site, http://www.nytimes.com/2010/11/28/weekinreview/28gibson.html).

106. The best book I know in this regard is *Silence* by the Japanese novelist Shusaku Endo (1923–96). See, for an excellent discussion, William T. Cavanaugh, "The God of Silence: Shusaku Endo's Reading of the Passion," *Commonweal*, March 13, 1998, 10–12.

107. See Pope John Paul II, *Veritatis Splendor*, §§90–94. The statement "it is not right to do what God's law qualifies as evil in order to draw some good from it" is taken from §91.

108. Thomas A. Cavanaugh, "Double-Effect Reasoning, Craniotomy, and Vital Conflicts: A Case of Contemporary Catholic Casuistry," *National Catholic Bioethics Quarterly* 11 (2011): 453–63, at 462–63.

109. Anscombe, *Intention*, 34.

110. I draw in the following from John Zeis, "What Contradicts Intention," *Proceedings of the American Catholic Philosophical Association* 86 (2012): 115–28, especially 123–27.

111. See Noonan, "An Almost Absolute Value in History," 58: "The principle of double effect was no doctrine fallen from heaven, but a method of analysis appropriate where two relative values were being compared."

112. That the wide form of the principle of choosing the lesser evil has lately been obscured, for whatever reason, is only more reason to look

at it again. The explanation, to speculate a bit, may have to do with the more or less consequentialist interpretation of the fourth condition of the PDE in terms of weighing good effects against bad effects. This interpretation was advanced in the twentieth century, in much qualified form, by so-called proportionalists. As the tradition of Catholic moral thought is antipathetic to consequentialism, more conservative representatives of the tradition reacted by magnifying the third condition of the PDE, with the result that any intentional doing of evil became nearly unthinkable. See, for precision on the consequentialism of proportionalists, Lisa Sowle Cahill, "Teleology, Utilitarianism, and Christian Ethics," *Theological Studies* 42 (1981): 610–29, especially 628–29. For an interesting discussion of the reaction of proponents of the so-called new natural law, see Daniel P. Sulmasy, "Double Effect Reasoning and Care at the End of Life: Some Clarifications and Distinctions," *Vera Lex* 6 (2005): 107–45, noting "a revisionist tendency to interpret the entire Catholic moral tradition through the PDE, even if it demands more of the faithful than the Tradition would demand" (124), in particular on the question of withholding and withdrawing an extraordinary means of treatment.

113. Austriaco, "Abortion in a Case of Pulmonary Arterial Hypertension," 514.

114. See, for example, Charles Camosy, *Beyond the Abortion Wars: A Way Forward for a New Generation* (Grand Rapids: Eerdmans, 2015), chap. 3. See, for criticism, my "The Wrong Description," review of *Beyond the Abortion Wars*, by Charles Camosy, *Commonweal*, May 15, 2015, 23–24.

CHAPTER 3

1. Lysaught, curiously, does not appeal to self-defense.

2. Judith Jarvis Thomson, "A Defense of Abortion," *Philosophy and Public Affairs* 1 (1971): 47–66, at 52. Thomson's paper, by the way, is well worth reading. See, for critical discussion, chapter 2 of my book *Parental Obligations and Bioethics: The Duties of a Creator* (New York: Routledge, 2013), 43–58.

3. Thomson, "A Defense of Abortion," 53–54.

4. Alan Donagan, *The Theory of Morality* (Chicago: The University of Chicago Press, 1977), 149.

5. Kevin L. Flannery, "Vital Conflicts and the Catholic Magisterial Tradition," *National Catholic Bioethics Quarterly* 11 (2011): 691–704, at 693.

6. Gareth B. Matthews, "Saint Thomas and the Principle of Double Effect," in *Aquinas's Moral Theory: Essays in Honor of Norman Kretzmann*, ed. Scott MacDonald and Eleonore Stump (Ithaca, NY: Cornell University Press, 1999), 63–78, at 63.

7. See David Albert Jones, "Magisterial Teaching on Vital Conflicts," *National Catholic Bioethics Quarterly* 14 (2014): 81–104, at 99: "There is surely a wide spectrum of opinion, not least among Thomists, as to how to characterize 'Aquinas's core insights.'"

8. Joseph M. Boyle Jr., "Toward Understanding the Principle of Double Effect," *Ethics* 90 (1980): 527–38, at 530.

9. Recall the formulation of the conditions by Joseph T. Mangan, in "An Historical Analysis of the Principle of Double Effect," *Theological Studies* 10 (1949): 41–61, at 43: "1) that the action in itself from its very object be good or at least indifferent; 2) that the good effect and not the evil effect be intended; 3) that the good effect be not produced by means of the evil effect; 4) that there be a proportionately grave reason for permitting the evil effect."

10. See ibid., 59.

11. Johannis Petri Gury, *Compendium Theologiae Moralis*, 14th ed. (Rome: Prati, 1901), vol. 1, "De actibus humanis," chap. 2, "De principiis actuum humanorum," article 1, §2, no. 9, p. 8: "Licet ponere causam bonam aut indifferentem, ex qua immediate sequitur duplex effectus, unus bonus, alter vero malus, si adsit proportionate gravis, et finis agentis sit honestus, pravum scilicet effectum non intendat."

12. Ibid., 8–9: "Requiritur ut bonus effectus saltem aeque immediate ex causa sequatur. Ratio est, quia is causa directe et immediate pravum habet effectum et nonnisi mediante illo pravo effectu bonus effectus provenit, tunc bonum ex malo quaeritur: porro nunquam fas est malum quantumvis leve, patrare ad bonum quodcumque procurandum; nam iuxta pervulgatum axioma ex Apostolo depromptum Rom. III.8.: *Numquam sunt facienda mala, ut eveniat bona.*"

13. Thomas Aquinas, *Summa Theologiae*, ed. Thomas Gilby, OP, bilingual ed. (New York: McGraw Hill/Blackfriars, 1975), II-II, q. 64, a. 7, pp. 40–2: "Nihil prohibet unius actus esse duos effectus, quorum alter solum sit in intentione, alius vero sit præter intentionem. Morales autem

actus recipiunt speciem secundum id quod intenditur, non autem ab eo quod est præter intentionem, cum sit per accidens, ut ex supra dictis patet. Ex actu igitur alicujus seipsum defendentis duplex effectus sequi potest: unus quidem conservatio propriæ vitæ; alius autem occisio invadentis. Actus ergo hujusmodi ex hoc quod intenditur conservatio propriæ vitæ, non habet rationem illiciti, cum hoc sit cuilibet naturale quod se conservet in esse quantum potest."

14. Cf. Alison McIntyre, "Doing Away with Double Effect," *Ethics* 111 (2001): 219–55, at 247–48.

15. John Finnis, "Object and Intention in Moral Judgments according to Aquinas," *The Thomist* 55 (1991): 1–27, at 25.

16. See Mangan, "An Historical Analysis of the Principle of Double Effect," 45. Mangan cites Leonard Lessius, Dominicus de Soto, and Gabriel Vasquez. Cf. John T. Noonan Jr., "An Almost Absolute Value in History," in *The Morality of Abortion: Legal and Historical Perspectives*, ed. John T. Noonan Jr. (Cambridge, MA: Harvard University Press, 1970), 1–59, at 24–26 (on Thomas) and 29–31 (on Tomás Sanchez and Lessius).

17. Joseph M. Boyle Jr., "*Praeter Intentionem* in Aquinas," *The Thomist* 42 (1978): 649–65, at 658.

18. Ibid., 660.

19. The text is *De malo* 1.3 ad 15; see Boyle, "*Praeter Intentionem* in Aquinas," 659, for a translation.

20. See Matthews, "Saint Thomas and the Principle of Double Effect," 74.

21. Thomas A. Cavanaugh, *Double-Effect Reasoning: Doing Good and Avoiding Evil* (Oxford: Oxford University Press, 2006), 10–11.

22. Ibid., 12.

23. By the way, a proponent of the new natural law's account of intentional action would counter that "exposing the attacker to the risk of death" is not an element in the chain of reasons that the agent intends. I thank John Zeis for this observation.

24. Mangan, "An Historical Analysis of the Principle of Double Effect," 44–45. Cf. Christopher Kaczor, "Double-Effect Reasoning from Jean Pierre Gury to Peter Knauer," *Theological Studies* 59 (1998): 297–316, at 308: "Historically, readers of Aquinas have been divided about the meaning and scope of intention both in general and specifically in ST 2-2, q. 64, a. 7."

25. See for citations Mangan, "An Historical Analysis of the Principle of Double Effect," 47.

26. Aquinas, *Summa Theologiae* II-II, q. 64, a. 7, p. 42: "Nec est necessarium ad salutem ut homo actum moderatæ tutelæ praetermittat ad evitandum occisionem alterius; quia plus tenetur homo vitæ suæ providere quam vitæ alienæ."

27. Ibid.: "Sed quia occidere hominem non licet nisi publica auctoritate propter bonum commune, ut ex supra dictis patet; illicitum est quod homo intendat occidere hominem ut seipsum defendat, nisi ei qui habet publicam auctoritatem, qui intendens hominem occidere ad sui defensionem refert hoc ad publicum bonum, ut patet in milite pugnante contra hostes, et in ministro judicis pugnante contra latrones."

28. Mangan, "An Historical Analysis of the Principle of Double Effect," 49.

29. Mangan, who holds that we can attribute to Aquinas the PDE, argues for this conclusion against Vincente M. Alonso, who in his 1937 doctoral dissertation for the Gregorian University, *El principio del doblo efecto en los comentadores de Santo Tomás de Aquino*, had denied that the third condition could be attributed to Aquinas. Josef Ghoos, "L'acte à double effet. Étude de théologie positive," *Ephemerides Theologicae Lovaniensis* 27 (1951): 30–52, comes to Alonso's support; James F. Keenan, "The Function of the Double Effect Principle," *Theological Studies* 54 (1993): 294–315, judges Ghoos's paper to have "proved" Mangan wrong (299).

30. Cf. Nicanor Pier Giorgio Austriaco, "Abortion in a Case of Pulmonary Arterial Hypertension: A Test Case for Two Rival Theories of Human Action," *National Catholic Bioethics Quarterly* 11 (2011): 503–18, at 504.

31. See ibid. Austriaco rejects conformity with Aquinas as the criterion of truth and proposes instead conformity with "the settled moral convictions of the Catholic tradition and the everyday commonplace experience of human action."

32. Thomson, "A Defense of Abortion," 53. See also her "Self-Defense," *Philosophy and Public Affairs* 20 (1991): 283–310, at 289–91, discussing cases of Substitution-of-a-Bystander, Use-of-a-Bystander, and Riding-Roughshod-over-a-Bystander. For what a bystander is and why bystanders are morally protected, see 298–99.

33. I draw some of the language here from Jeff McMahan, *Killing in War* (Oxford: Oxford University Press, 2009), 159 (on culpable threats) and 169 (on nonresponsible threats).

34. Ibid., 169. See also McMahan's *The Ethics of Killing: Problems at the Margins of Life* (Oxford: Oxford University Press, 2002), 405–7.

35. Charles Camosy, *Beyond the Abortion Wars: A Way Forward for a New Generation* (Grand Rapids: Eerdmans, 2015), 67–68.

36. See further David Rodin, *War and Self-Defense* (Oxford: Oxford University Press, 2002), 80–83.

37. See McMahan, *Killing in War*, 171. Thomson would call this a case of Riding-Roughshod-over-a-Bystander. Such cases have in fact been long discussed in Catholic moral theology; see in this regard John R. Connery, *Abortion: The Development of the Roman Catholic Perspective* (Chicago: Loyola University Press, 1977), 240. It seems, however, to be but a minority opinion in the tradition that the bystander may be run over; see Connery, *Abortion*, 162, on the French Jesuit Théophile Raynaud (1582–1663).

38. See further Lisa Sowle Cahill's excellent article, "Abortion and Argument by Analogy," *Horizons* 9 (1982): 271–87.

39. Noonan, "An Almost Absolute Value in History," 58. As Noonan comments, "A hardening position…was initiated with a series of responses from the Holy Office running from 1884 to 1902" (41). See further Connery, *Abortion*, 225–303, on the nineteenth-century controversy over fetal craniotomy and this controversy's resolution.

40. See Eric D'Arcy, *Conscience and Its Right to Freedom* (New York: Sheed and Ward, 1961), 130–31, on "the influential [Jesuit Antonio] Ballerini," with whom D'Arcy disagrees, but whose position he considers at least respectable. See further Noonan, "An Almost Absolute Value in History," 41–44; and Connery, *Abortion*, 217–22.

41. Noonan, "An Almost Absolute Value in History," 58. For discussion of the current state of "Magisterial Teaching on Vital Conflicts," see Jones's paper of that title, in particular 86–87 and 103.

42. Donagan, *The Theory of Morality*, 163.

43. Thomson, "Self-Defense," 293; cf. T. M. Scanlon, *Moral Dimensions: Permissibility, Meaning, Blame* (Cambridge, MA: Harvard University Press, 2008), 20 and 28–32.

44. See Scanlon, *Moral Dimensions*, 2–3 and 23. Scanlon also considers, though briefly, what he calls "the *predictive* significance of intent":

that is, the fact that what a person intends tells us about what he or she will do or at least seek to do (see 13). Let's say the enemy evacuates civilians from the vicinity of the munitions factory. A commander who intends to kill innocent civilians will likely act differently than a commander who does not have this intention.

CHAPTER 4

1. Ludwig Wittgenstein, *Culture and Value*, ed. G. H. Von Wright, trans. Peter Winch, bilingual ed. (Chicago: The University of Chicago Press, 1980), 15.

2. Jeff McMahan, *Killing in War* (Oxford: Oxford University Press, 2009), 1.

3. William Shakespeare, *Henry V*, ed. Claire McEachern (New York: Penguin, 1999), act 4, scene 1, p. 73.

4. Larissa MacFarquhar, "How to Be Good," *The New Yorker*, September 5, 2011, 43–53.

5. McMahan, *Killing in War*, 97.

6. See, for an overview, though it's already a decade old, David Rodin, "The Ethics of War: State of the Art," *Journal of Applied Philosophy* 23 (2006): 241–46.

7. McMahan, *Killing in War*, 120.

8. See, to begin with, Aquinas, *Summa Theologiae* II-II, q. 40, a. 1.

9. See, for example, the judgment of Gerald F. Powers, "The U.S. Bishops and War since the Peace Pastoral," *U.S. Catholic Historian* 27 (2009): 72–96, at 95: "While realism retained its dominant place in foreign policy, by the mid-1980s, the just war tradition was no longer considered anachronistic by secular elites, an uninvited guest at an exclusive party. The [U.S.] bishops played a singular role in this development."

10. James Turner Johnson, "Just War, as It Was and Is," *First Things*, January 2005, 14–24.

11. Leon Wieseltier, "Washington Diarist," *The New Republic*, March 25, 2013, 59. Wieseltier is writing here about the Syrian civil war and the reluctance of the administration of President Barack Obama to intervene militarily.

12. Virgil, *The Aeneid*, trans. Robert Fitzgerald (New York: Vintage, 1983), bk. 1, lines 394–98, pp. 13–14.

13. Daniel C. Maguire, "The Abnormality of War: Dissecting the 'Just War' Euphemisms and Building an Ethics of Peace," *Horizons* 33 (2006): 111–26, at 112. It is worth noting in this regard that "even the most conservative estimates of civilian casualties place the ratio [of civilians killed to combatants killed] at one-to-one." See Steve Coll, "The Unblinking Stare: The Drone War in Pakistan," *The New Yorker*, November 24, 2014, 98–109, at 100.

14. Maguire, "The Abnormality of War," 113.

15. Thomas Merton, *Peace in the Post-Christian Era*, ed. Patricia A. Burton (Maryknoll, NY: Orbis, 2004), 43.

16. See John Howard Yoder, *When War Is Unjust: Being Honest in Just-War Thinking*, 2nd ed. (Eugene, OR: Wipf & Stock, 1996), 3–4 and 71.

17. Consider the recent popularity of "stand-your-ground" laws, which represent an unprecedented extension of the ancient "castle doctrine" permitting the use of force, *if* necessary, to defend against an intruder in one's own home. See, for a lucid discussion, Stanley Fish, "Stand Your Ground, Be a Man," *New York Times*, July 22, 2013, available online through the *New York Times* Web site (http://opinion ator.blogs.nytimes.com/2013/07/22/stand-your-ground-be-a-man/).

18. United States Conference of Catholic Bishops, "Statement on Iraq," November 13, 2002, available online through the USCCB Web site (http://www.usccb.org/issues-and-action/human-life-and-dignity/ global-issues/middle-east/statement-on-iraq.cfm). To quote in part: "People of good will may differ on how to apply just war norms in particular cases, especially when events are moving rapidly and the facts are not altogether clear. Based on the facts that are known to us, we continue to find it difficult to justify the resort to war against Iraq, lacking clear and adequate evidence of an imminent attack of a grave nature. With the Holy See and bishops from the Middle East and around the world, we fear that resort to war, under present circumstances and in light of current public information, would not meet the strict conditions in Catholic teaching for overriding the strong presumption against the use of military force."

19. Oliver O'Donovan, *The Just War Revisited* (Cambridge: Cambridge University Press, 2003), 9. I have Americanized the quotation's spelling.

20. Paul J. Griffiths and George Weigel, "Who Wants War? An Exchange," *First Things*, April 2005, 10–12, at 10.

21. George Weigel, "Moral Clarity in a Time of War," *First Things*, January 2003, 20–27, at 21; "World Order: What Catholics Forget," *First Things*, May 2004, 31–38, at 37; and again with Griffiths, "Just War: An Exchange," *First Things*, April 2002, 31–36, at 34.

22. Griffiths and Weigel, "Who Wants War? An Exchange," 11.

23. Weigel, "Moral Clarity in a Time of War," 27.

24. Ibid.

25. Ibid. Cf. Michael Novak's "'Asymmetrical Warfare' and Just War," *National Review Online*, February 10, 2003, the text of an address that Novak presented that same day in Rome on the invitation of the United States' ambassador to the Holy See. Novak invoked "authentic Catholic doctrine on the just war" to remind "distant commentators" that "final judgment belongs to public authorities" who enjoy "moral priority of place." This text is available at http://www.nationalreview.com/article /205864/asymmetrical-warfare-just-war-michael-novak.

26. Rowan Williams and George Weigel, "War and Statecraft: An Exchange," *First Things*, March 2004, 14–22, at 17. Williams also called this Weigel's "really startling theological novelty" (ibid.).

27. Augustine, *The City of God against the Pagans*, ed. and trans. R. W. Dyson (Cambridge: Cambridge University Press, 1998), bk. 1, ch. 21, p. 33. See also, more fully, *Contra Faustum*, in *Nicene and Post-Nicene Fathers*, vol. 4, ed. Philip Schaff (Buffalo: Christian Literature Publishing Co., 1887), bk. 22, §75, http://www.newadvent.org/fathers/1406.htm.

28. See, for example, Thomas Hurka, "Proportionality in the Morality of War," *Philosophy and Public Affairs* 33 (2005): 34–66, at 35.

29. See David Rodin, *War and Self-Defense* (Oxford: Oxford University Press, 2002), 167: "*Jus in bello* is the product of the medieval chivalric code, the self-regulation of the warrior classes. *Jus ad bellum*, on the other hand, is the invention of churchmen and lawyers and represents a fundamental challenge to the assumptions build into chivalry," namely, that "military life and warfare are an acceptable and potentially noble form of activity."

30. Michael Walzer, *Just and Unjust Wars: A Moral Argument with Historical Illustrations*, 3rd ed. (New York: Basic Books, 2000), 21.

31. Ibid.

32. Ibid., 41.

33. Ibid., 37.

34. Ibid., 36.

35. Ibid.

36. Shakespeare, *Henry IV, Part One*, ed. M. A. Schaaber (New York: Penguin, 1970), act 4, scene 2, p. 108.

37. Cf. again *Henry V*, act 4, scene 1, p. 73.

38. McMahan, *Killing in War*, 112.

39. McMahan fleshes out this proposal in a 2012 paper titled "The Prevention of Unjust Wars," in *Reading Walzer*, ed. Yitzhak Benbaji and Naomi Sussman (New York: Routledge, 2014), 233–55. McMahan calls here for "moral vision as well as creativity in the design of new institutions" and questions whether "the frequent inability of soldiers...to reach reliable judgments about matters of *jus ad bellum*" ought simply to be considered "an unalterable feature of the moral landscape" (240). See, for some critical reflections on this proposal, Michael Walzer's "Response," in Benbaji and Sussman, *Reading Walzer*, 328–32, at 330–32.

40. McMahan, *Killing in War*, 59.

41. See Gordon Zahn's *In Solitary Witness: The Life and Death of Franz Jägerstätter*, 3rd ed. (Collegeville, MN: Liturgical Press, 1964).

42. McMahan, *Killing in War*, 136. See, for documentation, Zahn, *In Solitary Witness*, 57–58 and 75–76.

43. See Zahn, *In Solitary Witness*, 105.

44. McMahan, *Killing in War*, 8. Cf. Thomas Nagel, "War and Massacre," *Philosophy and Public Affairs* 1 (1972): 123–44, at 133: "Hostile treatment of any person must be justified in terms of something *about that person* which makes the treatment appropriate."

45. McMahan, "War Crimes and Immoral Action in War," in *The Constitution of the Criminal Law*, ed. R. A. Duff et al. (Oxford: Oxford University Press, 2013), 151–84, at 158.

46. McMahan, *Killing in War*, 12.

47. Ibid., 207–8.

48. Nagel, "War and Massacre," 140. "Contributions to [soldiers'] arms and logistics are contributions to this threat [soldiers pose]; contributions to their mere existence as men are not. It is therefore wrong to direct an attack against those who merely serve the combatants' needs as human beings, such as farmers and food suppliers."

49. David Rodin, "Justifying Harm," *Ethics* 122 (2011): 74–100, at 100. See for discussion 89–91.

50. McMahan, *Killing in War*, 208–9.

51. Ibid., 3.

52. Ibid., 95.

53. McMahan, "The Prevention of Unjust Wars," 238.

54. Tim O'Brien, *The Things They Carried* (New York: Mariner, 1990), 38. See, for a brief account of one of the horrors of this war, Seymour M. Hersh, "The Scene of the Crime: A Reporter's Journey to My Lai and the Secrets of the Past," *The New Yorker*, March 30, 2015, 53–61. Hersh too calls Vietnam "a war I had grown to hate" (54).

55. United States Conference of Catholic Bishops, *The Challenge of Peace: God's Promise and Our Response* (1983), §§232–33; *The Harvest of Justice Is Sown in Peace* (1993), pt. 1C, "The Centrality of Conscience." Both these documents are available online through the USCCB's Web site (http://www.usccb.org/upload/challenge-peace-gods-promise-our-response-1983.pdf and http://www.usccb.org/beliefs-and-teachings/what-we-believe/catholic-social-teaching/the-harvest-of-justice-is-sown-in-peace.cfm).

56. See here John Courtney Murray, "Remarks on the Moral Problem of War," *Theological Studies* 20 (1959): 40–61.

57. United States Conference of Catholic Bishops, *The Challenge of Peace*, §231.

58. *Gaudium et Spes*, §80. The document cites on this point John XXIII's 1963 encyclical *Pacem in Terris*; see its §§126–27. Both documents can be found on the Vatican's Web site (http://www.vatican.va/archive/hist_councils/ii_vatican_council/documents/vat-ii_const_19651207_gaudium-et-spes_en.html and http://w2.vatican.va/content/john-xxiii/en/encyclicals/documents/hf_j-xxiii_enc_11041963_pacem.html).

59. United States Conference of Catholic Bishops, *The Challenge of Peace*, §233; see also *Harvest of Justice*, pt. 1C.

60. United States Conference of Catholic Bishops, *The Challenge of Peace*, §233.

61. Interestingly, Michael Walzer, the foremost contemporary representative of the so-called conventional or orthodox account of the just war, also advocates provision for selective conscientious objection, though on different grounds from those the revisionists put forth. Walzer holds, "Democratic states suffer whenever conscience is coerced" and concludes that they ought to "tolerate refusals of service" that have a claim to be considered conscientious, which is to say following from "some more or less consistent pattern of interpersonal commitment and group action." See

his essay "Conscientious Objection," in *Obligations: Essays on War, Disobedience, and Citizenship* (Cambridge, MA: Harvard University Press, 1970), chap. 6, pp. 120–45, at 141. Walzer goes on to observe, insightfully, that "conscientious objection will almost certainly introduce...a pronounced class bias" inasmuch as "rates of group membership and participation climb startlingly" with the social scale (142).

62. See *Gillette v. United States*, 401 U.S. 437 (1971). Both the decision of the court, authored by Justice Thurgood Marshall, and the dissent by Justice William Douglas deserve reading. Justice Douglas's dissent in the associated case, *Negre v. Larsen et al.*, on certiorari to the United States Court of Appeals for the Ninth Circuit, focuses on "doctrines of the Catholic Church" and draws in particular on a petitioner's brief by "an authoritative lay Catholic scholar, Dr. John T. Noonan, Jr." (401 U.S. 437, 470). Interestingly, following Noonan, Douglas cites, among others, Vitoria and *Gaudium et Spes*.

63. Yoder, *When War Is Unjust*, 46.

64. I follow here Drew Christiansen, "A Roman Catholic Response," afterword to Yoder, *When War Is Unjust*, 102–17, at 113.

65. Cf. Rodin, *War and Self-Defense*, 169.

66. Christiansen, "A Roman Catholic Response," 113.

67. McMahan, "The Prevention of Unjust Wars," 238.

68. Cf. Seth Lazar's comment on Jeff McMahan, "Moral Wounds," *Boston Review* 38, no. 6 (November/December 2013): 27, available online through the *Boston Review*'s Web site (http://bostonreview.net/forum/moral-wounds/seth-lazar-moral-wounds-lazar): "McMahan concedes that malingering will occur only in wars where the combatants' own interests aren't directly at stake. Much of the world's population depends for its security not on their own militaries but on that of the United States. And given American power, no state is likely to directly threaten the U.S. mainland. If selective conscientious objection would lead to malingering when the United States is not directly threatened, then it would radically undermine the security of the world beyond American borders."

69. McMahan, "The Prevention of Unjust Wars," 254. A somewhat different worry applies to the use of drones. Arguably, "the very precision of drone technology raises the prospect for 'moral hazard.' The reduction in risks may tempt governments to order drones into action more frequently than they would conventional bombers or missiles. In other

words, drones may spare more innocents but they may also create more war." See Coll, "The Unblinking Stare," 108.

70. See Adil Ahmad Haque's comment on McMahan, "Moral Wounds," 28. Haque wrote only *she*; I have introduced both the masculine pronoun and the word *legitimate*.

71. Ibid.

72. See Rodin, *War and Self-Defense*, 170, for a critical discussion of Vitoria's position on this question.

73. See now Lawrence J. Korb's comment on McMahan, "Moral Wounds," 29.

74. See McMahan's "Moral Wounds," 18–23, at 21.

75. McMahan, "The Moral Case for Military Strikes against Syria," *Al-Jazeera America*, September 4, 2013, available online at http://america.aljazeera.com/articles/2013/9/4/the-moral-case-formilitarystrikesagainst syria.html.

76. O'Donovan, *The Just War Revisited*, 16–17.

77. See Shannon E. French's comment on McMahan, "Moral Wounds," 26.

78. See Charles J. Dunlap Jr.'s comment on McMahan, "Moral Wounds," 31.

79. Rodin, *War and Self-Defense*, 169. Rodin takes the analogy between soldiers and executioners not from Shannon French, but from Vitoria, and develops it to support the conclusion that "it would seem to be an act of the most extreme moral recklessness to adopt Vitoria's policy of 'in case of doubt, fight'" in light of the fact that, in any given war, "there is at least a 50 percent chance that [the soldier] is fighting on the unjust side" (170).

80. *Gillette v. United States*, 401 U.S. 437, 537 (1971).

81. See further Walzer, "Conscientious Objection," in *Obligations*, 128–38.

82. *Burns v. Wilson* 346 U.S. 137, 140 (1953).

83. See *Haig v. Agee*, 453 U.S. 280, 307 (1981), citing *Aptheker v. Secretary of State*, 378 U.S. 500, 509 (1964).

84. Cf. Dunlap's comment on McMahan, "Moral Wounds," 31. I learned of these cases through Dunlap, though his contribution does not make it clear that he is quoting several cases, not only *Gillette*.

85. See, just to begin with, McMahan's "Moral Wounds," 22, suggesting that, in order to deter malingering, "it would…be necessary to

impose penalties even on successful conscientious objectors.... Conscientious objectors might be required to do onerous tasks unrelated to the war and perhaps even refund some of the wages they had been paid while being trained for the work they now refuse to do."

86. *Haig v. Agee*, 453 U.S. 280, 307 (1981).

87. See memo 1 in *The Torture Papers: The Road to Abu Ghraib*, ed. Karen J. Greenberg and Joshua L. Dratel (New York: Cambridge University Press, 2005), 3–24, at 3 and 4 (the quotation from *Haig v. Agee* appears on 4).

88. Ibid., 24.

89. O'Donovan, *The Just War Revisited*, 9.

90. Christiansen, "A Roman Catholic Response," 116.

91. See note 79 above.

92. Walzer, "Response," in Benbaji and Sussman, *Reading Walzer*, 330, quoting McMahan, "The Prevention of Unust Wars," 237.

93. Ibid.

94. Ibid.

CHAPTER 5

1. Origen, *Contra Celsus*, in *Ante-Nicene Fathers*, vol. 4, ed. Alexander Roberts, James Donaldson, and A. Cleveland Coxe, trans. Frederick Crombie (Buffalo: Christian Literature Publishing Co., 1885), bk. 5, chap. 49, http://www.newadvent.org/fathers/0416.htm.

2. Augustine, *Of the Morals of the Catholic Church*, in *Nicene and Post-Nicene Fathers, First Series*, vol. 4, ed. Philip Schaff, trans. Richard Stothert (Buffalo: Christian Literature Publishing Co., 1887). chap. 31, §§65, 67, http://www.newadvent.org/fathers/1401.htm.

3. Augustine, *City of God against the Pagans*, ed. and trans. R. W. Dyson (Cambridge: Cambridge University Press, 1998), bk. 1, chap. 20, p. 33.

4. Aquinas, *Summa contra Gentiles*, trans. Fathers of the English Dominican Province (London: Burns, Oates & Washbourne, 1924), bk. 3, pt. 2, chap. 112, p. 92.

5. Even about whether animals will be redeemed! See Rick Gladstone, "Dogs in Heaven? Pope Francis Leaves Pearly Gates Open," *New York Times*, December 12, 2014, A1, available online through the

New York Times Web site (http://www.nytimes.com/2014/12/12/world/europe/dogs-in-heaven-pope-leaves-pearly-gate-open-.html?_r=0). But see also David Gibson, "Sorry, Fido. Pope Francis Did NOT Say Our Pets Are Going to Heaven," *Religion News Service*, December 12, 2014, available through the RNS Web site (http://www.religionnews.com/2014/12/12/sorry-fido-pope-francis-not-say-pets-going-heaven/).

    6. Tristram Stuart, *The Bloodless Revolution: A Cultural History of Vegetarianism from 1600 to Modern Times* (New York: W. W. Norton, 2006), 202.

    7. See, for a provocative discussion of pets, Mark Bittman, "Some Animals Are More Equal than Others," *New York Times*, March 15, 2011, available through the *New York Times* Web site (http://opinionator.blogs.nytimes.com/2011/03/15/some-animals-are-more-equal-than-others/).

    8. See Stuart, *The Bloodless Revolution*, 160.

    9. Jerome, *Against Jovinianus*, in *Nicene and Post-Nicene Fathers, Second Series*, vol. 6, ed. Philip Schaff and Henry Wace, trans. W. H. Fremantle, G. Lewis, and W. G. Martley (Buffalo: Christian Literature Publishing Co., 1893), bk. 2, chap. 15, http://www.newadvent.org/fathers/3009.htm.

    10. Stuart, *The Bloodless Revolution*, 152.

    11. Some might object that Tom Regan's work is what needs contending with. See, to begin with, his paper "The Case for Animals Rights," in *Animal Rights and Human Obligations*, ed. Tom Regan and Peter Singer, 2nd ed. (Englewood Cliffs, NJ: Prentice Hall, 1989), 105–14, and then, at much greater length, *The Case for Animal Rights* (Berkeley: The University of California Press, 1983). By way of response, inasmuch as Regan's work too depends on the argument from marginal cases—which is explained in this chapter's second section—I don't think it differs significantly from that of Rachels, Singer, and McMahan, on whom this chapter focuses.

    12. See, for example, Alfred J. Freddoso, "Good News, Your Soul Hasn't Died Quite Yet," *Proceedings of the American Catholic Philosophical Association* 75 (2001): 79–96.

    13. James Rachels, *Created from Animals: The Moral Implications of Darwinism* (Oxford: Oxford University Press, 1990), 1.

    14. Ibid.

    15. Ibid.

    16. Ibid., 4.

17. Ibid., 86.

18. Ibid., 97.

19. Cf. James B. Reichman, *Evolution, Animals "Rights," and the Environment* (Washington, DC: The Catholic University of America Press, 2000), 251–52.

20. Rachel, *Created from Animals*, 4.

21. See James Rachels, "Active and Passive Euthanasia," *New England Journal of Medicine* 292 (1975): 78–80.

22. Stuart, *The Bloodless Revolution*, 435.

23. Eva Feder Kittay, "At the Margins of Moral Personhood," *Ethics* 116 (2005): 100–31, at 126, citing documentation from the Nuremberg trials.

24. Mary Midgley, "Persons and Non-Persons," in *In Defence of Animals*, ed. Peter Singer (Oxford: Basil Blackwell, 1985), 52–62, at 60, also available online at http://www.animal-rights-library.com/texts-m/midgley01.htm.

25. Whether we're doing a good job at stewardship is another question....

26. Cora Diamond, "Eating Meat and Eating People," *Philosophy* 53 (1978): 465–79, at 478.

27. Peter Singer, "All Animals Are Equal," in Regan and Singer, *Animal Rights and Human Obligations*, 73–86, at 74.

28. See Hilde Lindemann Nelson, "What Child Is This?" *Hastings Center Report* 32, no. 6 (2002): 29–38, at 32–33.

29. As Rachels nicely writes, "Moral standing means that, from a moral point of view, you have claims that must be heard." See his paper "Drawing Lines," in *Animal Rights: Current Debates and New Directions*, ed. Cass R. Sunstein and Martha Nussbaum (Oxford: Oxford University Press, 2004), 162–74, at 164.

30. Ibid.

31. Jeff McMahan, *The Ethics of Killing: Problems at the Margins of Life* (Oxford: Oxford University Press, 2002), 204.

32. This commitment to the severely cognitively impaired, it should be noted, developed quite recently in human history.

33. McMahan, *The Ethics of Killing*, 214.

34. Rachels, *Created from Animals*, 173. Cf. McMahan, "Our Fellow Creatures," *The Journal of Ethics* 9 (2005): 353–80, at 354.

35. Rachels, *Created from Animals*, 173–74.

36. Stuart, *The Bloodless Revolution*, 340.

37. Singer, "Reflections," afterword to *The Lives of Animals*, by J. M. Coetzee, ed. Amy Gutmann (Princeton: Princeton University Press, 1999), 85–91, at 87.

38. Ibid., 87–88. Cf. Singer's *Animal Liberation: A New Ethics for Our Treatment of Animals* (New York: New York Review/Random House, 1975), 21–22.

39. McMahan, *The Ethics of Killing*, 190.

40. Ibid., 80.

41. Ibid., 195.

42. Rachels would likely argue toward this conclusion somewhat differently. In "Drawing Lines," he claims, "There is no such thing as moral standing *simpliciter*. Rather, moral standing is always moral standing with respect to some particular mode of treatment. A sentient being has moral standing with respect to not being tortured. A self-conscious being has moral standing with respect to not being humiliated. An autonomous being has moral standing with respect to not being coerced. And so on" (170). In brief, some beings have more, some less to stand on.

43. McMahan, *The Ethics of Killing*, 218. Cf. "Our Fellow Creatures," 354.

44. See McMahan, "Cognitive Disability, Misfortune, and Justice," *Philosophy and Public Affairs* 25 (1996): 3–35, at 35.

45. Dante Alighieri, *Inferno*, trans. Allen Mandelbaum, bilingual edition (New York: Bantam, 1980), canto XXXIII, line 75, p. 304. Notoriously, the Italian, "Poscia, più che 'l dolor, poté 'l digiuno" may be understood to mean either that Ugolino's fasting overwhelmed his grief, leading him too to die of hunger, or that his fasting overcame his grief, leading him to feed on his dead sons' flesh. Both Ugolino's dream that he recounts to Dante pilgrim and the fact that Dante meets Ugolino gnawing on the head of his captor, Archbishop Ruggieri, suggest to me the second interpretation, as does the fact that the Italian gives Ugolino shelter in this ambiguity. Surely Ugolino would not want to say, unambiguously, what he did.

46. See, in this regard, the valuable paper by David Sussman, "What's Wrong with Torture?" *Philosophy and Public Affairs* 33 (2005): 1–33.

47. Cf. McMahan, "Cognitive Disability, Misfortune, and Justice," 35.

48. See McMahan, *The Ethics of Killing*, 359–60, where he acknowledges that, on his theory, it would be morally permissible to kill a newborn infant with no living relations—its single mother is stipulated to have died in childbirth—in order to use its organs to save the lives of three older children, with families to boot. McMahan writes, "Many people will find this implication intolerable, and I confess that I cannot embrace it without significant misgivings and considerable unease" (360), but he does not repudiate it, or see it as giving reason to rethink his theory. See, on this point, Stephen Mulhall, "Fearful Thoughts," review of *The Ethics of Killing*, by Jeff McMahan, *London Review of Books* 24, no. 16 (August 22, 2002): 16–18, at 16, available online through the Web site of the *London Review* (http://www.lrb.co.uk/v24/n16/stephen-mulhall /fearful-thoughts).

49. Singer, *Animal Liberation*, 24.

50. McMahan, *The Ethics of Killing*, 221.

51. Ibid., 220. See also his "Cognitive Disability, Misfortune, and Justice," 33, where McMahan observes, correctly I think, that "a complete account of the morality of special relations must include a recognition that [some of] these relations are actually constitutive of certain areas of morality."

52. McMahan, "Our Fellow Creatures," 361.

53. McMahan, "Cognitive Disability, Misfortune, and Justice," 34.

54. Ibid.

55. McMahan, "Our Fellow Creatures," 361. See also *The Ethics of Killing*, 221.

56. McMahan, *The Ethics of Killing*, 221. See also "Our Fellow Creatures," 361.

57. McMahan, *The Ethics of Killing*, 221–22. See also "Our Fellow Creatures," 361.

58. Kittay, "At the Margins of Moral Personhood," 126.

59. Ibid., 116–17.

60. See, in this regard, Alexis Okeowo, "Freedom Fighter: Why Slavery Persists in Mauritania," *The New Yorker*, September 8, 2014, 38–46.

61. See, on the phenomenon of corruption of consciousness, R. G. Collingwood, *The Principles of Art* (Oxford: Oxford University Press, 1938), 217–21.

62. Cf. Shelley Burtt, "Is Inclusion a Civic Virtue? Cosmopolitanism, Disability, and the Liberal State," *Social Theory and Practice* 33 (2007): 557–78, at 572n27.

63. Cf. Mulhall, "Fearful Thoughts," 17–18 on personhood.

64. Cora Diamond, "Losing Your Concepts," *Ethics* 98 (1988): 255–77, at 266.

65. Diamond, "The Importance of Being Human," in *Human Beings*, ed. David Cockburn (Cambridge: Cambridge University Press, 1991), 36–62, at 62.

66. Diamond, "Eating Meat and Eating People," 469.

67. Ibid., 469–70.

68. See Eli Sagan, *Cannibalism: Human Aggression and Cultural Form* (New York: Harper & Row, 1974), chaps. 1–4, pp. 1–63.

69. Cf. ibid., xvi–xvii.

70. Is it why we give names to our pets?

71. Mulhall, "Fearful Thoughts," 18. Cf. Diamond, "The Importance of Being Human," 55, and "How Many Legs," in *Value and Understanding: Essays for Peter Winch*, ed. Raimond Gaita (London: Routledge, 1990), 149–78, at 176.

72. Kittay, "At the Margins of Moral Personhood," 127–28.

73. Ludwig Wittgenstein, *Philosophical Investigations*, trans. Elizabeth Anscombe, bilingual edition (Oxford: Basil Blackwell, 1958), pt. II, §11, p. 223.

74. See further John R. Searle, "Animal Minds," *Midwest Studies in Philosophy* 19 (1994): 206–19, at 213.

75. See further Alasdair MacIntyre, *Dependent Rational Animals: Why Human Beings Need the Virtues* (Chicago: Open Court, 1999), 34–41. Cf., from some years ago, the work of the biologist Jakob von Uexküll. Uexküll found that an organism's body plan "automatically establishes the animal's environment." Only a naïve anthropocentrism could suppose that "all sea animals," by way of example, "live in a world uniformly common to all. Closer study teaches us that each of these thousand-fold variant forms of life is in possession of an environment unique to it, which is reciprocally conditioned by the animal's body plan." Consequently, we can say that, "in the world of the earthworm, there are only earthworm-things, in the world of the dragonfly, there are only dragonfly-things, and so forth." Even more significantly, we can also say that an organism's behavior depends not only upon its biochemistry, neurophysiology, etc., but upon the form or struc-

ture of its bodily existence. For this structure opens the organism to its environment and to the possibility of meaningfully interacting with it. See Jakob von Uexküll, *Umwelt und Innenwelt der Tiere*, 2nd ed. (Berlin: Julius Springer, 1921), 4, 45.

76. It's an interesting question, put to me by Lydia Moland, whether the form of life of a group like ISIS is not just as alien to "us" as the form of life of a lion is. ISIS does not eat human beings, but apparently does see some human beings as fit for torture and desecration. Here's one difference: it seems that ISIS also sees what it's doing as shocking and appalling. It is being deliberately inhuman.

77. Elizabeth Anderson, "Animal Rights and the Values of Nonhuman Life," in Sunstein and Nussbaum, *Animal Rights*, 277–98, at 291. Some might want to distinguish between suffering and experiencing pain. I'm inclined to say, however, that an animal experiencing pain is suffering, though not in all the ways a human being might—about which there is a lot more to say.

78. Ibid., 291–92.

79. Ibid., 292.

80. Andrew Linzey, *Why Animal Suffering Matters: Philosophy, Theology, and Practical Ethics* (Oxford: Oxford University Press, 2009), 1.

81. Ibid., 37.

82. Ibid., 155.

83. Ibid., 154.

84. Ibid., 20–22.

85. Ibid., 23.

86. Ibid., 29.

87. John Sniegocki, "The Responsible Choice," *Commonweal*, September 14, 2007, 34.

88. Ibid.: "Many studies have shown that vegetarians have significantly lower rates of cancer, heart disease, diabetes, and other serious health problems."

89. Ibid.: "It takes, for example, an average of eight to twelve pounds of protein in the form of grains and beans fed to animals to produce one pound of animal protein." See further ecologist Jonathan Foley's "A Five-Step Plan to Feed the World," *National Geographic Magazine*, May 5, 2014, 26–59, at 45, available online through the National Geographic Web site (http://www.nationalgeographic.com/foodfeatures /feeding-9-billion/): "Today only 55 percent of the world's crop calories

feed people directly; the rest are fed to livestock (about 36 percent) or turned into biofuels and industrial products (roughly 9 percent). Though many of us consume meat, dairy, and eggs from animals raised on feed-lots, only a fraction of the calories in feed given to livestock make their way into the meat and milk that we consume. For every 100 calories of grain we feed animals, we get only about 40 new calories of milk, 22 calo-ries of eggs, 12 of chicken, 10 of pork, or 3 of beef. Finding more efficient ways to grow meat and shifting to less meat-intensive diets—even just switching from grain-fed beef to meats like chicken, pork, or pasture-raised beef—could free up substantial amounts of food across the world."

90. Sniegocki, "The Responsible Choice," 34. He writes, "Accord-ing to a recent UN report, the livestock industry is responsible for more greenhouse-gas emissions than all forms of transportation combined." See further Foley, "A Five-Step Plan To Feed the World," 35: "Agriculture is among the greatest contributors to global warming...largely from methane released by cattle and rice farms, nitrous oxide from fertilized fields, and carbon dioxide from the cutting of rain forests to grow crops or raise livestock. Farming is the thirstiest user of our precious water sup-plies and a major polluter, as runoff from fertilizers and manure disrupts fragile lakes, rivers, and coastal ecosystems across the globe. Agriculture also accelerates the loss of biodiversity. As we've cleared areas of grassland and forest for farms, we've lost crucial habitat, making agriculture a major driver of wildlife extinction."

91. Robert P. Heaney, "A Biological Approach," *Commonweal*, September 14, 2007, 34. Compare the so-called caveman or paleo diet.

92. Ibid.

93. Ibid.

94. Heaney, "Made for Meat," *Commonweal*, September 10, 2010, 2. He goes on here: "The fact that we now can provide through chemistry some of what plant foods lack is not very helpful. For many nutrients, there are no feasible supplemental sources. Nor would an individual sup-plementation strategy work for the poor and disadvantaged. Though doubtless well-intended, this approach, even if it worked, would be avail-able to only a privileged elite. Nor is it simply a question of the nutrient content of animal vs. plant foods. The human gastrointestinal tract is designed for an omnivorous diet—part animal, part plant. This is seen in the relative lengths of the small and large bowel. Similarly, our unique mix of bile acids is that of an omnivore, like the grizzly bear, and the human

intestine lacks the enzymes needed to break down many complex carbo-hydrates in otherwise protein-rich plant foods (like beans)."

95. See, in reply to Heaney, the dietitian Dulcie Ward, "Veganism Is Healthy," *Commonweal*, October 12, 2007, 37. The relevant literature is vast. For one more citation, see Dean Ornish, "The Myth of High-Protein Diets," *New York Times*, March 23, 2015, A21, available online through the *New York Times* Web site (http://www.nytimes.com/2015/03/23/opinion/the-myth-of-high-protein-diets.html).

96. I thank Greg Bassham for this point.

97. Linzey, *Animal Theology* (Urbana, IL: University of Illinois Press, 1994), 87.

98. See ibid., 123, 129, 135.

99. See, for example, Gretchen Reynolds, "Ask Well: Can Athletes Be Vegans?" *New York Times*, November 24, 2014, available online through the *New York Times* Web site (http://well.blogs.nytimes.com/2014/11/24/ask-well-can-athletes-be-vegans/).

100. But see McMahan, "The Meat Eaters," *New York Times*, September 19, 2010, likewise available through the *New York Times* Web site (http://opinionator.blogs.nytimes.com/2010/09/19/the-meat-eaters/).

101. David DeGrazia, *Taking Animals Seriously: Mental Life and Moral Status* (Cambridge: Cambridge University Press, 1996), 277.

102. Cf. Heaney, "A Biological Approach," 34: "We must confront the fact that all organisms eat other organisms—are utterly dependent upon doing so. That is one aspect of the arrangement of our world that caused [the South African mathematician and Quaker] George Ellis to see *kenosis* [that is, self-emptying] as the underlying principle of the cosmos." See, for a fascinating discussion of the problem of theodicy, Robert Merrihew Adams, "Existence, Self-Interest, and the Problem of Evil," *Noûs* 13 (1979): 53–65. See, too, the fascinating discussion of so-called plant neurobiology in Michael Pollan, "The Intelligent Plant: A Radical New Way of Understanding Flora," *The New Yorker*, December 23 and 30, 2013, 92–105, suggesting that plants have some share in sentience, long proffered by animal liberationists as the criterion of moral considerability.

103. See, for example, Alex Halberstadt, "Zoo Animals and Their Discontent," *New York Times Magazine*, July 6, 2014, 32ff., available online through the *New York Times* Web site (http://www.nytimes.com/2014/07/06/magazine/zoo-animals-and-their-discontents.html?ref=magazine&_r=4).

104. See peta.org.

105. Ruth Harrison, *Animal Machines: The New Factory Farming Industry* (London: Vincent Stuart, 1964), 3, quoted in Singer, *Animal Liberation*, 100.

106. Singer, "All Animals Are Equal," 79.

107. Nina Planck, *Real Food: What To Eat and Why* (New York: Bloomsburg, 2006), 91.

108. See further in this regard David Cloutier, *Walking God's Earth: The Environment and Catholic Faith* (Collegeville, MN: Liturgical Press, 2014), especially chapter 5, "Food and Fuel," 63–84.

109. Midgley, "Persons and Non-Persons," 60.

110. See, for recent discussions, Nicholas Kristof, "The Unhealthy Meat Market," *New York Times*, March 13, 2014, A27, http://www.nytimes.com/2014/03/13/opinion/kristof-the-unhealthy-meat-market.html; and "Is That Sausage Worth This?" *New York Times*, February 20, 2014, A21, http://www.nytimes.com/2014/02/20/opinion/kristof-is-that-sausage-worth-this.html.

111. Cf. John Zeis, "A Rawlsian Pro-Life Argument against Vegetarianism," *International Philosophical Quarterly* 53 (2013): 63–71, at 71.

112. Cell phones and computers make for clear examples.

113. See, for a valuable discussion of both the phenomenon of commodity distancing and how it facilitates modern-day slavery, Vincent J. Miller, "Slavery and Commodity Chains: Fighting the Globalization of Indifference," *America*, January 2, 2014, available online through the magazine's Web site (http://americamagazine.org/content/all-things/slavery-and-commodity-chains-fighting-globalization-indifference). Miller takes the phrase *the globalization of indifference* from Pope Francis's passionate and moving homily presented at Lampedusa, Italy, on July 8, 2013.

114. Zeis, "A Rawlsian Pro-Life Argument against Vegetarianism," 71.

115. See Cloutier, *Walking God's Earth*, 81.

116. See, if you don't believe it, Mark Bittman, "The True Cost of a Burger," *New York Times,* July 15, 2014, available online through the *New York Times* Web site (http://www.nytimes.com/2014/07/16/opinion/the-true-cost-of-a-burger.html).

117. Diamond, "Losing Your Concepts," 266.

CHAPTER 6

1. As the *New York Times* recently reported, "Although opposed by global health organizations, legalizing commercial donation is not the fringe position it once was. In July [of 2014], the American Society of Transplantation and the American Society of Transplant Surgeons called for pilot projects to test incentives for donation, potentially including cash payments." See Kevin Sack, "A Clash of Religion and Bioethics Complicates Organ Donation in Israel," *New York Times*, August 17, 2014, A17, also available online through the *New York Times* Web site (http://www.nytimes.com/2014/08/17/world/middleeast/a-clash-of-reli gion-and-bioethics-complicates-organ-donation-in-israel.html).

2. See Anne Phillips, *Our Bodies, Whose Property?* (Princeton: Princeton University Press, 2013), 106. Israel has long figured importantly in this trade. See not only Sack's "A Clash of Religion and Bioethics Complicates Organ Donation in Israel," but as well his "Kidneys for Sale," *New York Times*, August 17, 2014, A1, likewise available online (http://www.nytimes.com/2014/08/17/world/middleeast/transplant-brokers-in-israel-lure-desperate-kidney-patients-to-costa-rica.html).

3. Unlike Bentham, however, Mill holds that pleasures vary qualitatively and that the quality of a pleasure matters morally, so that a pleasure of a high quality might count for more than coarser pleasures of a greater quantity. So began the refinement and complexification of utilitarianism, which carries on today.

4. As I also noted in chapter 2, the claim that an action is identical with "the causing of each and every consequence to which the doer's agency in doing it extends" requires at least two qualifications. First, one's agency is cut short, so to speak, by the intervention of other agents. Second, one's agency does not extend to abnormal events. See, for discussion, Alan Donagan, *The Theory of Morality* (Chicago: The University of Chicago Press, 1977), 43–47.

5. Immanuel Kant, *Grundlegung zur Metaphysik der Sitten*, ed. Karl Vorländer, 3rd ed. (Hamburg: Felix Meiner, 1965), 52 (4:429); *Groundwork of the Metaphysics of Morals*, trans. Mary Gregor (Cambridge: Cambridge University Press, 1997), 38.

6. See, for close discussions of what it is to use someone merely as a means, Derek Parfit, *On What Matters*, ed. Samuel Scheffler (Oxford: Oxford University Press, 2011), vol. 1, 212–32; and T. M. Scanlon, *Moral*

Dimensions: Permissibility, Meaning, Blame (Cambridge, MA: Harvard University Press, 2008), 89–121.

7. Kant, *Grundlegung zur Metaphysik der Sitten*, 52 (4:429); *Groundwork of the Metaphysics of Morals*, 38. To quote, "*Handle so, daß du die Menschheit, sowohl in deiner Person als in der Person eines jeden anderen, jederzeit zugleich als Zweck, niemals bloß als Mittel brauchst*" (italics in the original).

8. See Joel Feinberg, *Harm to Self*, vol. 3 of *The Moral Limits of the Criminal Law* (New York: Oxford University Press, 1986), 68. Feinberg takes his inspiration from Mills's great *On Liberty* (1859).

9. Elizabeth Anderson, *Value in Ethics and Economics* (Cambridge, MA: Harvard University Press, 1993), 141. Cf. Michael Walzer, *Spheres of Justice: A Defense of Pluralism and Equality* (New York: Basic Books, 1983), 119–20.

10. Pope Leo XIII, *Rerum Novarum* (1891), §3, available online through the Vatican's Web site (http://w2.vatican.va/content/leo-xiii/en/encyclicals/documents/hf_l-xiii_enc_15051891_rerum-novarum.html).

11. Ibid., §43.

12. Ibid., §45.

13. Ibid., §§49–60. See further Micah Lott, "Labor Exploitation, Living Wages, and Global Justice: An Aristotelian Account," *Journal of Catholic Social Thought* 11 (2014): 329–59. As Lott notes, later papal encyclicals and ecclesial documents—including *Mater et Magistra*, *Pacem in Terris*, *Gaudium et Spes*, *Populorum Progressio*, *Laborem Exercens*, and *Centesimus Annus*—all affirm living wages "as a crucial benchmark for identifying just terms of labor" (331).

14. See Timothy Noah, "The 1 Percent Are Only Half the Problem," *New York Times*, May 18, 2013, available on the *New York Times* Web site (http://opinionator.blogs.nytimes.com/2013/05/18/the-1-percent-are-only-half-the-problem/).

15. Annie Lowrey, "Living on Minimum Wage," *New York Times*, June 15, 2013, available on the *New York Times* Web site (http://www.nytimes.com/interactive/2013/06/15/business/living-on-minimum-wage.html?_r=0).

16. James Surowiecki, "The Pay Is Too Damn Low," *The New Yorker*, August 12 and 19, 2013, 35.

17. See M. T. Anderson, "Clothed in Misery," *New York Times*, April 29, 2013, A19, likewise available online (http://www.nytimes.com/

2013/04/30/opinion/bangladeshs-are-only-the-latest-in-textile-factory-disasters.html).

18. "Le pape dénonce le 'travail d'esclave' au Bangladesh," *Agence France-Presse*, May 1, 2013, available online at http://www.lapresse.ca/international/asie-oceanie/201305/01/01-4646274-le-pape-denonce-le-travail-desclave-au-bangladesh.php.

19. Debra Satz, *Why Some Things Should Not Be for Sale: The Moral Limits of Markets* (Oxford: Oxford University Press, 2010), 3.

20. Ibid., 15.

21. Ibid., 23.

22. Ibid., 24.

23. By the way, "what money can't buy," the title of Sandel's book, figures as a heading in Walzer's *Spheres of Justice*, which was a pioneering work; see 97.

24. See, for discussion, Ahad J. Ghods and Shekoufeh Savaj, "Iranian Model of Paid and Regulated Living-Unrelated Kidney Donation," *Clinical Journal of the American Society of Nephrology* 1 (2006): 1136–45.

25. Sally Satel, "Why People Don't Donate Their Kidneys," *New York Times*, May 3, 2014, SR5 (Sunday Review), also available online (http://www.nytimes.com/2014/05/04/opinion/sunday/why-people-dont-donate-their-kidneys.html).

26. See, for example, Mark J. Cherry, *Kidney for Sale by Owner: Human Organs, Transplantation, and the Market* (Washington, DC: Georgetown University Press, 2005), 22–33.

27. Pope Benedict XVI, "Address of His Holiness Pope Benedict XVI to Participants at an International Congress Organized by the Pontifical Academy for Life," November 7, 2008, available online through the Vatican's Web site (https://w2.vatican.va/content/benedict-xvi/en/speeches/2008/november/documents/hf_ben-xvi_spe_20081107_acdlife.html).

28. See, for an account of the "intense debate on living organ transplantation that occurred in the Roman Catholic community in the 1950s," Thomas A. Shannon, "The Kindness of Strangers: Organ Transplantation in a Capitalist Age," *Kennedy Institute of Ethics Journal* 11 (2001): 285–303, at 286–96.

29. Aquinas, *Summa Theologiae*, vol. 38, pt. II-II q. 65 a. 1, pp. 48–50: "Dicendum quod cum membrum aliquod sit pars totius humani

corporis, est propter totum, sicut imperfectum propter perfectum. Unde disponendum est de membro humani corporis secundum quod expedit toti. Membrum autem humani corporis per se quidem utile est ad bonum totius corporis; per accidens tamen potest contingere quod sit nocivum, puta cum membrum putridum est totius corporis corruptivum. Si ergo membrum sanum fuerit, et in sua naturali dispositione consistens, non potest præscindi absque totius hominis detrimento."

30. United States Conference of Catholic Bishops, *Ethical and Religious Directives for Catholic Health Care Services*, 5th ed., §29, available online at http://www.usccb.org/issues-and-action/human-life-and-dignity/health-care/upload/Ethical-Religious-Directives-Catholic-Health-Care-Services-fifth-edition-2009.pdf.

31. Ibid.

32. Ibid., note 16.

33. Ibid., §30.

34. Cf. Richard A. McCormick, "Ambiguity in Moral Choice," in *Doing Evil to Achieve Good: Moral Choice in Conflict Situations*, ed. Richard A. McCormick and Paul Ramsey (Chicago: Loyola University Press, 1978), 7–53, at 45.

35. Pope John Paul II, "Address of His Holiness John Paul II to Participants of the First International Congress of the Society for Organ Sharing," June 20, 1991, §4, available online through the Vatican's Web site. Cf. Pope Benedict XVI, "Address…to Participants at an International Congress": "The possibility of organ sales…would greatly clash with the underlying meaning of the gift that would place it out of consideration, qualifying it as a morally illicit act."

36. See, for precision, Patrick Kain, "Kant's Defense of Human Moral Status," *Journal of the History of Philosophy* 47 (2009): 59–102. According to Kain, there is "substantial textual evidence that Kant ascribed basic moral status to all human beings" (61); what's more, he argued that human children are persons "from procreation" (63).

37. See, for an account of John Paul II's so-called personalist philosophy, Avery Dulles, "John Paul II and the Mystery of the Human Person," *America*, February 2, 2004, 10–22. As Dulles notes, "In *The Acting Person,* a work first published in Polish in 1969 before he became pope, [then-]Cardinal Wojtyla expounded a theory of the person as a self-determining agent that realizes itself through free and responsible action. Activity is not something strictly other than the person; it is the person

coming to expression and constituting itself. Persons, moreover, are essentially social and oriented to life in community. They achieve themselves as persons by interaction, giving to others and receiving from them in turn" (12).

38. See Pope Benedict XVI, *Deus Caritas Est* (2005), §5, available online at http://w2.vatican.va/content/benedict-xvi/en/encyclicals/documents/hf_ben-xvi_enc_20051225_deus-caritas-est.html.

39. Michael J. Sandel, *What Money Can't Buy: The Moral Limits of Markets* (New York: Farrar, Straus and Giroux, 2012), 93.

40. Ibid., 96.

41. Ibid., 111. Cf. Walzer, *Spheres of Justice*, 97: "If we attend to values, there are things that cannot be bought and sold."

42. Ibid., 112.

43. Ibid., 110.

44. See Matt Welch's contribution to the forum "How Markets Crowd Out Morals," *Boston Review* 37, no. 3 (May/June 2012): 20–21, at 21, available online through the *Boston Review*'s Web site (http://bostonreview.net/welch-morals-markets).

45. Ibid., 20.

46. Ibid.

47. Ibid.

48. See Satz's contribution to the forum "How Markets Crowd Out Morals," 22–23, at 23, likewise available at http://bostonreview. net/satz-egalitarian-response.

49. See again Welch's contribution to "How Markets Crowd Out Morals," 21.

50. Satz, "Voluntary Slavery and the Limits of the Market," *Law and Ethics of Human Rights* 3 (2009): 86–109, at 99. See *Why Some Things Should Not Be for Sale*, 180–81.

51. Ibid.

52. Satz, "The Moral Limits of Markets: The Case of Human Kidneys," *Proceedings of the Aristotelian Society* 108 (2008): 269–88, at 276. See *Why Some Things Should Not Be for Sale*, 201. Cf. Phillips, *Our Bodies, Whose Property?* 145–46.

53. Ibid., 275 (*Why Some Things Should Not Be for Sale*, 200).

54. Michael Finkel, "This Little Kidney Went to Market," *New York Times Magazine*, May 27, 2001, 26ff., at 32.

55. "After a surgeon has carved through skin, fat and several layers of muscle," Finkel writes, "getting at a kidney sometimes necessitates the partial extraction of the 12th rib." See ibid., 33. The development of laparoscopic techniques, however, obviates this need.

56. Satz, "The Moral Limits of Markets: The Case of Human Kidneys," 278.

57. See, for example, Elizabeth Anderson's "Is Women's Labor a Commodity?" *Philosophy and Public Affairs* 19 (1990): 71–92, reprinted with some changes in *Value in Ethics and Economics*, 168–89. For a summary discussion of Anderson's argument, see my *Parental Obligations and Bioethics*, 80–82.

58. Cf. Feinberg, *Harm to Self*, 69.

59. Satz, "The Moral Limits of Markets: The Case of Human Kidneys," 283–84.

60. Cf. Cecile Fabre, review of *Why Some Things Should Not Be for Sale*, by Debra Satz, *Ethics* 121 (2011): 469–75, at 475.

61. Satz, "The Moral Limits of Markets: The Case of Human Kidneys," 277. She says even less in this regard in *Why Some Things Should Not Be for Sale*; see 201.

62. Satz, "The Moral Limits of Markets," 283n24.

63. In technical terms, Satz's argument focuses on the *type* of action, not to begin with on *tokens* of that type.

64. See, for this account of autonomy, Anderson, *Value in Ethics and Economics*, 142.

65. Ibid., 141.

66. In technical terms again, Satz's argument must begin with tokens of the action. She cannot object to tokens only because of the effects of the type.

67. See, for example, Primo Levi, *The Drowned and the Saved*, trans. Raymond Rosenthal (New York: Vintage, 1989), 123–24, on the "iniquitous use that [the Nazis] made (not sporadically but with method) of the human body, as an object, an anonymous thing belonging to no one, to be disposed of in an arbitrary manner."

68. Consider bioethical controversies over abortion, access to health care, care of the radically disabled and those in persistent vegetative state, euthanasia, reproductive cloning, and research on human embryos. See here Daniel P. Sulmasy, "Dignity and Bioethics: History, Theory, and Selected Applications," in *Human Dignity and Bioethics*, ed. Edmund D.

Pellegrino, Adam Schulman, and Thomas W. Merrill (Notre Dame, IN: University of Notre Dame Press, 2009), 469–501, at 487–98.

69. Ruth Macklin, "Dignity Is a Useless Concept," *BMJ* 327 (2003): 1419–20.

70. See M. Therese Lysaught, "Respect: Or, How Respect for Persons Became Respect for Autonomy," *Journal of Medicine and Philosophy* 29 (2004): 665–80, at 675–76. See further F. Daniel Davis, "Human Dignity and Respect for Persons: A Historical Perspective on Public Bioethics," in Pellegrino et al., *Human Dignity and Bioethics*, 19–36, at 26–27.

71. See Feinberg, *Harm to Self,* 12: "Hard paternalism will accept as a reason for criminal legislation that it is necessary to protect competent adults, against their will, from the harmful consequences even of their fully voluntary choices and undertakings."

72. See further Parfit, *On What Matters*, 200–12. Cf. Feinberg, *Harm to Self,* 53.

73. Luke Harding, "Victim of Cannibal Agreed to Be Eaten," *The Guardian*, December 3, 2003, available online through *The Guardian*'s Web site (http://www.theguardian.com/world/2003/dec/04/germany .lukeharding).

74. There are, then, no "soft paternalist" grounds for intervention. See Feinberg, *Harm to Self,* 12: "Soft paternalism holds that the state has the right to prevent self-regarding harmful conduct…*when but only when* that conduct is substantially non-voluntary, or when temporary intervention is necessary to establish whether it is voluntary or not."

75. Cf. J. David Velleman, "A Right of Self-Termination?" *Ethics* 109 (1999): 606–28, at 612.

76. By the way, two kinds of respect should be distinguished: *recognition respect*, which "consists in giving appropriate consideration or recognition to some feature of its object in deliberating about what to do," and *appraisal respect*, which "consists in a positive appraisal of a person," as when we say that we respect someone because of this or that admirable quality of hers. See, for this distinction, Stephen Darwall, "Two Kinds of Respect," *Ethics* 88 (1977): 36–49, at 38, 39.

77. See, for a brief account of Kant's argument in his *Groundwork of the Metaphysics of Morals*, Susan M. Shell, "Kant's Concept of Human Dignity as a Resource for Bioethics," in Pellegrino et al., *Human Dignity and Bioethics*, 333–49, in particular 334–37. See further Thomas E. Hill Jr.,

"Servility and Self-Respect," *The Monist* 57 (1973): 87–104, articulating a Kantian account of the ground of duties to oneself.

78. I draw here and in the following from Velleman, "A Right of Self-Termination?" 611–15.

79. Satz, "The Moral Limits of Markets: The Case of Human Kidneys," 283n24.

80. Mark Twain, *Adventures of Huckleberry Finn*, in *Huck Finn; Pudd'nhead Wilson; No. 44, The Mysterious Stranger; and Other Writings* (New York: Library of America, 2000), 54.

81. Phillips, *Our Bodies, Whose Property?* 14, see also 19.

82. See, for a much closer discussion, my paper "When Words Fail Us: Reexamining the Conscience of Huckleberry Finn," *Journal of Aesthetic Education* 45 (2011): 1–22.

83. Twain, *Adventures of Huckleberry Finn*, 90–91.

84. Ibid., 93.

85. It should be noted, however, that Huck still has much room to grow at this point in the story. He comments next, "It was fifteen minutes before I could work myself up to go and humble myself to a nigger; but I done it, and I warn't ever sorry for it afterwards, neither" (ibid.). Huck's progress in acknowledging Jim's full humanity is painfully halting.

86. Sulmasy, "Dignity and Bioethics," 473. Sulmasy traces these three senses back to Cicero and Seneca, Thomas Hobbes, and Kant; see 470–72.

87. Tom Sawyer first plays a trick on Jim in the novel's second chapter.

88. See Lysaught, "Respect," 672, discussing Paul Ramsey's use of the term.

89. Virginia Woolf, *A Room of One's Own* (London: Harcourt Brace, 1929), 114.

90. Helmuth Plessner, *Lachen und Weinen. Eine Untersuchung nach den Grenzen menschlichen Verhaltens*, in vol. 7 of his *Gesammelte Schiften, Ausdruck und menschliche Natur*, ed. Günter Dux, Odo Marquard, and Elisabeth Ströker, et al. (Frankfurt am Main: Suhrkamp, 1982), 201–387, at 342; *Laughing and Crying: A Study of the Limits of Human Behavior*, trans. James Spencer Churchill and Marjorie Grene (Evanston, IL: Northwestern University Press, 1970), 37.

91. A critical condition for the possibility of human speech is that we learn to objectify our own voices. To this end, the intensive babbling

that is exhibited by young children is an important first step. Through babbling, a child becomes acquainted with her body—her lungs and larynx, the cavities of her mouth and nose, and her lips, tongue, and teeth—as an object under her control. See Adolf Portmann, *Biologische Fragmente zu einer Lehre vom Menschen* (Basel: Benno Schwabe, 1944), 74–5; cf. R. G. Collingwood, *The Principles of Art* (Oxford: Oxford University Press, 1938), 236–37.

92. Woolf, *A Room of One's Own*, 48.

93. Pope Benedict XVI, *Deus Caritas Est*, §5.

94. Plessner, *Lachen und Weinen*, 240; *Laughing and Crying*, 36.

95. See further my paper "The Science of Laughter: Helmuth Plessner's *Laughing and Crying* Revisited," *Continental Philosophy Review* 38 (2006): 41–69. Plessner's concept of eccentric positionality concerns, *not* the relation of body and mind as somehow distinct substances, but the *experience* of living as, in, and with a human body—experience that may be taken for granted and given little reflection, but whose worthiness for reflection is indicated immediately by the different locutions (as, in, with) that can be used to discuss it.

96. Satz, "The Moral Limits of Markets: The Case of Human Kidneys," 283–84.

97. Phillips, *Our Bodies, Whose Property?* 153.

98. Ibid., 9.

99. Walzer, *Spheres of Justice*, 102.

100. Another way to put my claim here is that the "rough and serviceable distinction" between other-regarding and self-regarding acts is not so serviceable after all. Some acts that appear primarily self-regarding, like selling oneself into slavery, diminish us all. Cf. Feinberg, *Harm to Self*, 56. Consider in this regard John Donne's poem "No Man Is an Island" (1624). Kant and Donne appear to agree in conceiving of human beings as *trustees* of humanity, duty-bound to preserve it. Cf. again Feinberg, *Harm to Self*, 94–97, where he memorably criticizes "Kant's notion of respect for persons" as "abstract and (oddly) impersonal," grounded in "a kind of internal Vatican City not subject to [a person's] sovereign control" (94).

101. See Velleman, "A Right of Self-Termination"? 619.

102. Phillips, *Our Bodies, Whose Property?* 120.

103. Cf. the dystopia in Kazuo Ishiguro's *Never Let Me Go* (New York: Knopf, 2005), at once like our world and unlike it.

104. Phillips, *Our Bodies, Whose Property?* 120.

105. Cf. here, interestingly, Todd David Whitmore, "Catholic Social Teaching: Starting with the Common Good," in *Living the Catholic Social Tradition: Cases and Commentary*, ed. Kathleen Maas-Weigert and Alexia K. Kelley (Lanham, MD: Rowman & Littlefield, 2005), 59–85, at 60, observing that the documents of the church's social justice tradition "stress that the [doctrine of the] *imago Dei*…is precisely about our imaging of the *triune*…God," with the upshot that "there is no dignity apart from the dignity we all have in relation to each other."

106. See Anderson, *Value in Ethics and Economics*, 141.

107. Ibid., xiii.

108. Ibid., 144.

109. Michael Walzer has claimed, "Whenever we ban the use of money [for a good], we do indeed establish a right—namely, that this particular good be distributed in some other way." See *Spheres of Justice*, 100. I think this claim is overstated—for example, when we ban the use of money for sex, do we establish a right that sex be distributed in some other way?—but it does seem to hold for organs. The question is then what other way is best.

110. Phillips, *Our Bodies, Whose Property?* 120.

111. See B. J. Boyarsky et al., "Potential Limitations of Presumed Consent Legislation," *Transplantation* 93 (2012): 136–40.

112. See the Room for Debate discussion "How Much for a Kidney?" *New York Times*, August 21, 2014, available online through the *New York Times* Web site (http://www.nytimes.com/roomfordebate/2014/08/21/how-much-for-a-kidney?).

113. Funeral costs might also be offered.

CHAPTER 7

1. See, for example, Richard Sorabji, *Moral Conscience through the Ages: Fifth Century BCE to the Present* (Chicago: The University of Chicago Press, 2014).

2. See *Dignitatis Humanae* (1965), §3, available online through the Vatican's Web site (http://www.vatican.va/archive/hist_councils/ii_vatican_council/documents/vat-ii_decl_19651207_dignitatis-humanae_en.html).

3. See *Gaudium et Spes* (1965), §16, likewise available online at http://www.vatican.va/archive/hist_councils/ii_vatican_council/docu ments/vat-ii_const_19651207_gaudium-et-spes_en.html. Further references to this document appear parenthetically in the body of the text.

4. *Homo sum: humani nihil a me alienum puto.*

5. Avery Dulles, "From Ratzinger to Benedict," *First Things*, February 2006, 24–29, at 28–29.

6. See, for insightful analyses of this polarization, Mary Ellen Konieczny, *The Spirit's Tether: Family, Work, and Religion among American Catholics* (Oxford: Oxford University Press, 2013); and Peter Steinfels, "Contraception and Honesty: A Proposal for the Next Synod," *Commonweal*, June 1, 2015, 12–19.

7. See Matthew Arnold, "Stanzas from the Grande Chartreuse" (1855), in *The Portable Matthew Arnold*, ed. Lionel Trilling (New York: Viking, 1949), 148–55, at 151, available online through the Poetry Foundation (http://www.poetryfoundation.org/poem/172861). I follow Thomas Albert Howard in using this verse to characterize the unfinished work of Vatican II. Howard writes, "On a host of issues, such as religious liberty and ecumenism, change has taken place. Other issues, however— the nature of church authority, priestly celibacy, the role of the Curia, the place of women—sometimes appear, in the words of Matthew Arnold," etc. See Howard's article "A Question of Conscience: The Excommunication of Ignaz von Döllinger," *Commonweal*, October 10, 2014, 14–20, at 14.

8. Michael G. Lawler and Todd A. Salzman, "Following Faithfully: The Catholic Way to Choose the Good," *America*, February 2, 2015, 16–20, at 16.

9. Ibid.

10. James T. Bretzke, *A Morally Complex World* (Collegeville, MN: Liturgical Press, 2004), 35. Cf., once upon a time, Avery Dulles, "Conscience and Church Authority," in *Conscience: Its Freedom and Limitations*, ed. William C. Bier (New York: Fordham University Press, 1971), 251–68, at 253: "The myth of an omniscient magisterium with a 'direct wire' to heaven is an illusion based on dark psychological tendencies."

11. Lawler and Salzman, "Following Faithfully," 17.

12. Joseph Ratzinger, *On Conscience: Two Essays* (Philadelphia/San Francisco: National Catholic Bioethics Center/Ignatius Press, 2007), 17.

See also 22: "The reduction of conscience to subjective certitude betokens at the same time a retreat from truth."

13. Lawler and Salzman, "Following Faithfully," 19.

14. Jean Porter, *Natural and Divine Law: Reclaiming the Tradition for Christian Ethics* (Grand Rapids: Eerdmans, 1999), 163.

15. Jason J. Howard, *Conscience in Moral Life: Rethinking How Our Convictions Structure Self and Society* (Landham, MD: Rowman & Littlefield, 2014), 18. See also Douglas C. Langston, *Conscience and Other Virtues* (University Park, PA: Pennsylvania State University Press, 2001), 77, 84.

16. Robert K. Vischer, *Conscience and the Common Good: Reclaiming the Space between Person and State* (Cambridge: Cambridge University Press, 2010), 3.

17. Cf. James Keenan, "Redeeming Conscience," *Theological Studies* 76 (2015): 129–47, at 134–35, who contrasts "the American use of conscience" over the last fifty years with the European experience of it. According to Keenan, "While Europe *collectively* faced itself in conscience" in the postwar period, "Americans *individually* invoked conscience to confront authorities" (135). That is, conscience became "the American option for opting out" (ibid.). This contrast is instructive, but it's important to recognize as well that "the American use of conscience" has European roots. What's more, the Canadian bishops, Americans themselves, initially responded to *Humanae Vitae* much as the European bishops did.

18. Jennifer A. Herdt, "Calvin's Legacy for Contemporary Reformed Natural Law," *Scottish Journal of Theology* 67 (2014): 414–35, at 420. I have Americanized the spelling. See also David Bosco, "Conscience as Court and Worm: Calvin and the Three Elements of Conscience," *Journal of Religious Ethics* 14 (1986): 333–55, at 342, 345.

19. See here the measured critique of "the modern period" of moral theology in Servais Pinckaers, *Morality: The Catholic View*, trans. Michael Sherwin (South Bend, IN: St. Augustine's Press, 2001), 40–41. Cf. John I. Jenkins, "The Challenge and Promise of Catholic Higher Education for Our Time," *Journal of Catholic Higher Education* 34, no. 1 (2015): 11–25.

20. Herdt, "Calvin's Legacy for Contemporary Reformed Natural Law," 420.

21. Ibid., 427.

22. See John Milton, *Paradise Lost*, ed. Gordon Teskey (New York: W. W. Norton, 2005), bk. 1, line 26, p. 4. See further Michael Walzer's insightful comments on "the Protestant conscience" in his essay "Conscientious Objection," in *Obligations: Essays on War, Disobedience, and Citizenship* (Cambridge, MA: Harvard University Press, 1970), 121–23.

23. Herdt, "Calvin's Legacy for Contemporary Reformed Natural Law," 423.

24. See Howard, *Conscience in Moral Life*, 9. Howard is a critic of the faculty view, which he presents as a product of "the Enlightenment confidence in our power to reason, along with the Protestant Reformation's perspective on our capacity to directly relate to God" (4). On his telling, these together provided "an unprecedented confidence in our moral power to discern right from wrong, and this confidence [became] encapsulated in the faculty view of conscience" (ibid.). The account of conscience developed by Bishop Joseph Butler (1692–1752) is a clear example (see 18). See further Butler, *Five Sermons*, ed. Stephen Darwall (Indianapolis: Hackett, 1983), 37–38 (first sermon) and 42–43 (second sermon), where Butler states, "Man hath the rule of right within; what is wanting is only that he honestly attend to it" (42).

25. Howard, *Conscience in Moral Life*, 19.

26. See, however, for the complexity of Newman's thought on conscience, Walter E. Conn, *Conscience and Conversion in Newman: A Developmental Study of Self in John Henry Newman* (Milwaukee: Marquette University Press, 2010).

27. Newman, *Discourses Addressed to Mixed Congregations* (London: Longmans, Green, 1906), discourse 5, "Saintliness the Standard of Christian Principle," http://newmanreader.org/works/discourses/index.html.

28. Ibid.

29. Ibid. Newman was not alone in both holding the faculty view of conscience and finding the conscience of his age wanting. So, too, writing at much the same time, did Samuel Clemens, but unlike Newman, Clemens turned a skeptic toward conscience, or at least was ambivalent toward it. See, in this regard, my paper "When Words Fail Us: Reexamining the Conscience of Huckleberry Finn," *Journal of Aesthetic Education* 45 (2011): 1–22. That Clemens conceived of conscience as an "agency within an agency" is vividly illustrated in his story "The Facts

Concerning the Recent Carnival of Crime in Connecticut" (1876), available online on the Web site of *The Atlantic* magazine (http://www.the atlantic.com/magazine/archive/1876/06/the-facts-concerning-the-recent-carnival-of-crime-in-connecticut/306240/). The narrator of the story is confronted by, and eventually succeeds in murdering, his conscience, which appears as a burlesque of himself.

30. Aquinas, *Summa Theologiae* I, q. 79, a. 12.

31. Ibid., a. 13. See, on the origins of the distinction between *synderesis* and *conscientia*, Timothy C. Potts, *Conscience in Medieval Philosophy* (Cambridge: Cambridge University Press, 1980), 10–11. Cf. Sorabji, *Moral Conscience through the Ages*, 59–67.

32. Ibid., I–II, q. 94, a. 2. Aquinas also suggests, in *De Veritate*, q. 17, a. 2, that *synderesis* supplies the principles to love God and not to do anything forbidden by God.

33. The analogy is common in the literature. See Ratzinger, *On Conscience*, 61, who follows here Robert Spaemann, and Eric D'Arcy, *Conscience and Its Right to Freedom* (New York: Sheed and Ward, 1961), 35.

34. Aquinas, *Summa Theologiae* I–II, q. 100, a. 4. As Jean Porter has explained Aquinas on this point, according to him, "anyone who grasps what it means to be someone, a potential neighbor, grasps the normative claim that one has on others" (personal communication, March 1, 2015). Cf., interestingly, Robert Spaemann, *Persons: The Difference between "Someone" and "Something,"* trans. Oliver O'Donovan (Oxford: Oxford University Press, 2006), 182: "To acknowledge personal status is already to express respect, which is the specific way in which persons are accessible to one another."

35. Herdt, "Calvin's Legacy for Contemporary Reformed Natural Law," 423.

36. Ibid., 424.

37. Aquinas, *Summa Theologiae*, ed. Thomas Gilby, bilingual ed. (New York: McGraw Hill/Blackfriars, 1975), vol. 28, I–II, q. 94, a. 4, p. 86: "Et ideo, si in communibus sit aliqua necessitas, quanto magis ad propria descenditur tanto magis invenitur defectus."

38. Cf. James Childress, "Appeals to Conscience," *Ethics* 89 (1979): 315–35, at 321.

39. See, for closer discussion, my paper "When Words Fail Us." As Elizabeth Anscombe remarked, "Butler exalts conscience, but appears

ignorant that a man's conscience may tell him to do the vilest things." See her "Modern Moral Philosophy," *Philosophy* 33 (1958): 1–19, at 2.

40. I follow here Howard, *Conscience in Moral Life*, 8, 144.

41. Ibid., 31.

42. Aquinas, *Summa Theologiae* I, q. 79, a. 13.

43. Christopher Kaczor, *A Defense of Dignity: Creating Life, Destroying Life, and Respecting the Rights of Conscience* (Notre Dame, IN: University of Notre Dame Press, 2013), 154.

44. Paul Ricoeur, *Oneself as Another*, trans. Kathleen Blamey (Chicago: University of Chicago Press, 1992), 318. See, for Ricoeur's reservations about Thomism, his *Freedom and Nature: The Voluntary and the Involuntary*, trans. Erazim V. Kohák (Evanston, IL: Northwestern University Press, 1966), 190–95.

45. Howard, *Conscience in Moral Life*, 53, 90.

46. Ricoeur, *Oneself as Another*, 353.

47. Howard, *Conscience in Moral Life*, 89. As Howard also observes, "The impetus of conscience is not to deny our personal concerns but [to] free us from what is *only* personal" (90).

48. Cf. Lisa Sowle Cahill, *Sex, Gender, and Christian Ethics* (Cambridge: Cambridge University Press, 1996), 2–3.

49. As Grisez, Boyle, and Finnis note, "An early version of the theory" appears in chapter 3 of Grisez's *Contraception and the Natural Law* (Milwaukee: Bruce, 1964), 46–75. See Germain Grisez, Joseph Boyle, and John Finnis, "Practical Principles, Moral Truths, and Ultimate Ends," *American Journal of Jurisprudence* 32 (1987): 99–151, at 148. For an account of the origins of the new natural law that does locate it with respect to recent moral and ecclesiological controversies, see David D. Kirkpatrick, "The Conservative-Christian Big Thinker," *New York Times Magazine*, December 16, 2009, 24ff. The figure on whom this article focuses is Robert George.

50. See, for example, Grisez, "The First Principle of Practical Reason: A Commentary on the *Summa theologiae*, 1–2, Question 94, Article 2," *Natural Law Forum* 10 (1965): 168–201.

51. Anscombe, "Modern Moral Philosophy," *Philosophy* 33 (1958): 1–19.

52. David Hume, *A Treatise of Human Nature*, ed. P. H. Nidditch, 2nd ed. (Oxford: Clarendon Press, 1978), bk. 2, pt. 3, sec. 3, p. 413.

53. Ibid., 414.

54. Ibid.

55. Ibid., bk. 3, pt. 1, sec. 1, p. 457.

56. Ibid.

57. Ibid.

58. Ibid., bk. 3, pt. 1, sec. 2, p. 470.

59. Ibid.

60. John Finnis, *Fundamentals of Ethics* (Washington, DC: Georgetown University Press, 1983), 26. See Hume, *An Enquiry Concerning the Principles of Morals*, in *Hume's Ethical Writings*, ed. Alastair MacIntyre (Notre Dame, IN: University of Notre Dame Press, 1965), sec. 1, pp. 27, 24.

61. Hume, *Treatise*, bk. 3, pt. 1, sec. 2, p. 471.

62. See Onora O'Neill, *Towards Justice and Virtue: A Constructive Account of Practical Reasoning* (Cambridge: Cambridge University Press, 1996), 31–32. As O'Neill nicely summarizes the strategy, "A new Science of Man will supposedly serve when the old Metaphysics of the Good fails." But as she also suggests, this strategy of "accommodat[ing], or at least postpon[ing], the intellectual crises of modernity" was bound to destruction, as it finally found at the hands of Nietzche. Hume claimed that the "internal sense or feeling" responsible for "pronounc[ing] characters and actions amiable or odious, praise-worthy or blameable" was by "nature…made universal in the species" and as such gave "a philosopher sufficient assurance, that he can never be mistaken in framing the catalogue" of praise or blame. See the *Enquiry*, sec. 1, pp. 26, 27. It is difficult to imagine that this faith did not seem dubious even in his time. But then Hume does sometimes seem to protest too much.

63. Grisez, Boyle, and Finnis, "Practical Principles, Moral Truths, and Ultimate Ends," 102.

64. See Hume, *Treatise*, bk. 3, pt. 1, sec. 1, pp. 469–70.

65. Grisez, Boyle, and Finnis, "Practical Principles, Moral Truths, and Ultimate Ends," 102. Purposes have "two aspects": "In one aspect a purpose is desired by reason of an intelligible good; in another aspect a purpose is desired as concrete and imaginable" (104). A purpose in the second sense is the object of emotional desire and is termed a *goal*.

66. Ibid., 103.

67. Ibid.

68. Unlike Aristotle, however, they do not postulate a highest good. The basic goods are instead incommensurable with one another; as the

authors put it, "The basic goods of diverse categories are called 'good' only by analogy" (ibid., 110).

69. Anscombe, *Intention*, 2nd ed. (Cambridge, MA: Harvard University Press, 1963), 57. Cf. Finnis, *Fundamentals of Ethics*, 2. Exhibit A might well be Hume, who claims in the *Treatise* that "reason is the discovery of truth or falsehood" and that "truth or falsehood consists in an agreement or disagreement either to the real relations of ideas, or to real existence and matter of fact." For him, then, "knowledge must be something that is judged as such by being in accordance with the facts." See Hume, *Treatise*, bk. 3, pt. 1, sec. 1, p. 458.

70. Aristotle, *Nicomachean Ethics*, bk. 1, chap. 1, p. 1, 1094a.

71. Grisez, Boyle, and Finnis, "Practical Principles, Moral Truths, and Ultimate Ends," 107.

72. See Finnis, *Fundamentals of Ethics*, 52.

73. In "Practical Principles, Moral Truths, and Ultimate Ends," these number seven: (1) life; (2) knowledge and aesthetic experience; (3) work and play; (4) harmony between and among individuals and groups of persons; (5) inner peace; (6) personal integrity; and (7) "harmony with some more than human source of meaning" in response to "tension with the wider reaches of reality" (1078).

74. Ibid., 147–48. It should be noted, however, that Grisez et al. acknowledge "a second thought on this point." For "it may be," they write, "that the intelligibility which specifies the will in making certain immoral choices merely is to use effective means to satisfy desires, hostile feelings, or other emotions, whose precise objects are not reducible to any of the basic human goods. If so, the basic human goods are not reasons for such immoral choices, but only serve to rationalize them" (148). The authors also claim that, even if this different analysis is correct, "we do not think the account of practical truth and moral truth we offer here would require very much revision." For my present purposes, I put this question aside.

75. Ibid., 106.

76. Ibid.

77. Ibid., 119.

78. Ibid., 120.

79. Ibid., 121.

80. Ibid.

81. Ibid.

82. Ibid.

83. Ibid., 125.

84. Milton, *Paradise Lost*, bk. 9, line 786, p. 218.

85. Mary Shelley, *Frankenstein*, ed. Paul J. Hunter (New York: W. W. Norton, 1996), vol. 1, chap. 3, p. 33.

86. Grisez, Boyle, and Finnis, "Practical Principles, Moral Truths, and Ultimate Ends," 125.

87. Ibid.

88. Grisez et al. also give us, at this point, a phenomenological account of the genesis of "the moral ought." It is "when practical knowledge is confronted with the tendency of feeling to restrict it by urging a possibility whose choice would fetter it [that] the is-to-be of practical knowledge [good is to be done and pursued] becomes ought-to-be" (ibid.). In other words, "The *directiveness* of practical knowledge *becomes normativity* because what is to be might not come to be and yet still rationally is to be." Accordingly, (with Hume) the moral *ought* cannot be derived "from any theoretical is," but (against Hume on most readings) it nonetheless is not "cut off from its roots in human nature. For the normativity of the moral *ought* is nothing but the integral directiveness of the is-to-be of practical knowledge" (127)—directing the person toward fulfillment of his or her nature as an animate, rational, social being.

89. Ibid., 129.

90. Ibid.

91. Ibid., 130.

92. Ibid., 131.

93. Ibid.

94. Jean Porter, *Nature as Reason: A Thomistic Theory of the Natural Law* (Grand Rapids: Eerdmans, 2005), 262.

95. Thomas Nagel, *The View from Nowhere* (Oxford: Oxford University Press, 1986), 139.

96. Grisez, Boyle, and Finnis, "Practical Principles, Moral Truths, and Ultimate Ends," 103.

97. Porter, *Nature as Reason*, 128. See also her *Natural and Divine Law*, 92–93.

98. Ibid.

99. Ibid.

100. Ibid., 129.

101. See, for discussion, Alan Donagan, *The Theory of Morality* (Chicago: The University of Chicago Press, 1977), 78, 175. A moral theory that does not recognize a morally significant difference between "the suicide of Captain Oates, in Scott's antarctic expedition, in order not to retard his companions," and the "sacrifice" and cannibalization of a boy, the offense in the case of *R. v. Dudley and Stephens*, lest all the castaways on a boat die—examples discussed by Donagan—has, at the very least, some explaining to do. Tacitly recognizing this problem, Boyle has claimed that "actions like that of Captain Oates need not be suicide, but can be described as a side effect of choices to do other things (e.g., removing oneself from the group), which have death as a predictable result"; but, as Nigel Biggar has observed, this "redescription" of what Oates did strains credulity. See Boyle, "Sanctity of Life and Suicide: Tensions and Developments within Common Morality," in *Suicide and Euthanasia: Historical and Contemporary Themes*, ed. Baruch Brody (Dordrecht: Kluwer, 1989), 221–50, at 233, and Biggar, "Conclusion," in *The Revival of Natural Law: Philosophical, Theological and Ethical Responses to the Finnis-Grisez School*, ed. Nigel Biggar and Rufus Black (Aldershot, UK: Ashgate, 2000), 283–94, at 288–90.

102. Cf. Alfonso Gómez-Lobo, *Morality and the Human Goods: An Introduction to Natural Law Ethics* (Washington, DC: Georgetown University Press, 2002), 14. See also Kirkpatrick, "The Conservative-Christian Big Thinker," on the twists and turns of Robert George's case against same-sex marriage.

103. See Grisez, *Difficult Moral Questions*, vol. 3 of *The Way of the Lord Jesus*, http://www.twotlj.org/G-3-V-3.html. These questions include (to cite several chosen at random): "May a woman take a job handling complaints evasively?" (question 125); "Should the family of someone marrying invalidly participate in the wedding?" (question 36); "May a pathologist examine tissue from immoral procedures?" (question 71).

104. Grisez, Boyle, Finnis, and William E. May, "'Every Marital Act Ought to Be Open to New Life': Toward a Clearer Understanding," *The Thomist* 52 (1988): 365–426, at 366.

105. Ibid., 366, 372.

106. Ibid., 371.

107. Ibid., 373–74.

108. Ibid., 373, 374. They might go on, as they do in the article that I have been quoting, we are sorry to have to tell you, too, that "it is logi-

cally impossible for a contraceptive act to be a marital act." For "if marriage is defined, as the Church does define it, as a human friendship whose specifying common good includes the procreation of children"—well, contraceptive acts reject this good, which is to say the good of life, and so falsify marriage, which is to say attack this good as well (415). Whether Grisez et al. correctly define marriage "as the Church does define it," however, is by no means clear. Grisez et al. present the good of procreation as, in Lisa Cahill's words, one of "the intrinsic aspects of the being of a marriage itself"; they do not consider whether marriage is to be understood instead as itself a good "ordered to the further, distinct goods of procreation and family," which is an understanding suggested by the traditional Augustinian language of the goods of marriage. See Cahill, "Grisez on Sex and Gender: A Feminist Theological Perspective," in Biggar and Black, *The Revival of Natural Law*, 242–61, at 246–47.

109. Grisez, Finnis, and Boyle, "Every Marital Act Ought to Be Open to New Life," 371. Grisez et al. operate in this article with what Jonathan Glover has called "the immigration queue model" of unconceived potential children; see Glover, *Choosing Children: Genes, Disability and Design* (Oxford: Oxford University Press, 2006), 42. As would-be immigrants line up to enter a country, potential children line up to enter life. The problem with this model, obviously, is that, whereas would-be immigrants already do exist, potential children do not. Moreover, the philosophical anthropology implicit in this model is certainly not Thomist.

110. Cf. David Leal, "Respect for Life in Germain Grisez's Moral Theology," in Biggar and Black, *The Revival of Natural Law*, 203–22, at 214. I imagine the typical maxim of married Catholic couples who use contraception to be something like the following: because of the needs of our children, the limits on our resources, and our professional and other goals in life, we seek to prevent conception of a child when sexually expressing our love to one another, though we are committed to welcoming a child should one be conceived despite our use of contraception. The typical maxim of married Catholic couples who practice natural family planning would presumably be, *mutatis mutandis*, much the same.

111. Which means (stipulating that the couple are married) that they also did not commit a nonmarital act even as Grisez et al. define marriage. See note 108 above. Cf. Donagan, *The Theory of Morality*, 106–7 and

167. See also Paul Ramsey, *Fabricated Man: The Ethics of Genetic Control* (New Haven: Yale University Press, 1970), 34.

112. Joseph M. Boyle Jr., "Aquinas, Kant, and Donagan on Moral Principles," *New Scholasticism* 58 (1984): 391–408, at 407.

113. Aquinas, *Summa Theologiae* I–II, q. 94, a. 4.

114. As the notes indicate, I have learned much from Jean Porter's *Natural and Divine Law* and *Nature as Reason*, among other works of hers.

115. Cf. Rosalind Hursthouse, "Virtue Theory and Abortion," *Philosophy and Public Affairs* 20 (1991): 223–46, at 226.

116. Cf. Aquinas, *Summa Theologiae* I–II q. 21, a. 2 and II-II, q. 141, a. 6.

117. Ibid., vol. 41, II–II, q. 108, a. 2., p. 120: "Unde patet quod virtutes perficiunt nos ad prosequendum debito modo inclinationes naturales quæ pertinent ad jus naturale."

118. Grisez, Boyle, and Finnis, "Practical Principles, Moral Truths, and Ultimate Ends," 130.

119. Cf. Alasdair MacIntyre, *Whose Justice? Which Rationality?* (Notre Dame, IN: University of Notre Dame Press, 1988), 176–77, contrasting the modern "assumption that the acquisition of an ability to make correct moral judgments...does not require the substantial acquisition of the virtues as a prerequisite" with Aristotle's view that "the development of a capacity for sound practical reasoning which will guide one both to judge truly and to act rightly is...inseparable from an education in the exercise of the moral virtues." See for further precision about Aquinas's own view 177–81.

120. Porter, *Nature as Reason*, 262.

121. Porter, "Does the Natural Law Provide a Universally Valid Morality?" in *Intractable Disputes about the Natural Law: Alasdair MacIntyre and Critics*, ed. Lawrence S. Cunningham (Notre Dame, IN: University of Notre Dame Press, 2009), 53–95, at 78.

122. I follow here Porter, *Nature as Reason*, 163. Cf. again Nagel, *Mind and Cosmos: Why the Materialist Neo-Darwinian Conception of Nature Is Almost Certainly False* (Oxford: Oxford University Press, 2012), 119–20.

123. Rosalind Hursthouse, *On Virtue Ethics* (Oxford: Oxford University Press, 1999), 36. Hursthouse calls these "rules of virtue ethics" or "v-rules."

124. Ibid., 33.

125. Ibid., 164.

126. Immanuel Kant, *Grundlegung zur Metaphysik der Sitten*, ed. Karl Vorländer, 3rd ed. (Hamburg: Felix Meiner, 1965), 28 (4:408); *Groundwork of the Metaphysics of Morals*, trans. Mary Gregor (Cambridge: Cambridge University Press, 1997), 21.

127. Jeff McMahan, "Moral Intuition," in *The Blackwell Guide to Ethical Theory*, ed. Hugh LaFollette and Ingmar Persson, 2nd ed. (West Sussex, UK: Wiley-Blackwell, 2013), 103–20, at 117.

128. I paraphrase here Lisa Cahill, *Sex, Gender, and Christian Ethics*, 3.

129. Ibid., 46.

130. Hursthouse, *On Virtue Ethics*, 228.

131. See, for development, Alasdair MacIntyre, *Dependent Rational Animals: Why Human Beings Need the Virtues* (Chicago: Open Court, 1999); and, from a more explicitly political perspective, Eva Feder Kittay, *Love's Labor: Essays on Women, Equality, and Dependency* (New York: Routledge, 1999).

132. Porter, "Does the Natural Law Provide a Universally Valid Morality?" in Cunningham, *Intractable Disputes about the Natural Law*, 91.

133. See, for an outstanding example, Anne Fadiman, *The Spirit Catches You and You Fall Down: A Hmong Child, Her American Doctors, and the Collision of Two Cultures* (New York: Farrar, Straus and Giroux, 1997).

134. Alasdair MacIntyre, *After Virtue*, 2nd ed. (Notre Dame, IN: University of Notre Dame Press, 1984), 222.

135. See, for further discussion, Porter, *Natural and Divine Law*, 284–93, contrasting the views of theologians like John Howard Yoder, Stanley Hauerwas, and John Milbank, "who argue that the foundational Christian value is not equality but non-violence" (284) with a medieval natural lawyer like William of Auxerre (circa 1150–1231), who operates with "the presupposition that if there is an apparent conflict between the gospel and the natural law, it is possible to reconcile them dialectically" (292).

136. I have learned here from Jennifer Herdt's paper "The Role of Guilt in the Development of Virtue" (presentation, Conference on Virtue and Its Development, Notre Dame, IN, May 21, 2014).

137. Thomas Hobbes, *De Cive*, ed. Howard Warrender (Oxford: Oxford University Press, 1983), chapter XIV.1, p. 168; see for discussion Stephen Darwall, *The Second-Person Standpoint: Morality, Respect, and*

Accountability (Cambridge, MA: Harvard University Press, 2006), 12–13, 289.

138. Cf. Darwall, *The Second-Person Standpoint*, 49, 257.

139. Anscombe, "Modern Moral Philosophy," 5.

140. Ibid.

141. Ludwig Wittgenstein, *Philosophical Investigations*, trans. Elizabeth Anscombe, bilingual edition (Oxford: Basil Blackwell, 1958), pt. 1, §115, p. 48.

142. See Anscombe, "Modern Moral Philosophy," 13.

143. Darwall, *The Second-Person Standpoint*, 106. See, for Suárez himself, *Moral Philosophy from Montaigne to Kant: An Anthology*, ed. J. B. Schneewind, vol. 1 (Cambridge: Cambridge University Press, 1990), 67–87.

144. Ibid.

145. Anscombe, "Modern Moral Philosophy," 6.

146. See Sorabji, *Moral Conscience through the Ages*, 20.

147. I paraphrase here Josef Fuchs, *Christian Morality: The Word Becomes Flesh*, trans. Brian McNeil (Washington, DC: Georgetown University Press, 1987), 121. It should be noted that a Kantian might counter that we experience ourselves in conscience as *self*-legislating. Whether that makes sense is a question for readers to pursue beyond this book. Thanks to Lydia Moland for raising it.

148. Ibid., 122. The nonbeliever, it should be acknowledged, could counter that religion is the reification of the experience of conscience.

149. I follow here Darwall, *The Second-Person Standpoint*, 105, 146.

150. As the preceding notes indicate, the idea that the moral point of view is "an impartially regulated second-person stance" is represented most prominently today by Darwall; see *The Second-Person Standpoint*, 102. Another important work in this regard is T. M. Scanlon's *What We Owe to Each Other* (Cambridge, MA: Harvard University Press, 1998), which develops his contractualist view that "thinking about right and wrong is, at the most basic level, thinking about what could be justified to others on grounds that they, if appropriately motivated, could not reasonably reject" (5). In the continental tradition, the principal figure to consider in this regard is Emmanuel Lévinas.

151. Darwall, *The Second-Person Standpoint*, 105.

152. Cf. Kant, *Grundlegung zur Metaphysik der Sitten*, 10 (4:393); *Groundwork of the Metaphysics of Morals*, 7.

153. See further, just to begin with, Ricoeur, *Oneself as Another*, 170–71.

154. I draw here from Porter, *Nature as Reason*, 144.

155. Bernard Williams, "Evolution, Ethics, and the Representation Problem," in *Making Sense of Humanity and Other Philosophical Papers 1982–1993* (Cambridge: Cambridge University Press, 1995), 100–10, at 110.

156. See, for a fascinating place to begin, Nagel's *Mind and Cosmos: Why the Materialist Neo-Darwinian Conception of Nature Is Almost Certainly False* (Oxford: Oxford University Press, 2012). Nagel's principal interlocutor here on matters of morality is Sharon Street; see first, among her fine papers, "A Darwinian Dilemma for Realist Theories of Value," *Philosophical Studies* 127 (2006): 109–66. The argument is insightfully joined by Micah Lott in "Explaining Value: Nagel on Normative Realism and the Teleology of Evolution," *Expositions: Interdisciplinary Studies in the Humanities* 8, no. 2 (2014): 26–37. Finally, I have written a rather different kind of introduction in "The Ethics of Metaethics: On Thomas Nagel's *Mind and Cosmos*," *Expositions: Interdisciplinary Studies in the Humanities* 8, no. 2 (2014): 1–10.

BIBLIOGRAPHY

Adams, Robert Merrihew. "Existence, Self-Interest, and the Problem of Evil." *Noûs* 13 (1979): 53–65.

Alighieri, Dante. *Inferno.* Translated by Allen Mandelbaum. Bilingual edition. New York: Bantam, 1980.

Alter, Robert, trans. *The Five Books of Moses.* New York: W.W. Norton, 2004.

Anderson, Elizabeth. "Animal Rights and the Values of Nonhuman Life." In *Animal Rights: Current Debates and New Directions,* edited by Cass R. Sunstein and Martha Nussbaum, 277–98. Oxford: Oxford University Press, 2004.

———. "Is Women's Labor a Commodity?" *Philosophy and Public Affairs* 19 (1990): 71–92.

———. *Value in Ethics and Economics.* Cambridge, MA: Harvard University Press, 1993.

Anscombe, Elizabeth. "Action, Intention and 'Double Effect.'" *Proceedings of the American Catholic Philosophical Association* 56 (1982): 12–25.

———. *Intention.* 2nd ed. Cambridge, MA: Harvard University Press, 1963.

———. "Modern Moral Philosophy." *Philosophy* 33 (1958): 1–19.

Aquinas, Thomas. *Summa contra Gentiles.* 5 vols. Translated by the Fathers of the English Dominican Province. London: Burns, Oates & Washbourne, 1924.

———. *Summa Theologiae.* 61 vols. Edited by Thomas Gilby. Bilingual ed. New York: McGraw Hill/Blackfriars, 1964–81.

Aristotle. *Nicomachean Ethics.* Translated by Joe Sachs. Newburyport, MA: Focus Publishing, 2002.

Arnold, Matthew. *The Portable Matthew Arnold*. Edited by Lionel Trilling. New York: Viking, 1949.

Augustine. *The City of God against the Pagans*. Edited and translated by R. W. Dyson. Cambridge: Cambridge University Press, 1998.

————. *Contra Faustum*. In *Nicene and Post-Nicene Fathers, First Series*, vol. 4, edited by Philip Schaff, translated by Richard Stothert. Buffalo: Christian Literature Publishing Co., 1887. http://www.newadvent.org/fathers/1406.htm.

————. *Of the Morals of the Catholic Church*. In *Nicene and Post-Nicene Fathers, First Series*, vol. 4, edited by Philip Schaff, translated by Richard Stothert. Buffalo: Christian Literature Publishing Co., 1887. http://www.newadvent.org/fathers/1401.htm.

Austin, J. L. *Philosophical Papers*. Edited by J. O. Urmson and G. J. Warnock. 3rd ed. Oxford: Oxford University Press, 1979.

Austriaco, Nicanor Pier Giorgio. "Abortion in a Case of Pulmonary Arterial Hypertension: A Test Case for Two Rival Theories of Human Action." *National Catholic Bioethics Quarterly* 11 (2011): 503–18.

Bernardin, Joseph. *The Seamless Garment: Writings on the Consistent Ethic of Life*. Edited by Thomas A. Nairn. Maryknoll, NY: Orbis, 2008.

Biggar, Nigel. "Conclusion." In *The Revival of Natural Law: Philosophical, Theological and Ethical Responses to the Finnis-Grisez School*, edited by Nigel Biggar and Rufus Black, 283–94. Aldershot, UK: Ashgate, 2000.

Bosco, David. "Conscience as Court and Worm: Calvin and the Three Elements of Conscience." *Journal of Religious Ethics* 14 (1986): 333–55.

Boswell, John. *The Kindness of Strangers: The Abandonment of Children in Western Europe from Late Antiquity through the Renaissance*. New York: Pantheon, 1988.

Boyarsky, B. J., E. C. Hall, N. A. Deshpande, R. L. Ros, R. A. Montgomery, D. M. Steinwachs, and D. L. Segev. "Potential Limitations of Presumed Consent Legislation." *Transplantation* 93 (2012): 136–40.

Boyle, Joseph M., Jr., "Aquinas, Kant, and Donagan on Moral Principles." *New Scholasticism* 58 (1984): 391–408.

————. "*Praeter Intentionem* in Aquinas." *The Thomist* 42 (1978): 649–65.

———. "Sanctity of Life and Suicide: Tensions and Developments within Common Morality." In *Suicide and Euthanasia: Historical and Contemporary Themes*, edited by Baruch Brody, 221–50. Dordrecht: Kluwer, 1989.

———. "Toward Understanding the Principle of Double Effect." *Ethics* 90 (1980): 527–38.

———. "Who Is Entitled to Double Effect?" *Journal of Medicine and Philosophy* 16 (1991): 475–94.

Brague, Rémi. *Europe, la voie romaine*. Paris: Gallimard, 1992.

———. *On the God of the Christians (and on One or Two Others)*. Translated by Paul Seaton. South Bend, IN: St. Augustine's Press, 2013.

Brann, Eva. "A Call to Thought." *The St. John's Review* 45 (1999): 108–18.

Bretzke, James T. *Handbook of Roman Catholic Moral Terms*. Washington, DC: Georgetown University Press, 2013.

———. "The Lesser Evil." *America*, March 26, 2007, 16–18.

———. *A Morally Complex World*. Collegeville, MN: Liturgical Press, 2004.

Buckley, Michael J. *At the Origins of Modern Atheism*. New Haven: Yale University Press, 1987.

———. *Denying and Disclosing God: The Ambiguous Progress of Modern Atheism*. New Haven: Yale University Press, 2004.

Burrell, David B. "Perspectives in Catholic Philosophy II." In *Teaching the Tradition: Catholic Themes in Academic Disciplines*, edited by John J. Piderit and Melanie Morey, 85–106. Oxford: Oxford University Press, 2012.

Burtt, Shelley. "Is Inclusion a Civic Virtue? Cosmopolitanism, Disability, and the Liberal State." *Social Theory and Practice* 33 (2007): 557–78.

———. "Which Babies? Dilemmas of Genetic Testing." *Tikkun* 16, no. 1 (January/February 2001): 45–47.

Butler, Joseph. *Five Sermons*. Edited by Stephen Darwall. Indianapolis: Hackett, 1983.

Cahill, Lisa Sowle. "Abortion and Argument by Analogy." *Horizons* 9 (1982): 271–87.

———. "Grisez on Sex and Gender: A Feminist Theological Perspective." In *The Revival of Natural Law: Philosophical,*

Theological and Ethical Responses to the Finnis-Grisez School, edited by Nigel Biggar and Rufus Black, 242–61. Aldershot, UK: Ashgate, 2000.

———. *Sex, Gender, and Christian Ethics*. Cambridge: Cambridge University Press, 1996.

———. "Teleology, Utilitarianism, and Christian Ethics." *Theological Studies* 42 (1981): 610–29.

Camosy, Charles. *Beyond the Abortion Wars: A Way Forward for a New Generation*. Grand Rapids: Eerdmans, 2015.

Cavadini, John C. "Why Study God? The Role of Theology at a Catholic University." *Commonweal*, October 11, 2013, 12–18.

Cavanaugh, Thomas A. "Double-Effect Reasoning, Craniotomy, and Vital Conflicts: A Case of Contemporary Catholic Casuistry." *National Catholic Bioethics Quarterly* 11 (2011): 453–63.

———. *Double-Effect Reasoning: Doing Good and Avoiding Evil*. Oxford: Oxford University Press, 2006.

Cavanaugh, William T. "The God of Silence: Shusaku Endo's Reading of the Passion." *Commonweal*, March 13, 1998, 10–12.

Cherry, Mark J. *Kidney for Sale by Owner: Human Organs, Transplantation, and the Market*. Washington, DC: Georgetown University Press, 2005.

Christiansen, Drew. "A Roman Catholic Response." Afterword to *When War Is Unjust: Being Honest in Just-War Thinking*, by John Howard Yoder, 102–17. 2nd ed. Eugene, OR: Wipf & Stock, 1996.

Clark, Peter A. "Methotrexate and Tubal Pregnancies: Direct or Indirect Abortion?" *Linacre Quarterly* 16 (2000): 7–24.

Cloutier, David. "Introduction: The Trajectories of Catholic Sexual Ethics." In *Leaving and Coming Home: New Wineskins for Catholic Sexual Ethics*, edited by David Cloutier, 1–26. Eugene, OR: Wipf and Stock, 2010.

———. *Walking God's Earth: The Environment and Catholic Faith*. Collegeville, MN: Liturgical Press, 2014.

Coleman, Gerald D. "Direct and Indirect Abortion in the Roman Catholic Tradition: A Review of the Phoenix Case." *HEC Forum* 25 (2013): 127–43.

Coll, Steve. "The Unblinking Stare: The Drone War in Pakistan." *The New Yorker*, November 24, 2014, 98–109.

Collingwood, R. G. *The Principles of Art*. Oxford: Oxford University Press, 1938.

Conn, Walter E. *Conscience and Conversion in Newman: A Developmental Study of Self in John Henry Newman*. Milwaukee: Marquette University Press, 2010.

Connery, John R. *Abortion: The Development of the Roman Catholic Perspective*. Chicago: Loyola University Press, 1977.

Curran, Charles. "Natural Law and Contemporary Moral Theory." In *Contraception: Authority and Dissent*, edited by Charles Curran, 151–75. New York: Herder and Herder, 1969.

Dahlstrom, Daniel O. "Philosophy as an Opening for Faith." *Journal of Catholic Higher Education* 34, no. 1 (2015): 27–41.

D'Arcy, Eric. *Conscience and Its Right to Freedom*. New York: Sheed and Ward, 1961.

Darwall, Stephen. *The Second-Person Standpoint: Morality, Respect, and Accountability*. Cambridge, MA: Harvard University Press, 2006.

———. "Two Kinds of Respect." *Ethics* 88 (1977): 36–49.

Davis, Daniel F. "Human Dignity and Respect for Persons: A Historical Perspective on Public Bioethics." In *Human Dignity and Bioethics*, edited by Edmund D. Pellegrino, Adam Schulman, and Thomas W. Merrill, 19–36. Notre Dame, IN: University of Notre Dame Press, 2009.

DeGrazia, David. *Taking Animals Seriously: Mental Life and Moral Status*. Cambridge: Cambridge University Press, 1996.

Diamond, Cora. "Eating Meat and Eating People." *Philosophy* 53 (1978): 465–79.

———. "How Many Legs." In *Value and Understanding: Essays for Peter Winch*, edited by Raimond Gaita, 149–78. London: Routledge, 1990.

———. "The Importance of Being Human." In *Human Beings*, edited by David Cockburn, 36–62. Cambridge: Cambridge University Press, 1991.

———. "Losing Your Concepts." *Ethics* 98 (1988): 255–77.

Donagan, Alan. "Moral Absolutism and the Double-Effect Exception: Reflections on Joseph Boyle's 'Who Is Entitled to Double Effect?'" *Journal of Medicine and Philosophy* 16 (1991): 495–509.

———. *The Theory of Morality*. Chicago: The University of Chicago Press, 1977.

Dougherty, M. V. *Moral Dilemmas in Medieval Thought: From Gratian to Aquinas*. Cambridge: Cambridge University Press, 2011.

Dulles, Avery. "Conscience and Church Authority." In *Conscience: Its Freedom and Limitations*, edited by William C. Bier, 251–68. New York: Fordham University Press, 1971.

————. "Faith and Reason: From Vatican I to John Paul II." In *The Two Wings of Catholic Thought: Essays on Fides et Ratio*, edited by David Ruel Foster and Joseph W. Koterski, 193–208. Washington, DC: Catholic University of America Press, 2003.

————. "From Ratzinger to Benedict." *First Things*, February 2006, 24–29.

————. "John Paul II and the Mystery of the Human Person." *America*, February 2, 2004, 10–22.

Emerson, Ralph Waldo. *The Complete Writings of Ralph Waldo Emerson*. Vol. 1. New York: W. H. Wise, 1929.

Fabre, Cecile. Review of *Why Some Things Should Not Be for Sale*, by Debra Satz. *Ethics* 121 (2011): 469–75.

Faggioli, Massimo. *Vatican II: The Battle for Meaning*. New York: Paulist Press, 2012.

Feigl, Herbert. "Logical Empiricism." In *Readings in Philosophical Analysis*, edited by Herbert Feigl and Wilfrid Sellars, 3–26. New York: Appleton-Century-Crofts, 1949.

Feinberg, Joel. *Harm to Self*. Vol. 3 of *The Moral Limits of the Criminal Law*. New York: Oxford University Press, 1986.

Ferry, David, trans. *Gilgamesh*. New York: Farrar, Straus and Giroux, 1993.

Finkel, Michael. "This Little Kidney Went to Market." *New York Times Magazine*, May 27, 2001, 26ff.

Finnis, John. *Fundamentals of Ethics*. Washington, DC: Georgetown University Press, 1983.

————. "Object and Intention in Moral Judgments According to Aquinas." *The Thomist* 55 (1991): 1–27.

————. "Reflections and Responses." In *Reason, Morality, and Law: The Philosophy of John Finnis*, edited by John Keown and Robert P. George, 459–584. Oxford: Oxford University Press, 2013.

Finnis, John, Germain Grisez, and Joseph Boyle. "'Direct' and 'Indirect': A Reply to Critics of Our Action Theory." *The Thomist* 65 (2001): 1–44.

Flannery, Kevin L. "John Finnis on Thomas Aquinas on Human Action." In *Reason, Morality, and Law: The Philosophy of John Finnis*, edited by John Keown and Robert P. George, 118–32. Oxford: Oxford University Press, 2013.

———. "Vital Conflicts and the Catholic Magisterial Tradition." *National Catholic Bioethics Quarterly* 11 (2011): 691–704.

Foley, Jonathan. "A Five-Step Plan to Feed the World." *National Geographic Magazine*, May 5, 2014, 26–59.

Foot, Philippa. *Virtues and Vices and Other Essays in Moral Philosophy*. Berkeley: University of California Press, 1978.

Ford, John C. "The Morality of Obliteration Bombing." *Theological Studies* 5 (1944): 261–309.

Freddoso, Alfred J. "Good News, Your Soul Hasn't Died Quite Yet." *Proceedings of the American Catholic Philosophical Association* 75 (2001): 79–96.

Freedman, Lori, and Tracy A. Weitz. "The Politics of Motherhood Meets the Politics of Poverty." *Contemporary Sociology* 41 (2012): 36–42.

Fuchs, Josef. *Christian Morality: The Word Becomes Flesh*. Translated by Brian McNeil. Washington, DC: Georgetown University Press, 1987.

———. *Moral Demands and Personal Obligations*. Translated by Brian McNeil. Washington, DC: Georgetown University Press, 1993.

Gazzaniga, Michael S. "Human Being Redux." *Science* 304 (2004): 388–89.

George, Robert P., and Christopher Tollefsen. *Embryo: A Defense of Human Life*. New York: Doubleday, 2008.

Ghods, Ahad J., and Shekoufeh Savaj. "Iranian Model of Paid and Regulated Living-Unrelated Kidney Donation." *Clinical Journal of the American Society of Nephrology* 1 (2006): 1136–45.

Ghoos, Josef. "L'acte à double effet. Étude de théologie positive." *Ephemerides Theologicae Lovanienses* 27 (1951): 30–52.

Gilbert, Scott F. "When 'Personhood' Begins in the Embryo: Avoiding a Syllabus of Errors." *Birth Defects Research* Part C 84 (2008): 164–73.

Gilson, Étienne. *The Spirit of Mediæval Philosophy*. Translated by A. H. C. Downes. New York: Charles Scribner's Sons, 1940.

Glover, Jonathan. *Choosing Children: Genes, Disability and Design*. Oxford: Oxford University Press, 2006.

Gómez-Lobo, Alfonso. *Morality and the Human Goods: An Introduction to Natural Law Ethics*. Washington, DC: Georgetown University Press, 2002.

Greenberg, Karen J., and Joshua L. Dratel, ed. *The Torture Papers: The Road to Abu Ghraib*. New York: Cambridge University Press, 2005.

Griffiths, Paul J., and George Weigel. "Just War: An Exchange," *First Things*, April 2002, 31–36.

————. "Who Wants War? An Exchange." *First Things*, April 2005, 10–12.

Grisez, Germain. *Contraception and the Natural Law*. Milwaukee: Bruce, 1964.

————. "The First Principle of Practical Reason: A Commentary on the *Summa theologiae*, 1–2, Question 94, Article 2." *Natural Law Forum* 10 (1965): 168–201.

————. "Toward a Consistent Natural-Law Ethics of Killing." *The American Journal of Jurisprudence* 15 (1970): 64–96.

————. *The Way of the Lord Jesus*. 3 vols. http://www.twotlj.org/index.html.

Grisez, Germain, Joseph Boyle, and John Finnis. "Practical Principles, Moral Truths, and Ultimate Ends." *American Journal of Jurisprudence* 32 (1987): 99–151.

Grisez, Germain, Joseph Boyle, John Finnis, and William E. May. "'Every Marital Act Ought to Be Open to New Life': Toward a Clearer Understanding." *The Thomist* 52 (1988): 365–426.

Gury, Johannis Petri. *Compendium Theologiae Moralis*. Vol. 1. 14th ed. Rome: Prati, 1901.

Halberstadt, Alex. "Zoo Animals and Their Discontent." *New York Times Magazine*, July 6, 2014, 32ff.

Hare, R. M. "Is Medical Ethics Lost?" *Journal of Medical Ethics* 19 (1993): 69–70.

Harrison, Beverly Wildung, and Shirley Cloyes. "Theology and Morality of Procreative Choice." In *Making the Connections: Essays in Feminist Social Ethics*, by Beverly Wildung Harrison, edited by Carol S. Robb, 115–34. Boston: Beacon Press, 1985.

Harrison, Ruth. *Animal Machines: The New Factory Farming Industry*. London: Vincent Stuart, 1964.

Hart, H. L. A. *Punishment and Responsibility: Essays in the Philosophy of Law*. Oxford: Oxford University Press, 1968.

Heidegger, Martin. *Phänomenologie und Theologie*. Frankfurt am Main: Vittorio Klostermann, 1970.

Herdt, Jennifer A. "Calvin's Legacy for Contemporary Reformed Natural Law." *Scottish Journal of Theology* 67 (2014): 414–35.

Hersh, Seymour M. "The Scene of the Crime: A Reporter's Journey to My Lai and the Secrets of the Past." *The New Yorker*, March 30, 2015, 53–61.

Hill, Thomas E., Jr. "Servility and Self-Respect." *The Monist* 57 (1973): 87–104.

Himes, Michael J. "'Finding God in All Things': A Sacramental Worldview and Its Effects." In *As Leaven in the World: Catholic Perspectives on Faith, Vocation, and the Intellectual Life*, edited by Thomas M. Landy, 91–103. Franklin, WI: Sheed & Ward, 2001.

Hobbes, Thomas. *De Cive*. Edited by Howard Warrender. Oxford: Oxford University Press, 1983.

Howard, Jason J. *Conscience in Moral Life: Rethinking How Our Convictions Structure Self and Society*. Landham, MD: Rowman & Littlefield, 2014.

Howard, Thomas Albert. "A Question of Conscience: The Excommunication of Ignaz von Döllinger." *Commonweal*, October 10, 2014, 14–20.

Hume, David. *An Enquiry Concerning the Principles of Morals*, in *Hume's Ethical Writings*. Edited by Alastair MacIntyre. Notre Dame, IN: University of Notre Dame Press, 1965.

———. *A Treatise of Human Nature*. Edited by P. H. Nidditch. 2nd ed. Oxford: Clarendon Press, 1978.

Hurka, Thomas. "Proportionality in the Morality of War." *Philosophy and Public Affairs* 33 (2005): 34–66.

Hursthouse, Rosalind. "Discussing Dilemmas." *Christian Bioethics* 14 (2008): 141–50.

———. *On Virtue Ethics*. Oxford: Oxford University Press, 1999.

———. "Virtue Theory and Abortion." *Philosophy and Public Affairs* 20 (1991): 223–46.

Jenkins, John I. "The Challenge and Promise of Catholic Higher Education for Our Time." *Journal of Catholic Higher Education* 34, no. 1 (2015): 11–25.

Jerome. *Against Jovinianus*. In *Nicene and Post-Nicene Fathers, Second Series*, vol. 6, edited by Philip Schaff and Henry Wace, translated by

W. H. Fremantle, G. Lewis, and W. G. Martley. Buffalo: Christian Literature Publishing Co., 1893. http://www.newadvent.org/fathers/3009.htm.

Johnson, James Turner. "Just War, As It Was and Is." *First Things*, January 2005, 14–24.

Jonas, Hans. *The Phenomenon of Life: Toward a Philosophical Biology.* Evanston, IL: Northwestern University Press, 2001.

Jones, David Albert. "Magisterial Teaching on Vital Conflicts." *National Catholic Bioethics Quarterly* 14 (2014): 81–104.

Jonsen, Albert R., and Stephen Toulmin. *The Abuse of Casuistry: A History of Moral Reasoning.* Berkeley: University of California Press, 1988.

Kaczor, Christopher. *A Defense of Dignity: Creating Life, Destroying Life, and Respecting the Rights of Conscience.* Notre Dame, IN: University of Notre Dame Press, 2013.

———. "Double-Effect Reasoning from Jean Pierre Gury to Peter Knauer." *Theological Studies* 59 (1998): 297–316.

———. *The Ethics of Abortion: Women's Rights, Human Life, and the Question of Justice.* Routledge: New York, 2011.

Kain, Patrick. "Kant's Defense of Human Moral Status." *Journal of the History of Philosophy* 47 (2009): 59–102.

Kant, Immanuel. *Groundwork of the Metaphysics of Morals.* Translated by Mary Gregor. Cambridge: Cambridge University Press, 1997.

———. *Grundlegung zur Metaphysik der Sitten.* Edited by Karl Vorländer. 3rd ed. Hamburg: Felix Meiner, 1965.

Kasper, Walter. "Merciful God, Merciful Church." By Matthew Boudway and Grant Gallicho. *Commonweal*, June 13, 2014, 14–19.

Kaveny, M. Cathleen. "Appropriation of Evil: Cooperation's Mirror Image." *Theological Studies* 61 (2000): 280–313.

———. "Toward a Thomistic Perspective on Abortion and the Law in Contemporary America." *The Thomist* 55 (1991): 343–96.

Keenan, James F. "Applying the Seventeenth-Century Casuistry of Accommodation to HIV Prevention." *Theological Studies* 60 (1999): 492–512.

———. "The Function of the Double Effect Principle." *Theological Studies* 54 (1993): 294–315.

———. "Redeeming Conscience." *Theological Studies* 76 (2015): 129–47.

————. "The Return of Casuistry." *Theological Studies* 57 (1996): 123–38.

Kenny, Anthony. "Intention and Side Effects: The Mens Rea for Murder." In *Reason, Morality, and Law: The Philosophy of John Finnis*, edited by John Keown and Robert P. George, 109–17. Oxford: Oxford University Press, 2013.

Kirkpatrick, David D. "The Conservative-Christian Big Thinker." *New York Times Magazine*, December 16, 2009, 24ff.

Kittay, Eva Feder. "At the Margins of Moral Personhood." *Ethics* 116 (2005): 100–31.

————. *Love's Labor: Essays on Women, Equality, and Dependency* (New York: Routledge, 1999)

Knauer, Peter. "La détermination du bien et du mal moral par le principe du double effet." *Nouvelle revue théologique* 87 (1965): 356–76.

Kolodny, Niko. "Scanlon's Investigation: The Relevance of Intent to Permissibility." *Analytic Philosophy* 52 (2011): 100–23.

Konieczny, Mary Ellen. *The Spirit's Tether: Family, Work, and Religion among American Catholics*. Oxford: Oxford University Press, 2013.

Langston, Douglas C. *Conscience and Other Virtues*. University Park, PA: Pennsylvania State University Press, 2001.

Lawler, Michael G., and Todd A. Salzman. "Following Faithfully: The Catholic Way to Choose the Good." *America*, February 2, 2015, 16–20.

Leal, David. "Respect for Life in Germain Grisez's Moral Theology." In *The Revival of Natural Law: Philosophical, Theological and Ethical Responses to the Finnis-Grisez School*, edited by Nigel Biggar and Rufus Black, 203–22. Aldershot, UK: Ashgate, 2000.

Lee, Patrick. *Abortion and Unborn Human Life*. 2nd ed. Washington, DC: The Catholic University of America Press, 2010.

Levi, Primo. *The Drowned and the Saved*. Translated by Raymond Rosenthal. New York: Vintage, 1989.

Linzey, Andrew. *Animal Theology*. Urbana, IL: University of Illinois Press, 1994.

————. *Why Animal Suffering Matters: Philosophy, Theology, and Practical Ethics*. Oxford: Oxford University Press, 2009.

Lott, Micah. "Explaining Value: Nagel on Normative Realism and the Teleology of Evolution." *Expositions: Interdisciplinary Studies in the Humanities* 8, no. 2 (2014): 26–37.

————. "Labor Exploitation, Living Wages, and Global Justice: An Aristotelian Account." *Journal of Catholic Social Thought* 11 (2014): 329–59.

Luker, Kristin. *Abortion and the Politics of Motherhood*. Berkeley: University of California Press, 1984.

Lysaught, M. Therese. "Moral Analysis of Procedure at Phoenix Hospital." *Origins* 40 (2011): 537–49.

————. "Respect: Or, How Respect for Persons Became Respect for Autonomy." *Journal of Medicine and Philosophy* 29 (2004): 665–80.

MacFarquhar, Larissa. "How to Be Good." *The New Yorker*, September 5, 2011, 43–53.

MacIntyre, Alasdair. *After Virtue*. 2nd ed. Notre Dame, IN: University of Notre Dame Press, 1984.

————. *Dependent Rational Animals: Why Human Beings Need the Virtues*. Chicago: Open Court, 1999.

————. *God, Philosophy, Universities: A Selective History of the Catholic Philosophical Tradition*. Lanham, MD: Rowman & Littlefield, 2009.

————. *Whose Justice? Which Rationality?* Notre Dame, IN: University of Notre Dame Press, 1988.

Macklin, Ruth. "Dignity Is a Useless Concept." *BMJ* 327 (2003): 1419–20.

Magill, Gerard. "Threat of Imminent Death in Pregnancy: A Role for Double-Effect Reasoning." *Theological Studies* 72 (2011): 848–76.

Maguire, Daniel C. "The Abnormality of War: Dissecting the 'Just War' Euphemisms and Building an Ethics of Peace." *Horizons* 33 (2006): 111–26.

Mahoney, John. *The Making of Moral Theology: A Study of the Roman Catholic Tradition*. Oxford: Oxford University Press, 1987.

Mangan, Joseph T. "An Historical Analysis of the Principle of Double Effect." *Theological Studies* 10 (1949): 41–61.

Marion, Jean-Luc. "'Christian Philosophy': Hermeneutic or Heuristic?" In *The Question of Christian Philosophy Today*, edited by Francis J. Ambrosio, 247–64. New York: Fordham University Press, 1999.

————. *Dieu sans l'être*. Paris: Presses universitaires de France, 1991.

Maritain, Jacques. *An Essay on Christian Philosophy*. Translated by Edward H. Flannery. New York: Philosophical Library, 1955.

Marquis, Donald B. "Four Versions of Double Effect." *Journal of Medicine and Philosophy* 16 (1991): 515–44.

Matthews, Gareth B. "Saint Thomas and the Principle of Double Effect." In *Aquinas's Moral Theory: Essays in Honor of Norman Kretzmann*, edited by Scott MacDonald and Eleonore Stump, 63–78. Ithaca, NY: Cornell University Press, 1999.

McCormick, Richard A. "Ambiguity in Moral Choice." In *Doing Evil to Achieve Good: Moral Choice in Conflict Situations*, edited by Richard A. McCormick and Paul Ramsey, 7–53. Chicago: Loyola University Press, 1978.

McIntyre, Alison. "Doing Away with Double Effect." *Ethics* 111 (2001): 219–55.

McKenna, George. "On Abortion: A Lincolnian Position." *The Atlantic Monthly*, September 1995, 51–68.

McMahan, Jeff. "Cognitive Disability, Misfortune, and Justice." *Philosophy and Public Affairs* 25 (1996): 3–35.

———. *The Ethics of Killing: Problems at the Margins of Life*. Oxford: Oxford University Press, 2002.

———. *Killing in War*. Oxford: Oxford University Press, 2009.

———. "Moral Intuition." In *The Blackwell Guide to Ethical Theory*, edited by Hugh LaFollette and Ingmar Persson, 103–20. 2nd ed. West Sussex, UK: Wiley-Blackwell, 2013.

———. "Moral Wounds." *Boston Review* 38, no. 6 (November/December 2013): 18–23.

———. "'Our Fellow Creatures.'" *The Journal of Ethics* 9 (2005): 353–80.

———. "The Prevention of Unjust Wars." In *Reading Walzer*, edited by Yitzhak Benbaji and Naomi Sussman, 233–55. New York: Routledge, 2014.

———. "War Crimes and Immoral Action in War." In *The Constitution of the Criminal Law*, edited by R. A. Duff, Lindsay Farmer, S. E. Marshall, Massimo Renzo, and Victor Tadros, 151–84. Oxford: Oxford University Press, 2013.

Merton, Thomas. *Peace in the Post-Christian Era*. Edited by Patricia A. Burton. Maryknoll, NY: Orbis, 2004.

Merton, Thomas, and Czesław Miłosz. *Striving towards Being: The Letters of Thomas Merton and Czesław Miłosz*. Edited by Robert Faggen. New York: Farrar, Straus and Giroux, 1996.

Michon, Cyrille. "Faith and Reason: Aquinas's Two Strategies." In *Faith and Reason: The Notre Dame Symposium 1999*, edited by Timothy L. Smith, 283–300. South Bend, IN: St. Augustine's Press, 2001.

Midgley, Mary. "Persons and Non-Persons." In *In Defence of Animals*, edited by Peter Singer, 52–62. Oxford: Basil Blackwell, 1985.

Milton, John. *Paradise Lost*. Edited by Gordon Teskey. New York: W.W. Norton, 2005.

Morey, Melanie M., and John J. Piderit. *Catholic Higher Education: A Culture in Crisis*. Oxford: Oxford University Press, 2006.

Mulhall, Stephen. "Fearful Thoughts." Review of *The Ethics of Killing*, by Jeff McMahan. *London Review of Books* 24, no. 16 (August 22, 2002): 16–18.

Murray, John Courtney. "Remarks on the Moral Problem of War." *Theological Studies* 20 (1959): 40–61.

Nagel, Thomas. *Mind and Cosmos: Why the Materialist Neo-Darwinian Conception of Nature Is Almost Certainly False*. Oxford: Oxford University Press, 2012.

———. *The View from Nowhere*. Oxford: Oxford University Press, 1986.

———. "War and Massacre." *Philosophy and Public Affairs* 1 (1972): 123–44.

National Catholic Bioethics Center. "Commentary on the Phoenix Situation." *Origins* 40 (2011): 549–51.

Nelson, Hilde Lindemann. "What Child Is This?" *Hastings Center Report* 32, no. 6 (2002): 29–38.

Newman, John Henry. *Discourses Addressed to Mixed Congregations*. London: Longmans, Green, 1906. http://newmanreader.org/works/discourses/index.html.

———. *An Essay on the Development of Christian Doctrine*. London: Longmans, Green, 1909. http://www.newmanreader.org/works/development/.

———. *The Idea of a University*. London: Longmans, Green, 1907. http://www.newmanreader.org/works/idea/.

———. "A Letter Addressed to the Duke of Norfolk on Occasion of Mr. Gladstone's Recent Expostulation." In *Certain Difficulties Felt by Anglicans in Catholic Teaching*. Vol. 2. London: Longmans, Green, 1900. http://newmanreader.org/works/anglicans/volume2/gladstone/index.html.

Nietzsche, Friedrich. *On the Genealogy of Morality*. Translated by Maudemarie Clark and Alan J. Swensen. Indianapolis: Hackett, 1998.

Noonan, John T., Jr. "An Almost Absolute Value in History." In *The Morality of Abortion: Legal and Historical Perspectives*, edited by John T. Noonan Jr., 1–59. Cambridge, MA: Harvard University Press, 1970.

————. *A Church That Can and Cannot Change*. Notre Dame, IN: University of Notre Dame Press, 2005.

————. "Development in Moral Doctrine." *Theological Studies* 54 (1993): 662–77.

————. "Transparency in Theology." In *The Foundation of Freedom*, edited by William Hund and Margaret Monahan Hogan, 23–28. Portland: The University of Portland Press, 2006.

O'Brien, Dennis, Peter Steinfels, and Cathleen Caveny. "Can We Talk about Abortion? An Exchange." *Commonweal*, September 23, 2011, 12–19.

O'Brien, Matthew B., and Robert C. Koons. "Objects of Intention: A Hylomorphic Critique of the New Natural Law Theory." *American Catholic Philosophical Quarterly* 86 (2012): 655–703.

O'Brien, Tim. *The Things They Carried*. New York: Mariner, 1990.

O'Donovan, Oliver. *The Just War Revisited*. Cambridge: Cambridge University Press, 2003.

Okeowo, Alexis. "Freedom Fighter: Why Slavery Persists in Mauritania." *The New Yorker*, September 8, 2014, 38–46.

O'Malley, John W. *Four Cultures of the West*. Cambridge, MA: Harvard University Press, 2004.

O'Neill, Onora. *Towards Justice and Virtue: A Constructive Account of Practical Reasoning*. Cambridge: Cambridge University Press, 1996.

Origen. *Contra Celsus*. In *Ante-Nicene Fathers*. Vol. 4. Edited by Alexander Roberts, James Donaldson, and A. Cleveland Coxe. Translated by Frederick Crombie. Buffalo: Christian Literature Publishing Co., 1885. http://www.newadvent.org/fathers/0416.htm.

Orsy, Ladislas. "Magisterium: Assent and Dissent." *Theological Studies* 48 (1987): 473–97.

Padawer, Ruth. "The Two-Minus-One Pregnancy." *New York Times Magazine*, August 10, 2011, 22ff.

Parfit, Derek. *On What Matters*. 2 vols. Edited by Samuel Scheffler. Oxford: Oxford University Press, 2011.

Parikh, Mahendra N. "Destructive Operations in Obstetrics." *Journal of Obstetrics and Gynecology of India* 56, no. 2 (March–April 2006): 113–14.

Pascal, Blaise. *Oeuvres completes*. Edited by Michel Le Guern. Vol. 1. Paris: Gallimard, 1998.

———. *Pensées*. Edited by Léon Brunschvicg. Paris: Garnier-Flammarion, 1976.

Peach, Andrew. "Late- vs. Early-Term Abortion: A Thomistic Analysis." *The Thomist* 71 (2007): 113–41.

Phillips, Anne. *Our Bodies, Whose Property?* Princeton: Princeton University Press, 2013.

Pinckaers, Servais. *Morality: The Catholic View*. Translated by Michael Sherwin. South Bend, IN: St. Augustine's Press, 2001.

Planck, Nina. *Real Food: What to Eat and Why*. New York: Bloomsburg, 2006.

Plessner, Helmuth. *Lachen und Weinen. Eine Untersuchung nach den Grenzen menschlichen Verhaltens*. Vol. 7 of *Gesammelte Schiften, Ausdruck und menschliche Natur*. Edited by Günter Dux, Odo Marquard, and Elisabeth Ströker, et al. Frankfurt am Main: Suhrkamp, 1982.

———. *Laughing and Crying: A Study of the Limits of Human Behavior*. Translated by James Spencer Churchill and Marjorie Grene. Evanston, IL: Northwestern University Press, 1970.

Pollan, Michael. "The Intelligent Plant: A Radical New Way of Understanding Flora." *The New Yorker*, December 23 and 30, 2013, 92–105.

Pope, Alexander. *The Rape of the Locke and Other Poems*. Edited by Geoffrey Tillotson. Vol. 2 of *The Poems of Alexander Pope*. London: Methuen, 1940.

Pope Francis. "A Big Heart Open to God." By Antonio Spadaro. Translated by Massimo Faggioli, Sarah Christopher Faggioli, Dominic Robinson, Patrick J. Howell, and Griffin Oleynick. *America*, September 30, 2013, 15–38.

Porter, Jean. "Does the Natural Law Provide a Universally Valid Morality?" In *Intractable Disputes about the Natural Law: Alasdair MacIntyre and Critics*, edited by Lawrence S. Cunningham, 53–95. Notre Dame, IN: University of Notre Dame Press, 2009.

———. *Natural and Divine Law: Reclaiming the Tradition for Christian Ethics.* Grand Rapids: Eerdmans, 1999.

———. *Nature as Reason: A Thomistic Theory of the Natural Law.* Grand Rapids: Eerdmans, 2005.

Portmann, Adolf. *Biologische Fragmente zu einer Lehre vom Menschen.* Basel: Benno Schwabe, 1944.

Powers, Gerald F. "The U.S. Bishops and War since the Peace Pastoral." *U.S. Catholic Historian* 27 (2009): 72–96.

Potts, Timothy C. *Conscience in Medieval Philosophy.* Cambridge: Cambridge University Press, 1980.

Prusak, Bernard G. "The Ethics of Metaethics: On Thomas Nagel's *Mind and Cosmos.*" *Expositions: Interdisciplinary Studies in the Humanities* 8, no. 2 (2014): 1–10.

———. "The Idea of a Catholic College: Charism, Curricula, and Community." *Journal of Catholic Higher Education* 34, no. 1 (2015): 1–9.

———. *Parental Obligations and Bioethics: The Duties of a Creator.* New York: Routledge, 2013.

———. "The Science of Laughter: Helmuth Plessner's *Laughing and Crying* Revisited." *Continental Philosophy Review* 38 (2006): 41–69.

———. "When Words Fail Us: Reexamining the Conscience of Huckleberry Finn." *Journal of Aesthetic Education* 45 (2011): 1–22.

———. "The Wrong Description." Review of *Beyond the Abortion Wars: A Way Forward for a New Generation*, by Charles Camosy. *Commonweal*, May 15, 2015, 23–24.

Quinn, Warren. "Abortion: Identity and Loss." *Philosophy and Public Affairs* 13 (1984): 24–54.

———. "Actions, Intentions, and Consequences: The Doctrine of Double Effect." *Philosophy and Public Affairs* 18 (1989): 334–51.

Rachels, James. "Active and Passive Euthanasia." *New England Journal of Medicine* 292 (1975): 78–80.

———. *Created from Animals: The Moral Implications of Darwinism.* Oxford: Oxford University Press, 1990.

———. "Drawing Lines." In *Animal Rights: Current Debates and New Directions*, edited by Cass R. Sunstein and Martha Nussbaum, 162–74. Oxford: Oxford University Press, 2004.

Ramsey, Paul. *Fabricated Man: The Ethics of Genetic Control.* New Haven: Yale University Press, 1970.

Ratzinger, Joseph. *On Conscience: Two Essays*. Philadelphia/San Francisco: National Catholic Bioethics Center/Ignatius Press, 2007.

Regan, Tom. *The Case for Animal Rights*. Berkeley: The University of California Press, 1983.

————. "The Case for Animals Rights." In *Animal Rights and Human Obligations*, edited by Tom Regan and Peter Singer, 105–14. 2nd ed. Englewood Cliffs, NJ: Prentice Hall, 1989.

Reichman, James B. *Evolution, Animals "Rights," and the Environment*. Washington, DC: The Catholic University of America Press, 2000.

Ricoeur, Paul. *Freedom and Nature: The Voluntary and the Involuntary*. Translated by Erazim 'V. Kohák. Evanston, IL: Northwestern University Press, 1966.

————. *Oneself as Another*. Translated by Kathleen Blamey. Chicago: University of Chicago Press, 1992.

Rodin, David. "The Ethics of War: State of the Art." *Journal of Applied Philosophy* 23 (2006): 241–46.

————. "Justifying Harm." *Ethics* 122 (2011): 74–100.

————. *War and Self-Defense*. Oxford: Oxford University Press, 2002.

Sagan, Eli. *Cannibalism: Human Aggression and Cultural Form*. New York: Harper & Row, 1974.

Sandel, Michael J. *The Case against Perfection*. Cambridge, MA: Harvard University Press, 2007.

————. "How Markets Crowd Out Morals." *Boston Review* 37, no. 3 (May-June 2012): 13–18.

————. *What Money Can't Buy: The Moral Limits of Markets*. New York: Farrar, Straus and Giroux, 2012.

Satz, Debra. "The Moral Limits of Markets: The Case of Human Kidneys." *Proceedings of the Aristotelian Society* 108 (2008): 269–88.

————. "Voluntary Slavery and the Limits of the Market." *Law and Ethics of Human Rights* 3 (2009): 86–109.

————. *Why Some Things Should Not Be for Sale: The Moral Limits of Markets*. Oxford: Oxford University Press, 2010.

Scanlon, T. M. *Moral Dimensions: Permissibility, Meaning, Blame*. Cambridge, MA: Harvard University Press, 2008.

————. *What We Owe to Each Other*. Cambridge, MA: Harvard University Press, 1998.

Schneewind, J. B., ed. *Moral Philosophy from Montaigne to Kant: An Anthology*. Vol. 1. Cambridge: Cambridge University Press, 1990.

Searle, John R. "Animal Minds." *Midwest Studies in Philosophy* 19 (1994): 206–19.

Shakespeare, William. *Henry IV Part One*. Edited by M.A. Schaaber. New York: Penguin, 1970.

———. *Henry V*. Edited by Claire McEachern. New York: Penguin, 1999.

Shanley, Brian J. "Perspectives in Catholic Philosophy I." In *Teaching the Tradition: Catholic Themes in Academic Disciplines*, edited by John J. Piderit and Melanie Morey, 65–83. Oxford: Oxford University Press, 2012.

Shannon, Thomas A. "The Kindness of Strangers: Organ Transplantation in a Capitalist Age." *Kennedy Institute of Ethics Journal* 11 (2001): 285–303.

Shell, Susan M. "Kant's Concept of Human Dignity as a Resource for Bioethics." In *Human Dignity and Bioethics*, edited by Edmund D. Pellegrino, Adam Schulman, and Thomas W. Merrill, 333–49. Notre Dame, IN: University of Notre Dame Press, 2009.

Shelley, Mary. *Frankenstein*. Edited by Paul J. Hunter. New York: W.W. Norton, 1996.

Shields, Jon A. "The Politics of Motherhood Revisited." *Contemporary Sociology* 41 (2012): 43–48.

Simmel, Georg. *On Individuality and Social Forms*. Edited by Donald N. Levine. Chicago: The University of Chicago Press, 1971.

Singer, Peter. "All Animals Are Equal." In *Animal Rights and Human Obligations*, edited by Tom Regan and Peter Singer, 73–86. 2nd ed. Englewood Cliffs, NJ: Prentice Hall, 1989.

———. *Animal Liberation: A New Ethics for Our Treatment of Animals*. New York: New York Review/Random House, 1975.

———. "Reflections." In *The Lives of Animals*, by J. M. Coetzee, edited by Amy Gutmann, 85–91. Princeton: Princeton University Press, 1999.

Smith, Christian, and Kyle Longest, Jonathan Hill, and Kari Christoffersen. *Young Catholic America: Emerging Adults in, out of, and Gone from the Church*. Oxford: Oxford University Press, 2014.

Sokolowski, Robert. *The God of Faith and Reason: Foundations of Christian Theology*. Washington, DC: The Catholic University of America Press, 1995.

Sorabji, Richard. *Animal Minds and Human Morals: The Origins of the Western Debate*. Ithaca, NY: Cornell University Press, 1993.

————. *Moral Conscience through the Ages: Fifth Century BCE to the Present*. Chicago: The University of Chicago Press, 2014.

Spaemann, Robert. *Persons: The Difference between "Someone" and "Something."* Translated by Oliver O'Donovan. Oxford: Oxford University Press, 2006.

Steinfels, Peter. "Beyond the Stalemate: Fifty Years after 'Roe.'" *Commonweal*, June 14, 2013, 12–18.

————. "Contraception and Honesty: A Proposal for the Next Synod." *Commonweal*, June 1, 2015, 12–19.

Street, Sharon. "A Darwinian Dilemma for Realist Theories of Value." *Philosophical Studies* 127 (2006): 109–66.

Stuart, Tristram. *The Bloodless Revolution: A Cultural History of Vegetarianism from 1600 to Modern Times*. New York: W.W. Norton, 2006.

Sulmasy, Daniel P. "Dignity and Bioethics: History, Theory, and Selected Applications." In *Human Dignity and Bioethics*, edited by Edmund D. Pellegrino, Adam Schulman, and Thomas W. Merrill, 469–501. Notre Dame, IN: University of Notre Dame Press, 2009.

————. "Double Effect Reasoning and Care at the End of Life: Some Clarifications and Distinctions." *Vera Lex* 6 (2005): 107–45.

————. "'Reinventing' the Rule of Double Effect." In *The Oxford Handbook of Bioethics*, edited by Bonnie Steinbock, 114–49. Oxford: Oxford University Press, 2007.

Sussman, David. "What's Wrong with Torture?" *Philosophy and Public Affairs* 33 (2005): 1–33.

Swindal, James C. and Harry J. Gensler. *The Sheed & Ward Anthology of Catholic Philosophy*. Lanham, MD: Rowman & Littlefield, 2005.

Thomson, Judith Jarvis. "A Defense of Abortion." *Philosophy and Public Affairs* 1 (1971): 47–66.

————. "Self-Defense." *Philosophy and Public Affairs* 20 (1991): 283–310.

Twain, Mark [Samuel Clemens]. *Huck Finn; Pudd'nhead Wilson; No. 44, The Mysterious Stranger; and Other Writings*. New York: Library of America, 2000.

Uexküll, Jakob von. *Umwelt und Innenwelt der Tiere*. 2nd ed. Berlin: Julius Springer, 1921.

Vacek, Edward. "Conditions May Apply: Relativity without Relativism." *Commonweal*, March 11, 2011, 14–17.

Velleman, J. David. "A Right of Self-Termination?" *Ethics* 109 (1999): 606–28.

Virgil. *The Aeneid*. Translated by Robert Fitzgerald. New York: Vintage, 1983.

Vischer, Robert K. *Conscience and the Common Good: Reclaiming the Space between Person and State*. Cambridge: Cambridge University Press, 2010.

Walzer, Michael. *Just and Unjust Wars: A Moral Argument with Historical Illustrations*. 3rd ed. New York: Basic Books, 2000.

———. *Obligations: Essays on Disobedience, War, and Citizenship*. Cambridge, MA: Harvard University Press, 1970.

———. "Response." In *Reading Walzer*, edited by Yitzhak Benbaji and Naomi Sussman, 328–32. New York: Routledge, 2014.

———. *Spheres of Justice: A Defense of Pluralism and Equality*. New York: Basic Books, 1983.

Webster, John. "God and Conscience." In *The Doctrine of God and Theological Ethics*, edited by Alan J. Torrance and Michael Banner, 147–65. New York: T & T Clark, 2006.

Weigel, George. "Moral Clarity in a Time of War." *First Things*, January 2003, 20–27.

———. "World Order: What Catholics Forget." *First Things*, May 2004, 31–38.

Whitmore, Todd David. "Catholic Social Teaching: Starting with the Common Good." In *Living the Catholic Social Tradition: Cases and Commentary*, edited by Kathleen Maas-Weigert and Alexia K. Kelley, 59–85. Lanham, MD: Rowman & Littlefield, 2005.

Williams, Bernard. *Making Sense of Humanity and Other Philosophical Papers 1982–1993*. Cambridge: Cambridge University Press, 1995.

Williams, Rowan, and George Weigel. "War and Statecraft: An Exchange." *First Things*, March 2004, 14–22.

Wiman, Christopher. "'Being Prepared for Joy.'" By Anthony Domestico. *Commonweal*, May 2, 2014, 11–16.

Wittgenstein, Ludwig. *Culture and Value*. Edited by G. H. Von Wright. Translated by Peter Winch. Bilingual ed. Chicago: The University of Chicago Press, 1980.

———. *Philosophical Investigations*. Translated by Elizabeth Anscombe. Bilingual edition. Oxford: Basil Blackwell, 1958.

Woolf, Virginia. *A Room of One's Own*. London: Harcourt Brace, 1929.

Yoder, John Howard. *When War Is Unjust: Being Honest in Just-War Thinking*. 2nd ed. Eugene, OR: Wipf & Stock, 1996.

Zahn, Gordon. *In Solitary Witness: The Life and Death of Franz Jägerstätter*. 3rd ed. Collegeville, MN: Liturgical Press, 1964.

Zeis, John. "Killing Innocents and the Doctrine of Double Effect." *Proceedings of the American Catholic Philosophical Association* 78 (2005): 133–44.

———. "A Rawlsian Pro-Life Argument against Vegetarianism." *International Philosophical Quarterly* 53 (2013): 63–71.

———. "What Contradicts Intention." *Proceedings of the American Catholic Philosophical Association* 86 (2012): 115–28.

INDEX